Bedeviled

SUNY series in Islam

Seyyed Hossein Nasr, editor

Bedeviled

Jinn Doppelgangers in Islam and Akbarian Sufism

DUNJA RAŠIĆ

SUNY
PRESS

Cover Art: Instructions for performing an exorcism, from an eighteenth-century North African travelling physician's handbook. British Library (Or.6557, f041r).

Published by State University of New York Press, Albany

Printed in the United States of America

For information, contact State University of New York Press, Albany, NY
www.sunypress.edu

Library of Congress Cataloging-in-Publication Data

Name: Rašić, Dunja, author.
Title: Bedeviled : jinn doppelgangers in Islam and Akbarian Sufism / Dunja Rašić.
Description: Albany : State University of New York Press, [2024]. | Series: SUNY series in Islam | Includes bibliographical references and index.
Identifiers: LCCN 2023029847 | ISBN 9781438496894 (hardcover : alk. paper) | ISBN 9781438496900 (ebook) | ISBN 9781438496887 (pbk. : alk. paper)
Subjects: LCSH: Jinn. | Devil—Islam. | Good and evil—Religious aspects—Islam. | Sufism—Doctrines.
Classification: LCC BP166.89 .R375 2024 | DDC 297.2/17—dc23/eng/20230712
LC record available at https://lccn.loc.gov/2023029847

10 9 8 7 6 5 4 3 2 1

Everything exists in pairs, one set against the other and He made nothing that is incomplete.

—Sirach 42:24

Contents

List of Illustrations ix

Acknowledgments xi

Transcription and Transliteration System xiii

Chapter 1 Neither of the East, nor of the West 1

Chapter 2 Signs on the Horizons 27

Chapter 3 The Devil Within 81

Chapter 4 The Red Death 103

Notes 131

Bibliography 175

Index 201

Illustrations

Figures

1.1	The animal form of the demoness Tābiʿa/ ʾUmm al-Ṣibyān.	13
1.2	ʾUmm al-Ṣibyān assuming the form of a cat.	14
2.1	Ṭīṭān, the jinni with the head of a goat, the body of human, and legs of an elephant.	37
2.2	Conjuror burning incense to be able to see and summon jinn.	41
2.3	*Siʿlāh,* a forest jinni.	47
2.4	*Dalhāth* attacking a ship.	48
2.5	A ghoul falls off a horse, allowing the man to escape. Three other jinn also lurk nearby.	50
2.6	Jinn were thought to be capable of transforming arid lands into fertile soil.	59
2.7	A sigil containing an image of a jinni from the Banū al-Qāwāʿid tribe.	66
2.8	Mars and the jinn-king of Mars.	69
2.9	Jinn slaves working at the baths of Tiberias.	72
3.1	Ibn ʿArabī's diagram of the Great City.	82
3.2	The tree of Zaqqum.	90

Table

Acknowledgments

Many people have helped me to make this book a reality, beginning with Ejaz Ahmad, my *deus ex machina* in summer 2022. Dozens of other people have also provided help, whether professional or personal, during the years I have worked on this book—and I especially thank Stephen Hirtenstein, James Peltz, and Nikola Pantić. Without their knowledge, support, and generosity, I would not have gotten far. I would also like to express my gratitude to my two readers (Reviewer A and Reviewer B) for the State University of New York Press, for their reports that went well beyond the call of duty. Finally, my thanks go to my husband, Alex Stahl, and my family, for their unfailing encouragement, love, and brilliance. Together, we saw this project to the end.

Transcription and Transliteration System

Name	Orthographic symbol	Transliteration system
alif	ا	ā
bāʾ	ب	b
tāʾ	ت	t
thāʾ	ث	th
jīm	ج	j
ḥāʾ	ح	ḥ
khāʾ	خ	kh
dāl	د	d
dhāl	ذ	dh
rāʾ	ر	r
zāy	ز	z
sīn	س	s
shīn	ش	sh
ṣād	ص	ṣ
ḍād	ض	ḍ
ṭāʾ	ط	ṭ
ẓāʾ	ظ	ẓ
ʿayn	ع	ʿ
ghayn	غ	gh
fāʾ	ف	f
qāf	ق	q
kāf	ك	k
lām	ل	l
mīm	م	m
nūn	ن	n
hāʾ	ه	h
wāw	و	w
yāʾ	ي	y

Chapter 1

Neither of the East, nor of the West

> Then He said to me: "Light is a veil and darkness is a veil. You'll be aware of what is the most beneficial at the line between them. Follow this line closely—and if you arrive at the point in which it originates, make it disappear in the sunset prayer."
>
> —Ibn ʿArabī[1]

The surah *al-Baqarah* attests that both *the East and the West belong to God. Wherever you turn is the face of God* (Qur'an 2:115). The Akbarian school of Islamic mysticism followed this ayah to the letter. Akbarians were well aware that God's face sometimes takes a hideous form. However, they also maintained that ugly things can lead to beautiful outcomes.[2] Reprehensible forms of existence were seen among Akbarians as an opportunity for spiritual growth as well as a threat. A prominent supporter of the Akbarian school in Timurid Persia was even rumored to have said: "I turn away from God who doesn't disclose Himself in a cat or dog!"[3] This book examines the face of God reflected in jinn doppelgangers. These cat-eyed jinn were said to prefer to disclose themselves in the form of a black dog.

1.1. Ibn ʿArabī and the Marvels of Existence

The Akbarian school follows the teaching of Muḥyī al-Dīn Ibn ʿArabī. A member of the Tayy aristocracy, Ibn ʿArabī was born in Spain in 1165 AD. However, he spent half of his life traveling through the Middle East, and he died in Damascus in 1240 AD. For this reason, he was once compared to a blessed tree that is neither of the East nor of the West since it equally belongs to both.[4] Medieval scholars principally acknowledged Ibn ʿArabī as a *muḥaddith,* a specialist in the Islamic normative tradition. Later on, he was also recognized as a mystic and poet—and the greatest of all Muslim philosophers.[5] By his own account, he wrote over 250 works, 84 of which survive today. The significance of these works cannot be overstated. Such was the impact of his teachings that Takeshita divided the Islamic cultural history to the period before and after Ibn ʿArabī.[6] The major, divisive role he played in Islamic culture is attested by the vast body of polemical literature he inspired. To his followers, Ibn ʿArabī was the Greatest Shaykh (*al-shaykh al-ʾakbar*), the Reviver of Faith (*muḥyiddin*), and the Seal of Sainthood (*khatam al-wilāya*). In the eyes of his detractors, Ibn ʿArabī was an infidel who neglected jihad so that he could battle with evil spirits and his soul instead.[7] Al-Sīnūbī said: "His school of thought (*madhhab*) is a great calamity. Believers, hold fast to Sharia so that you avoid being misled . . . The author of *Fuṣūṣ* [i.e. Ibn ʿArabī] was one of the greatest scholars and the leader among shaykhs at first. Then, towards the end of his life, he became the leader of infidels like the Devil himself, who was first the leader and the first among angels and then became the first among infidels."[8]

The enmity towards Ibn ʿArabī among the early modern scholars tends to be associated with Ibn Taymiyya's (d. 1328) rising influence in Syria and Egypt. In spite of the fact that the orthodoxy of Ibn ʿArabī's teachings had been questioned before Ibn Taymiyya's time, Ibn Taymiyya's refutations still played a major role in shifting the public opinion against Ibn ʿArabī.[9] On his side, Ibn Taymiyya was convinced that Ibn ʿArabī's teachings opposed the basic principles of Islam. He furthermore accused Ibn ʿArabī of seeing God in every living being and every form of existence. Hinting that evil, ugliness, and imperfection were also God—and of God—such claims were unacceptable for Ibn Taymiyya. In contrast, Ibn ʿArabī maintained that the world of nature is imbued with the Divine presence. His teachings were chiefly based on a *ḥadīth qudsī,* which reads: "I was a hidden treasure and I loved to be known. Hence, I created the world to make Myself known."[10] Whereas most medieval jurisprudents agreed that the *ḥadīth qudsī* has a dubious chain of transmissions, Ibn ʿArabī claimed he received the assurance of its soundness by the means of revelation (*kashf*).[11] He found further support to his teachings in the surah *Fuṣṣilat*: *We will show them Our signs on the horizons and within themselves until it becomes clear to them what is true* (Q 41:53). The joint authority of the Qur'an, *sunnah,* and Ibn ʿArabī's mystical insights thus led him to the conclusion that the Divine is always imminent within the mundane.

> He created us only to worship Him and to know Him. If we gaze, it is upon Him; if we hear, it is from Him; if we use our intelligence, it is towards Him; if we reflect, it is upon Him; if we know, it is Him; if we have faith, it is in Him. For it is He who is revealed in every face, sought in every sign, gazed upon by every eye, worshipped in every object of worship and pursued in the invisible and the visible.[12]

To marvel at God's creation was seen as an act of piety in medieval Islam. This is to be attributed to the fact that the Qur'an instructs believers to *observe carefully all that is in the heavens and on earth* (Q 10:101). Hence, al-Ghazālī (d. 1111) maintained that the best way to gain knowledge of God is by observing the things He created and by contemplating the wonders (*ʿajāʾib*) of His works.[13] Wonders and the state of wonder were identified as the roots of philosophical inquiries by Plato and Aristotle.[14] Descartes noted that wonder is the first of passions. Its roots are novelty and ignorance. Like Descartes, al-Qazwīnī (d. 1283) pointed out that humans tend to lose the ability to wonder as they grow older and accumulate knowledge and experience. Al-Qazwīnī furthermore observed that the perfect symmetry of a beehive will in most cases prove to be insufficient to arouse a genuine interest in natural philosophy. The wonders of nature are more likely to inspire religious devotion. This is especially the case with fantastic beasts and strange plants which, according to al-Qazwīnī, can always induce the tongue to sing praises of God.[15] Comparable teachings could also be found among scholastics. For example, Thomas of Chobham (d. 1236) taught that the world was created to serve as a book of lessons to mankind. "There is no creature," Chobham recorded, "which may not preach that the God who created it is powerful and that the God who gave it its order and form is wise and that the God who conserves it in being is merciful. And—speaking in a wider sense—there is no creature in which we may not contemplate some property belonging to it which may lead us to imitate God or some property which may move us to flee from the Devil."[16] The quoted excerpt from Chobham's *Summade arte praedicandi* evokes al-Jāḥiẓ's (d. 868) definition of zoology. Al-Jāḥiẓ defined zoology as a branch of religious studies, whose goal is to demonstrate the existence of God by focusing on the wisdom inherent in His creation.[17] Like Ibn ʿArabī, he taught that the world was created in such a way that even the movement patterns of worms in the ground can point a way to God.[18] He nevertheless advised his students against limiting their spiritual practices to witnessing the marvels of nature. Ibn ʿArabī identified two major risks with this approach. The first risk is the result of the great diversity and vastness of the world of nature. Ibn ʿArabī feared this plenitude could distract a Seeker, causing them to lose sight of their primary objectives.[19] Nonetheless, he held the beauty of nature in high regard. The Islamic normative tradition speaks of the Beautiful God—and Ibn ʿArabī believed that some of His beauty is reflected in the world He created. "Whoever loves God for His beauty, which is nothing other than the beauty which can be contemplated in the universe, [let him remember that] God gave it existence in accordance with His own form, so that in this same way, he who loves the world for its beauty loves God alone, since Divine reality has no place of transcendence and manifestation except the cosmos."[20]

Ibn ʿArabī referred to the Islamic normative tradition to underline that God is beautiful, merciful, and kind. However, He was also described as the Deceiver (*al-Mākir*), the One who Leads Astray (*al-Mudhill*). These Names are also embodied in the world He created. The possibility of encountering embodiments of these Names was identified as the second, greater risk with seeking God among the marvels of existence. For Ibn ʿArabī believed there are species in the universe which seek to obstruct a Seeker from reaching unity with the Divine.[21] One of these species are jinn.

1.2. *Hic sunt dracones*! Jinn Studies—the State of Field

Jinn were regularly featured in zoological compendiums and travel literature (*ʾadab al-riḥlāt*) as of the ninth century AD. Al-Bīrūnī (d. 1048) even claimed to have found records of the jinn folk in the works of Aristotle and Mani.[22] However, this is likely to be attributed to the faulty translations he read. The earliest examples of jinn narratives had been transmitted among Bedouins before the onset of Islam. These were the tales of poetic contests, wondrous encounters, and monsters lurking at the frontiers of society, at the far edge of the world. Throughout the centuries, Bedouins of the old Arabia have feared the power of jinn to mislead and enrapture. With the rise of Islam, old legends have changed in tone and content. Nevertheless, jinn narratives continue to challenge the common notions of what is spirit, animal, miraculous, and mundane. In this regard, jinn are the epitome of Park's definition of marvels of nature. Marvels, Park noted, share a common tendency to cluster at the margins of the known world. Jinn fulfill this criterion. As al-Masʿūdī (d. 956) explained: "Many people believe that *nasnās* [a subspecies of one-legged jinn] live in China and other distant kingdoms. Whereas some people say that *nasnās* can be found in the East, others claim that they can be found in the West. People of the East claim that *nasnās* live in the West and the people of the West claim that they live in the East. Every nation speaks of the existence of jinn in countries far distant from their own."[23]

Invisible and incorporeal, jinn inhabit the visible, material world. Their natural habitat was thought to be the direct outcome of Divine retribution. God, the All-Merciful, was not particularly merciful towards jinn. Having grown tired of their sins, He first had them exiled to the most isolated corners of Earth. Later on, jinn were also found to be guilty of eavesdropping at heaven's door and recounting Divine secrets to humans. As a punishment, God confined jinn to the world of gross matter.[24] Jinn are, however, closer in nature to the spiritual World of Malakūt (*ʿalām al-malakūt*) and the World of Jabarūt (*ʿalām al-jabarūt*). Ibn ʿArabī thus had them described as strangers to the world of nature.[25] The material world was referred to in Ibn ʿArabī's works as the East, the place of the rising Sun. Contrasting the East, the West stands for all that is hidden and unseen (*al-ghayb*). Ibn ʿArabī's perception of the East and the West corresponds to the Qur'anic notions of *ẓāhir* and *bāṭin*. Having analyzed the etymology of these terms, Lory pointed out that whereas the term *ẓāhir* refers to *ẓahr* (the human back), the term *bātin* is etymologically linked to the word *baṭn* (belly). Lory cautioned that the visible, apparent aspect of human lives is actually "the backside of reality, the less interesting part of it. The 'belly' of reality, the organism that gives life to it, is hidden from perception and common sense."[26] The invisible jinn were described in Ibn ʿArabī's works as the creatures of *barzakh*. Ibn ʿArabī used this term as a synonym for the intermediate World of Jabarūt. However, the term *barzakh* could also stand for the borderlines between black and white, life and death, positive and negative, known and the Unknown. In other words, *barzakh* is a border between two extremes, where their seemingly irreconcilable attributes are balanced out and combined with one another. Neither of the East, nor of the West, jinn populate borders between shade and sunlight.[27] A successful contribution to jinn studies can thus be seen as an act of exploring (and breaching) boundaries. As Nathan explains:

> If religion builds groups, participates in the foundation of social spaces and contributes to the intelligence of those who are weak and destitute, the world of jinn engages those who venture into the exploration of margins, of the reverse side, of the lines of lines. Religion establishes order; the world of the jinn recovers those excluded from this order, heals them, and reintegrates them into the world. If religion builds the walls, the world of jinn digs cracks in them, constantly explores the faults, enlarges the cavities and proposes ways of settling in permanently.[28]

Jinns' ambiguous nature matches Park's second main criterion for determining what constitutes marvels of nature. Apart from their tendency to nest at the frontiers of society, "they [also] constitute a distinct ontological category, the preternatural, suspended between the mundane and the miraculous."[29] The third, additional criterion was brought forth by Bynum, who argued that the very function of wonders is predicated upon an uncanny reality as one "can only marvel at something that is, at least in some sense, there."[30] On his side, Ibn ʿArabī was adamant that jinn exist. He also believed that people who have no knowledge of the Unseen will come to an evil end. That said, throughout the centuries, there were several notable attempts to challenge the existence of jinn. For instance, al-Jāḥiẓ believed that jinn narratives reflect Bedouins' fear of deserts (*bilād al-waḥsh*), solitude (*ʾinfirād*), and isolation from their fellow men (*buʿd min al-ʾins*). In wilderness, consumed with fear of the unknown, a Bedouin's imagination would play tricks on him, causing him to hear the whispers of jinn:

> Young people grow up with these ideas and children become familiar with them through the course of the upbringing. Once a man finds himself alone in the middle of night, in the middle of vast deserts, he would remember these stories. If he is of a lying sort and likes to boast, he could even write poems about the experience. He would say: "I saw a ghoul." Or: "I talked to a *siʿlāh*." Later on, he would say: ". . . and I had it killed!" He could then take things further by saying: "I befriended it." Going even further, one could say: "Actually, I married a jinni" [. . . However, only Bedouins and the uneducated indulge themselves with such poems and tales.[31]

Al-Jāḥiẓ maintained that most jinn sightings can be dismissed as fabrications or delusions of the feeble-minded. Notable attempts to provide a rational explanation for jinn encounters were also conducted by Ibn Qutaybah (d. 889) and Ibn Rushd (d. 1198).[32] These attempts mostly fell on deaf ears. Convincing the world that he does not exist was said to be the greatest ruse of the Devil in Christianity. In contrast, jinn were thought to be prone to afflicting humans who doubted their existence with madness, sometimes killing them in retribution.[33] It goes without saying that the wrath of the jinn folk would not be a major impediment to skeptics questioning their existence. Their main cause for concern was the fear of being accused of idolatry. For instance, Ibn Ḥazm (d. 1064) proclaimed: "The one who denies the existence of jinn or comes up with interpretations denying them a place in the external world is a disbelieving polytheist (*kāfir mushrik*), whose blood and wealth can be lawfully claimed (*ḥalāl al-dam wal-māl*)."[34] Ibn Ḥazm's stand was based on the fact that the Islamic normative tradition affirms the existence of jinn. To question their existence would thus mean challenging the authority of the Qur'an and *sunnah*. Throughout the centuries, few skeptics had the courage to do so. As a result, as early as the seventh century AD, jinn became an integral part of the Islamic worldview.[35]

The natural habitat, social structures, and anatomy of the jinn folk have been discussed within a great variety of scientific disciplines. From the Balkan Peninsula to Zanzibar and Indonesia, theologians, jurisprudents (*fuqahā'*), historians, philosophers, and zoologists have contributed to jinn studies. As of the nineteenth century, jinn were diligently studied with regard to folk medicine and popular religion. Zwemer, Meier, and Hadromi-Allouche subsequently expanded these studies by examining how jinn were described in Islamic orthodoxy and in classical literature. However, al-Zain dismissed most studies on the topic as unsophisticated and naïve, describing one of them as "simply quotation upon quotation of Qur'anic verses and prophetic tradition, hadith that mention jinn and demons without any interpretation or analysis whatsoever."[36] Contemporary Arab and Muslim studies, al-Zain maintained, expand on works of their predecessors—but rarely innovate.[37] Nevertheless, the Islamic normative tradition also served as the foundation of al-Zain's works on jinn. This was unavoidable in the light of the fact that the Qur'an and *sunnah* are the primary sources in Islamic studies—to the point where some scholars argued that it would be improper to ponder about jinn beyond what Allah and His Messenger have informed us of them.[38] Medieval and early modern works on jinnealogy[39] thus rarely ventured beyond the Islamic normative tradition. Contemporary scholarly inquiries are often hindered by a general discomfort of researchers when dealing with the topic. "Jinn are perceived by Westerners as both slippery and pagan or superstitious," Badeen and Krawietz observed.[40] *Kitāb 'ākām al-marjān*, the earliest surviving work on jinnealogy by Badr al-Dīn al-Shiblī (d. 1367), thus was dismissed by Zwemer as "a door to a world of grovelling superstition and demonolatry."[41] In contrast, Nawfal noted, Muslim scholars find jinn fascinating but repugnant. Nawfal believed this is to be attributed to the fact that humans associate jinn with hell, suffering, and torment.[42] The fact that classical works on jinnealogy are yet to be tracked down, cataloged, and placed in context was identified by Schöller as the main reason for the general lack of progress in jinn studies.[43] Whereas jinn have received little scholarly attention, they play a fairly important role in the daily lives of Muslims. Padwick, however, noted that people still tend to speak of jinn by allusions so as not to draw their attention.[44] It was always easier to ignore jinn than to tackle them directly.

1.3. Jinn Narratives and the Scope of the Present Study

This book was originally envisioned as an in-depth study of the widespread notions of jinn in Muslim cultures and societies. However, all too soon it became clear that no book could provide a comprehensive overview of jinn narratives. The sheer volume of written sources makes this task impossible.[45] We therefore decided to limit our research to jinn doppelgangers (*qarīn*, pl. *quranāʾ*). "Among all the superstitions in Islam, there is none more curious in its origin and character than the belief in the *Qarin* or *Qarina*," reads the opening sentence of Zwemer's research paper "The Familiar Spirit or Qarina."[46] Zwemer's pioneering research on jinn doppelgangers begins with a cursory overview of the relevant hadith and ayahs. This was intended as a general introduction for his study on Egyptian folklore. Zwemer published his findings in 1919. A handful of studies have been published on the topic since, with each of them focusing on oral traditions.[47] Having compared the notions of jinn in oral and written traditions, Nünlist concluded that no separate demonology evolved in folk religion.[48] Whereas this is the case with most subspecies of jinn, Nünlist's observation is factually incorrect with regard to *quranāʾ*.

In the Islamic normative tradition and in writings of the elite, a *qarīn* was generally understood to be a jinni companion and a doppelganger of human beings. Each qarīn was thought to be conceived at the same time as its human. When a child is born, a qarīn enters its heart, "the way air fills an empty bowl."[49] A qarīn will whisper to the child from then on, tempting it to indulge in its passions and to follow its whims. But if a human—in spite of the qarīn's efforts—proves to be pious, honorable, and just, their qarīn will convert to Islam and guide them through the mysteries of life. An evil jinni thus becomes the follower of a noble imam. Possible antecedents and origins of these beliefs are a matter of debate among scholars. For instance, Fahd, Hoyland, Nasser, Basharin, and Gallorini maintained that the belief in doppelgangers was widespread in pre-Islamic Arabia. Gallorini furthermore argued that the pre-Islamic legends of quranāʾ have served as a direct inspiration for the Islamic notions of angels and jinn.[50] In contrast, van Vloten surmised that the belief in quranāʾ postdates the rise of Islam. Van Vloten believed that the Prophet came up with the stories of wicked doppelgangers as a part of his efforts to curb the social influence of seers.[51] Seers and poets of old Arabia have been suspected of keeping close and friendly relations with the jinn folk. Zādih (d. 1495) noted that "divination is the way human souls communicate with the souls of jinn."[52] The Prophet argued it would be pointless to honor a seer for the accuracy of their predictions since they rely on jinn for help: "Every word they say which happens to be true is what a jinni stealthily snatched [from heavens] and poured into the ears of his friend. A seer then mixes that word with one hundred lies" (*Ṣaḥīḥ al-Bukhārī* #7561). It is, however, doubtful whether the ethereal companions of Bedouin seers can be universally identified with quranāʾ. For instance, Wellhausen argued that, before the onset of Islam, the common people were not generally presumed to have a jinni companion. It was only through subsequent generalizations that people were led to believe that each person has a qarīn of their own.[53] Zwemer's work on doppelgangers proposed two alternative theories explaining the origins of the notions of qarīn in writings of the elite. His first theory argued that the belief in quranāʾ was inspired by the animistic religions of pre-Islamic Arabia and Egypt.[54] This theory was likely based on Smith's disputed work on the Bedouin animistic cults. Since jinn prefer to disclose themselves in animal form, Smith argued that the jinn folk can be identified as an animal species, each of which was worshipped by a certain tribe. For instance, quranāʾ were known for their tendency to appear in the form of a black dog.[55] Henninger and Westermarck later demonstrated that Smith's theory is inconclusive. As a result, Zwemer's first theory received little scholarly attention.[56] His second theory had a greater impact in the field. This theory argued that the antecedents of the belief in quranāʾ can be found in *Pert Em Heru, The Egyptian Book of the Dead*, and in the ancient Egyptian belief in *ka* doubles.

On the authority of Budge, Zwemer identified *ka* as "an abstract individuality or personality [of a man, which is] endowed with all his characteristic attributes."[57] Among the prominent supporters of this theory were Hornblower, Blackman, Ridgeway, and al-Shamy. These four scholars argued that the belief in *ka* doubles still exists in Egypt as a variant of the belief in quranāʾ. Al-Shamy linked the Islamic concept of a qarīn being born at the same time as its human to the ancient Egyptian reliefs depicting the god Khnum modeling a royal child and its *ka* simultaneously, so that the two could be born together.[58] Al-Safi's field research offered further evidence that *ka* and qarīn are indistinguishable in folk religion.[59] However, this cannot be taken as a definitive proof that the prophet Muhammad was familiar with the ancient Egyptian religion. For, as Meier pointed out, comparable beliefs in companion spirits can also be found in Mazdeism, Manicheism, and in the works of Plato, Plutarch, and Virgil, each of whom might have been an (in)direct source of inspiration for the Prophet.[60] Whereas the existence of jinn was almost universally acknowledged in Islamic culture, the belief in doppelgangers met with firmer opposition. For instance, al-Suyūṭī (d. 1505) argued it would be impossible for a jinni to enter the human heart. His reasoning was based on the fact that the spiritual substances jinn are made of cannot be mixed with coarse human bodies:

> Physicians maintain that nothing can enter a human being, by which is meant all the inhabitants of the earth. He replied: "That is a mere babble, for the Prophet has said: 'Verily the Devil runs within a human being just as his blood runs within him.' " But I, the author of this work, maintain that the bodies of jinns are subtle bodies and that it is impossible for the humors of jinns to mix with human souls in the manner that blood and phlegm mix in human bodies with all their impurities.[61]

Here it ought to be taken into consideration that al-Suyūṭī did not doubt the existence of jinn. This is evident form his *Laqṭ al-marjān fī ʾaḥkām al-jānn,* which was envisioned as a comprehensive study on the jinn folk. Al-Suyūṭī's skepticism was only reserved for quranāʾ. Somehow, al-Suyūṭī found it easier to study (and oppose) monsters lurking at the frontiers of society than to face the devil within the human heart. Most scholars, however, relied on the authority of hadith to affirm the existence of quranā'. For instance, a sound hadith informs us that the Prophet taught that each of his followers "has a qarīn from among the jinn."[62] Another well-cited hadith reads: "the Devil runs in the blood-stream of Adam's descendants" (*Ṣaḥīḥ Muslim* #1188). The Qur'anic revelation also contains several references to quranā', e.g. that God will assign evil companions (quranā') to those who are forgetful of their Lord (Q 41:25, 43:36). *"I had a companion (*qarīn*) on the Earth,"* says one of the inhabitants of the paradise in the surah *aṣ-Ṣāffāt*, *"who used to say: 'Are you one of those who believe that we will be brought to judgement after we die and become dust and bones?' God will then ask if you'd care to see [his fate]—and lo and behold, one will see his* qarīn *in the midst of hellfire and say: 'By God, you almost had me ruined!'"* (Q 37:51–56). Another ayah, however, implies that each person's qarīn will testify against them on the Judgment Day (Q 50:27). Surah *an-Nisā'* explicitly identifies quranā' as evil spirits: *He who takes a devil as his companion (*qarīnan*)—what an evil companion he has!* (Q 4:38). The belief in quranā' appears to have been widespread in the Arab Middle East as late as the twentieth century. Conducted in 1924, Padwick's field research indicates no jinn were as feared among the common folk as quranā'.[63] Nevertheless, jinn doppelgangers remain among the least studied subspecies of jinn. This is especially the case when written traditions are concerned.

Oral traditions have received more scholarly attention. Evil doppelgangers of the Islamic normative tradition were gradually transformed in folk imagination into the demoness Qarīna: succubus, seductress, and murderer of pregnant women and children. Whereas each doppelganger was thought to be conceived at the same time as its human, Palestinians believe that Qarīna is as old as the world. Canaan thought that the belief in Qarīna among the common folk was inspired by the tales of Lilith, the first wife of Adam. Like Lilith, Qarīna has been accused of causing miscarriages. She thus was known as the Puerperal Demoness.[64] Her other names are 'Umm al-Ṣibyān and Tābiʿa.[65] Folktales typically describe Qarīna as an old woman, gray of hair, with fiery eyes and merged eyebrows. She would sometimes appear as a dark woman cradling a human figure in her arms.[66] When disclosing herself in animal form, Qarīna often resembles a cow (figure 1.1).

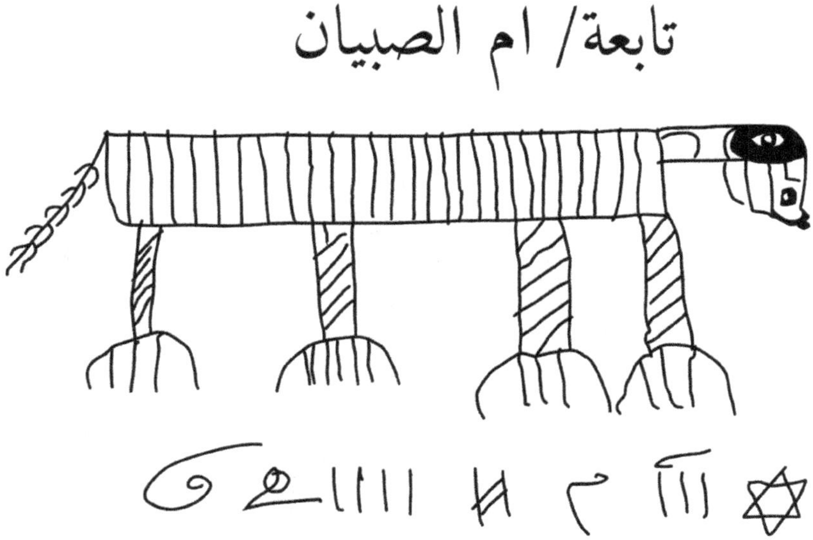

Figure 1.1. The animal form of the demoness Tābiʿa/ʾUmm al-Ṣibyān. Drawing by the author based on ʾAbū Jāmūs, al-Qurʿah al-kubrā (MS USJ 00277), ff. 38.

This is not to say that Qarīna was incapable of assuming a beautiful form when it suited her. Albeit evil, this demoness would sometimes fall in love with humans. She would then appear to her lovers as a beautiful woman. But if a man were to reject her advances, Qarīna would make him sterile. In Iraqi folklore, some men were even rumored to have been married to Qarīna. Strange dreams and nocturnal emissions were often attributed to the encounters with their demonic spouse.[67] It is doubtful whether Qarīna can be identified as a jinni: folk tales are inconclusive in this regard. Even so, the natural habitat and behavior of this demoness have little in common with jinn doppelgangers, as described in the Islamic normative tradition. The main difference between a qarīn and Qarīna is reflected in the fact that Qarīna's cruelty is not reserved for a single person. Jinn are disgusted with menstrual blood which seems to attract Qarīna—which is another major difference between a qarīn and Qarīna.[68] Garbage heaps, hearths, thresholds, and latrines were all said to be Qarīna's domain. In Egypt, there is belief that, past nightfall, Qarīna dwells in the body of a cat (figure 1.2). Zwemer noted that, for this reason, neither Copts nor Muslims would dare to beat or injure a cat after dark.[69]

In contrast, a qarīn lives only in the bloodstream of humans. With the notable exceptions of Syrian and Dagestani folklore, folk traditions have mostly substituted a qarīn for Qarīna.[70] Discrepancies between the oral and written tradition led Winkler to dismiss written

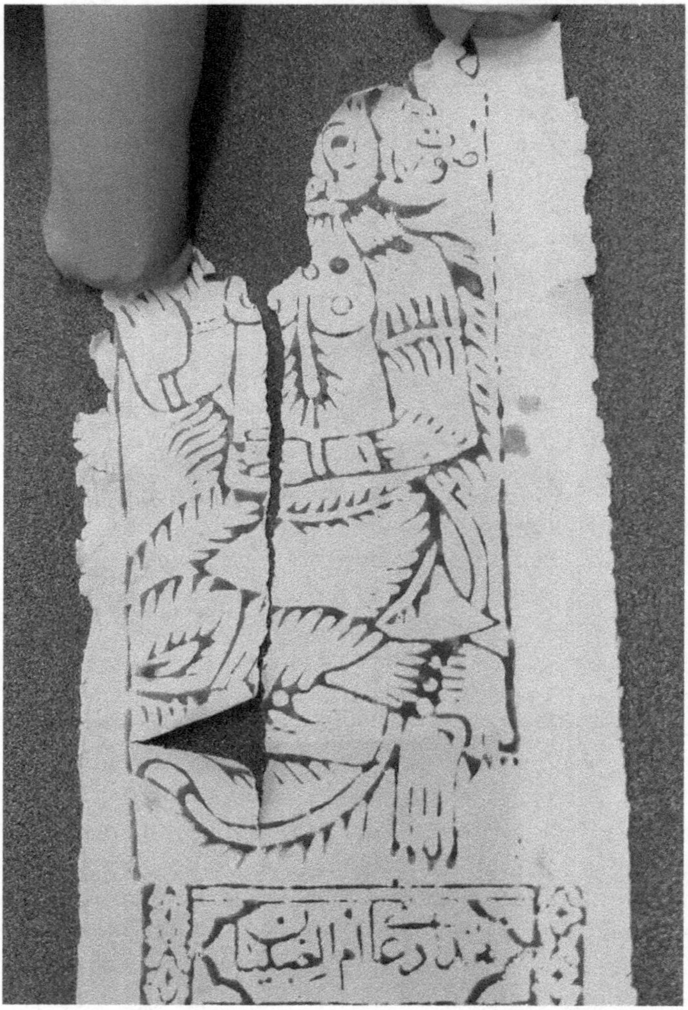

Figure 1.2. ʾUmm al-Ṣibyān assuming the form of a cat. *Source*: MS Or 506. David Eugene Smith Collection at RBML, Columbia. Used with permission.

sources on the topic as misinterpretations of the Qur'an. Winkler believed that the term qarīn in the Qur'an only meant to denote polytheists: mortal men who worshipped gods of old Arabia. He argued that all later-date accounts of jinn doppelgangers—including the *sunnah!*—can be rejected as "Yiddish," foreign elements imported from Babylonia.[71] In his otherwise detailed overview of folktales, customs, and the rituals performed to keep familiar spirits in check, Winkler deliberately ignored doppelgangers so that he could focus on the demoness. The present study adopts the opposite approach: we decided to give precedence to jinn doppelgangers, written traditions, and Ibn ʿArabī's works in particular.

The role of jinn in Ibn ʿArabī's teachings remains one of the least studied aspects of Akbarian Sufism until today. Although he was sympathetic to folk piety, Ibn ʿArabī adhered to the Islamic normative tradition in his writings. Hence, he identified qarīn as a devil (*shayṭān*) within the blood and hearts of humans.[72] Ibn ʿArabī wrote on jinn in substantial detail, documenting the character and behavior of this species. However, by his own admission, Ibn ʿArabī was less interested in amassing curious tales than in interpreting them.

> The story of ʿAmr al-Jinnī, God have mercy of him, is very famous. ʿAmr was killed by a whirlwind, he was seen in a whirlwind, he was scattered by it and left for dead. He died soon afterwards; only to be integrated as a worshipper among the jinn. If we were to write a book consisting of quoted reports and stories, we would have mentioned some of it—a glimpse perhaps! However, this book was intended for the understanding of meanings (*maʿāna*). You should look in literary histories and in poetry for jinn stories instead.[73]

Even though Ibn ʿArabī's works contain information on social structures, anatomy, and culture of the jinn folk, these were not his main research interests with regard to quranāʾ. Ibn ʿArabī's inquiries on doppelgangers mostly focused on the problem of evil, predestination, and the step-levels of spiritual elevation. These issues belong to the science of meanings (*ʿilm al-maʿāna*), which builds and expands on the Islamic normative tradition in search of the meanings of the Divine Names like *al-Mudhill*, the One Who Leads Astray. Jinn doppelgangers were seen as an embodiment of this Name in Akbarian Sufism.[74] The figure of an evil jinni tempter did not exist alone or in isolation in Ibn ʿArabī's writings. Throughout the centuries, whispers of quranāʾ have served as a common excuse for excessive behavior in Muslim cultures and societies. Jinn doppelgangers were regularly blamed for impure thoughts, dark impulses, and human sins in general. The reasoning behind these narratives was simple: assuming that doppelgangers are the true cause of the evil commited by humans would imply that humans are inherently good by nature. Human tendency for blame-shifting thus led to quranāʾ being used as scapegoats for personal shortcomings. Such was also the fate of other subspecies of jinn.

Seemingly uniform, jinn narratives are far from monolithic. With each of them being a product of its time and location, these narratives reflect the changing social, political, and cultural realities of Muslim societies. However, one could speak of a general tendency to use jinn as examples of immoral conduct. Natural habitat, taxonomy, and social structures of the jinn folk were of minor concern for *ʿulamāʾ*. Religious scholars mostly relied on jinn stories to highlight what constitutes a socially (un)acceptable behavior. Similar tendencies can also be observed in popular culture. Grisly descriptions of jinn sightings in folklore and literature were chiefly intended as a control mechanism, with their purpose being to deter deviances from social and religious norms. Contrasting the scholastic notions of moral evil, jinn attacks were not generally perceived as a form of Divine retribution in Muslim cultures and societies.[75] Jinn were, however, said to be attracted by human vanity, envy, lust, and avarice. As a result, jinn narratives emphasize the necessity of (1) upholding a proper moral conduct and (2) adhering to certain religious practices which, when properly executed, would presumably keep jinn at bay. Believers were advised to be chaste, dress modestly, and eat only with their right hand, for whoever eats with their left hand, the Devil eats with them.[76] "Jābir reported that the Prophet said: 'Do not visit women whose husbands are away from home, for the devil [i.e. qarīn] circulates in your blood.' We asked whether this applies to him as well and he said: 'To me as well, but God helped me against it and made me safe from harm.'" (*Mishkāt al-Maṣābīḥ* #3119).

By the late ninth and the early tenth century, jinn were strongly associated with sexual depravity, illicit magic, and idolatry. The fear of Otherness, anti-Semitism, and misogyny emerge as implicit biases in jinn narratives. For example, jinn were rumored to frequent synagogues, where they would inflict believers with a magnificent sense of self-importance and pride, causing them to be prone to loneliness and quick to anger.[77] Churches were also said to be their turf. From time to time, the church jinn would make Christians forget human speech and refuse all guidance.[78] However, their preferred method of corrupting believers was to rely on women. Capricious, vile, and vain, women were said to be close in nature to jinn. Like doppelgangers, women were closely associated with yearnings and corruption of the lower soul. They were thus seen as natural allies of the jinn who sought to orchestrate the demise of pious men.[79] Nevertheless, like Jews and Christians, jinn were allowed to hold properties in Muslims states and cities.[80] Jinn narratives can thus be read as meditations on the society's reception of its foreign Other. Whatever one's persona rejects in Islamic culture has been cast on quranāʾ. Apart from negative character traits, the fear of sickness, injuries, and forces of nature were also projected on jinn.[81] In folk narratives, jinn were typically described as mischief-makers and bogies. As such, they were also regularly blamed for damaged clothes, souring milk, and troubled marriages in general. These trends were satirized in *Epistles of the Brethren of Purity* (ar. *Rasāʾil ʾikhwān al-safā*), where jinn jurists challenge human beings to bring forward a single person who has seen a jinni committing such deeds. One of these jurists said to the jinn king Bīwarāsp the Wise:

> You must know, then, that there are good and bad jinn, both Muslims and unbelievers, some pure and some profligate, just as there are among humans. The better jinn show indescribable loyalty to their leaders and kings, far beyond anything known to mortals of Adamite race. They follow their kings as the stars in the heavens follow that greatest of luminaries, the Sun . . . . Another sign of how well the jinn obey their leaders is what certain humans have found in traversing waste and desert places: if one descends into a wadi where he

> fears bewitchment by the jinn, and he hears their cries and clamor all about, he has but to call on their leaders and kings for protection and recite a verse or a word from the Qur᾿an, the Torah, or the Gospels, seeking in it protection from them and from any harm or hindrance wrought by them, and they will not disturb him as long as he remains in that place. So well do the jinn obey their chiefs that if some rebel jinni troubles an Adamite with madness, terror, confusion, or panic, and a human enchanter calls for help from the leader of that jinni's tribe, or from their king or his forces, they throng and rally around, doing just as they are commanded and forbidden with that person.
>
> The nature and moral character of human beings are the opposite. Their obedience to their lords and monarchs is mostly hypocritical grasping for money, investments, prizes and rewards. Once they are denied what they've been looking for, they engage in open defiance and rebellion, they shed their outward allegiance and bring strife, war, bloodshed and destruction to the land. Their treatment of their prophets and apostles of their Lord is no different. They reject their calls, denying obvious truths and proofs, and demanding miracles of them out of sheer perversity . . . The vast majority of humans are rude and blind. Even worse, human beings aren't satisfied 'til they assert their claim, with no proof or argument whatsoever, that they are rulers and that all others are their slaves.[82]

For this reason, the jurists concluded, jinn fled the realms of men and ran into deserts and wastelands. But the children of Adam "sought them everywhere and tried to catch them with every magic trick, witchcraft and sorcery they knew."[83] Since the surah *Saba*ʿ hints that God granted Solomon the ability to control jinn (Q 34:12–13), attempts to emulate Solomon's feats have mostly met with mild reprovals. Instructions on how to summon and enslave jinn commonly appear in Sufi literature and occult manuals. Ibn ʿArabī rejected these and similar practices on the grounds that Solomon asked God to grant him the power that is befitting of him alone. God fulfilled his request by granting him the power over jinn. Although the prophet Muhammad was also said to have possessed this power, Ibn ʿArabī maintained that the Prophet refrained from using it out of respect for Solomon.[84] The less courteous among Ibn ʿArabī's students were, however, warned that jinn cannot help them with their spiritual endeavors. Since God had them confined to the world of gross matter, jinn have no knowledge of Him. Hence, Ibn ʿArabī argued that only the lowest of Seekers, with no other means at their disposal, would throw in their lot with jinn. In contrast, wise men avoid the company of these creatures. Were a jinni to approach a Seeker of its own volition, Ibn ʿArabī advised to ignore it.[85] However, there is one species of jinn whose company cannot be avoided: a qarīn, the Devil Within. Like any other jinni, a qarīn has no knowledge of the Divine. Nevertheless, a Seeker can (in)directly benefit from their doppelganger by studying it.

1.4. Jinn Studies—The Benefits of Knowledge

Jinn studies were not motivated by unbridled curiosity in the Akbarian school. As a general rule, the direct contact and interactions with jinn were condemned among Akbarians. The main reason behind their inquiries into quranāʾ was a sense of self-preservation, for there was a general understanding among Sufis that most doppelgangers will seek to harm a Seeker if they can. Ibn ʿArabī believed that ignorance, denial, and fear of the Unknown are the greatest weapons at their disposal. This is why a qarīn must be subdued with knowledge.[86] Today, it is generally assumed that the knowledge of doppelgangers falls under the scope of jinnealogy. Ibn ʿArabī, however, maintained that only the uninitiated adhere to classifications of sciences. In contrast, People of God (*ʾahl allah*) realize that all things are connected and cannot be studied apart from one another. Jinn studies are thus (also) concerned with knowledge of the Creator. This knowledge was identified by Ibn ʿArabī as the source of all felicity. He furthermore argued that God created the universe "only so that the universe might get to know Him."[87] Ibn ʿArabī taught that true and useful knowledge always points a way to God. Jinn studies are not an exception in this regard. Whereas most living beings have inherent knowledge of God, humans and jinn were created in a state of ignorance.[88] They were thus ordered to seek Him—with doppelgangers standing in their way. Jinn doppelgangers—and evil jinn in general—were commonly referred to in the Akbarian school and in the Islamic normative tradition as a veil (*ḥijāb*) between the Creator and the created. For instance, a sound hadith attests that flying jinn form a veil between God in heaven and humans. The same hadith reports that evil jinn hover in front of the eyes of humans, preventing them from witnessing marvels of heaven and earth. God-fearing jinn were also said to be their target.[89] Even so, Ibn ʿArabī argued that contemplating a veil (jinn) can teach the veiled (humans) about the One who veils (God). "Some creatures are veils over other creatures. Even though veils are signifiers, they are signifiers by way of undifferentiation for the cosmos. In other words, the whole existence is nothing but a veil, the veiled and the One who veils."[90]

Among other things, jinn doppelgangers signify that the knowledge of God is inexhaustible.[91] Each Seeker, no matter how advanced, will always find new issues to contemplate with regard to Him. The reason why He created quranāʾ is one such issue. Both Akbarians and the *ʿulamāʾ* assumed that God is omniscient, omnipresent, and omnipotent. Ibn ʿArabī furthermore claimed that God is first and foremost kind. But although it is in His power to end all suffering, He assigned evil jinn to torture humans and lead them to sin. However, the fact that innocents suffer does not mean that God is unjust—Ibn ʿArabī made this clear.[92] Seekers were, however, advised to verify Ibn ʿArabī's teachings for themselves, rather than taking his word for granted. In other words, one ought to study quranāʾ to verify that God is merciful and just. To achieve this feat, a Seeker must comprehend the meaning of the Divine Name *al-Mudhill* and come to terms with its embodiments. Apart from doppelgangers, evil humans, the lower soul, and Iblis the Devil were identified as the main embodiments of this Name.[93] They all exist because God wants them to exist. Ibn ʿArabī's reasoning as to why jinn were created also mirrors his attempts to expound on the problem of evil in Islam.

Not only did Ibn ʿArabī try to make sense of evil—but he also went on to show how humans, jinn, and even the Devil himself might be saved from it. No other Seeker, Ibn ʿArabī boasted, has ever managed to get to the heart of this matter before him.[94] We will examine Ibn ʿArabī's meditations on the problem of evil and the Divine Name *al-Mudhill* in Chapter 4. Awn, who studied the role of Iblis in Akbarian Sufism, however, questioned the necessity of studying individual Names. Awn argued that Ibn ʿArabī and his followers had but one goal in mind: to return to the One, where all is One. At this stage of spiritual development, heaven and hell, reward and punishment, and Iblis the Tempter "become empty concepts."[95] The perfect balance, unity, and knowledge of the Divine Names can only be achieved by the Perfect Human (*al-ʾinsān al-kāmil*). To reach this step-level, a Seeker must free themselves from effects and influences of individual Names. Among other things, this would mean dealing with their doppelganger—for whereas Iblis, women, and other embodiments of the Name *al-Mudhill* can be avoided, each person has a qarīn of their own. Although the taming of their qarīn is insufficient to transform a human into the Perfect Human, each Seeker must perform this feat. "For if there is anything of himself veiling a man from seeing the whole, he has committed a crime against himself and he is not the Perfect Human."[96]

In spite of the fact that Ibn ʿArabī's works contain instructions on how to summon a qarīn and deal with it directly, his recommended approach was to tame a doppelganger indirectly, through soul work. Sufi works often made no distinction between the act of taming a qarīn and the pacification of the lower soul (*al-nafs al-ʾammārah*). Both these processes were referred to among Sufis as the Red Death and/or the Greater Jihad (*al-jihād al-ʾakbar*). Although Ibn ʿArabī preferred the terms Jihad of the Soul (*jihād al-nafs*) and the Conquest of the City (*fatḥ al-madīna*) to *al-jihād al-ʾakbar*,[97] he was also among those who emphasized correspondences between human beings and the universe. In other words, he believed that each human is the world in small (*ʿālam ṣaghīr*): a perfect, abridged copy of the great world (*ʿālam kabīr*). All forms, realities, Names, and attributes of God were brought together and manifested in the human form.

> What is man? An all-embracing isthmus, the form of creatures and of God placed within him. He is a copy in synopsis whose content is the Essence of God and

> His ineffable Attributes. Connected to the subtleties of the World of Power, inclusive of the verities of the World of Dominion, His inward is drowned in the sea of Unity, his outward dry-lipped on the shore of separation. There is not one of the Attributes of God which is not manifest in his essence. He is knowing, hearing and seeing, speaking, willing, alive and powerful in the same way, of the realities of the Universe, everything is incorporated within him: Take the heavens or the elements, or take minerals, plants and animals; The form of good and bad are written within him, the behavior of a devil and beast are kneaded in him. If he was not the mirror of the Face of the Everlasting, why did the angels prostrate themselves to him? He is the reflection of the beauty of the Immaculate Presence. If Iblis cannot fathom this, so what?[98]

This is not to say that Ibn ʿArabī used jinn doppelgangers as an allegory of the abased human soul. Metaphorical interpretations of Islamic doctrines were seen among Akbarians as a sign of corrupt intelligence and a lack of knowledge in general.[99] Microcosm and macrocosm were rather thought to be analogous to one another. Hence, the same method can be used to tame both jinn and the soul, so that a human can be transformed into the Perfect Human. Whether one should seek this perfection was a matter of debate among Sufis. For instance, ʾAbū Ṭālib al-Makkī (d. 996) advised his student not to yearn for perfection lest they become as arrogant as the devil they are trying to subdue.[100] ʾAḥmad al-Ghazālī (d. 1126), however, noted: "Whoever does not learn of God's unity from a devil is an infidel."[101] Then there were scholars who argued that it is pointless to aspire to become the Perfect Human since each person's fate is predetermined. Whereas those who are marked for success will subdue their qarīn, those who are destined to fail will fall into hellfire. Such fatalism was strongly condemned by Ibn ʿArabī, for he maintained that if God did not intend for a human being to reach perfection, that person would not yearn for it either.[102] Ibn ʿArabī believed that the transformation of a human into the Perfect Human occurs as a Seeker advances in knowledge. In the ideal case, a Seeker will advance in jinn studies by the means of a divine revelation. However, as no Seeker can dictate the content of a revelation they receive, al-Ghazālī advised consulting saints and prophets on the problem of evil, the meanings (*ma ʿnā*) of jinn, and the reason why jinn hate humans.[103] This is the theoretical approach of a religious scholar. In contrast, magicians relied on practical manuals when attempting to seal their doppelgangers. Ibn ʿArabī took the middle course: he argued that a qarīn cannot be exorcised, sealed, nor subdued with theoretical knowledge. Instead, one must follow the example of the Prophet and convert their qarīn to Islam.[104] That way, a doppelganger can also enter the heavenly gardens. Saving a creature which is set on destroying a Seeker was not entirely motivated by compassion in Akbarian Sufism. Self-interest and a sense of self-preservation also played a role in the process, not in the least since Ibn ʿArabī taught that one can only save their qarīn by saving themselves. To do so, one must combine spiritual work with knowledge.

The knowledge and practice of Sufism were compared by Ali to the wings of a bird. To ascend, a Seeker must make use of both.[105] Knowing there is an evil spirit in their blood is not sufficient to protect a Seeker from the machinations of their doppelganger. Each Seeker must convert their doppelganger to Islam to prevent it from causing harm. Barring a direct intervention from God, knowledge on how jinn think and act, as well as familiarity with their strengths and weaknesses, are prerequisites for the success of the procedure. In other words, a Seeker must use their knowledge of jinn to avoid a qarīn's traps and transform their doppelganger into something harmless—and enlightened. The first three chapters of the present study deal with theoretical knowledge. Ibn ʿArabī, who was more interested in spiritual practices, advised his students to seek theoretical knowledge of jinn in poetry and literature. Whereas Ibn ʿArabī presumed his students were already familiar with the stories he was referring to, this is not the case with a twenty-first century reader. The scattered reports on jinn, their culture and society in poetry and literature, largely remain *terra incognita* even in academic circles—and the information on doppelgangers in particular is not readily available to Arabic and non-Arabic speakers. We will therefore need to retell the old stories before supplying them with Ibn ʿArabī's interpretations. Although we originally planned to follow Ibn ʿArabī's advice, we ultimately decided against limiting our research to literary histories. Medieval, early modern, and contemporary works of religious scholars, philosophers, zoologists, and historians who were writing on jinn were thus also among our sources.

Contemporary academic studies on doppelgangers proved to be scarce. To the best of our knowledge, there are only five other works on the topic: Zwemer's "The Familiar Spirit or Qarina" (1919), Blackman's "The Karīn and Karīneh" (1926), Winkler's book *Salomo und die Ḳarīna* (1931), Parman's essay "The Demon as Human Double" (2004), and Perdigon's "Bleeding Dreams" (2015). Each of the aforementioned studies focuses on oral traditions.[106] In contrast, the present study centers around the surviving works of Ibn ʿArabī. Anthropological and ethnographic studies on popular religion and the demoness Qarīna were of minor importance to our research. We were, however, aiming to supplement Ibn ʿArabī's writings on doppelgangers with contrasting views of other cultural and religious figures. Akbarians, Hanbalis, Ashʿarites, and the Shia thinkers we cited did not always agree with one another when interpreting Qur'anic verses and the relevant *hadith* on doppelgangers. The present study does not venture a judgment on the legitimacy of divergent schools of Islam, nor does it aim to present Ibn ʿArabī's teachings as the only legitimate worldview in Muslim cultures and societies. We were rather aiming to document the richness and diversity of jinn narratives, with the intention of placing Ibn ʿArabī's works in context, as well as laying the foundations for future research in the field.

Even though there are numerous reports of quranāʾ in poetry and literature, few scholars have attempted to clarify what are jinn and jinn doppelgangers in particular. Hence, one of our main tasks will be to pinpoint the definition of doppelgangers and to determine how they differ from angels, humans, animals, and other subspecies of jinn. This will serve as a foundation for an in-depth analysis of the role of quranāʾ in Akbarian Sufism. Akbarians typically divided reality into three great books: Qur'an, the World, and a Human. The chapter-structure of the present study was inspired by this division. We already discussed how doppelgangers were described in the Qur'an in this chapter (Chapter 1 "Neither of the East, nor of the West"). Chapter 2, "Signs on the Horizons," pivots on the macrocosmic dimension of evil. In other words, this chapter will examine jinn doppelgangers as one of the six species in the universe. Chapter 2 begins with an attempt to pinpoint Ibn

ʿArabī's definition of jinn (§2.1). The following subchapters will focus on the character traits and anatomy (§2.2), origins (§2.3), taxonomy (§2.4), and culture (§2.6) of the jinn folk and jinn doppelgangers in particular. The second chapter of the present study will furthermore seek to demonstrate how a qarīn differs from jinn companions, guardian spirits, and other subspecies of jinn (§2.5). The Brethren of Purity, however, argued it would be impossible to conduct research on spiritual beings without the knowledge of the soul. Ibn ʿArabī also adopted this approach when jinn are concerned. Microcosmic and macrocosmic perspective were not in opposition in his works. Thus, he concurrently identified jinn as spiritual beings and the invisible part of human minds and bodies.[107] To study a doppelganger is to study the soul and vice versa. Ibn ʿArabī's reasoning was based on the fact that the Creator promised He will provide believers with *signs on the horizons and within themselves until it becomes clear to them what is true* (Q 41:53).

Whereas Chapter 2 pivots on signs on the horizons, Chapter 3, "The Devil Within," will focus on the microcosmic dimension of evil. These complementary chapters deal with theoretical knowledge and the twofold notion of jinn in Akbarian Sufism. In contrast, Chapter 4, "The Red Death," examines the spiritual practices which were used to subdue quranāʾ. The fourth chapter of the present study builds and expands on the first three chapters, like spiritual practices build on theoretical knowledge. It should, however, be noted that, throughout the centuries, not a few Sufis advocated the opposite approach to theoretical knowledge, spiritual practices, and jinn. Such was the case of al-Ghazālī, who compared jinn studies to a man pondering what is the form, color, and length of a snake crawling all over him. Al-Ghazālī noted it would be better for that man to simply hurl the snake away and be done with it.[108] However, not all snakes can be avoided, chased away, or killed. A qarīn is one such snake, which thrives on evil in the human heart. In *Mathnawī*, Rūmī's devil thus warns Muʿāwiya that he won't be able to avoid evil until he understands the roots of evil. Iblis can only tempt—but the true danger lies within the human heart.[109] Whereas classical works on jinnealogy have sought out the monsters lurking at the frontiers of society, the present study is dedicated to the Devil Within.

Chapter 2

Signs on the Horizons

> God gave all He has to a man only as a bridge to pass over. Blessed is he who passes this bridge in safety.
>
> —Ibn ʿArabī[1]

Defining the nature of invisible jinn has long posed a problem for researchers. It is, however, necessary to determine what jinn are before establishing a definition of quranāʾ. One cannot define jinn doppelgangers without a working definition of jinn—for the taxonomic category of subspecies ranks below that of a species. Besides, most things that can be said about quranāʾ also apply to jinn in general. In spite of the fact that morphological and behavioral variations between jinn subspecies are minor, the devil is in the details. In other words, pinpointing the details which set quranāʾ apart from other subspecies of jinn will help us form a clear notion of the Devil Within. A working definition of quranāʾ is the prerequisite for any sort of inquiries into their culture, social structures, and behavior. That being said, it should be noted that the present study does not aim to establish the universally applicable definition of quranāʾ. For, as Ibn ʿArabī proudly pointed out, Sufis ascribe different meaning to well-established terms.[2] Our definition of quranāʾ is based on the surviving works of Ibn ʿArabī. Albeit delimited, this definition will bring us one step closer to understanding the role of doppelgangers in Akbarian Sufism.

2.1. Etymology of the Unseen

Jinn were typically described as mischievous, solitary creatures which do not encourage contact and curiosity. Nevertheless, the link between human society and the world of demons was recognized by Lory as one of the central tenets of esoteric knowledge in Islam. Lory also noted that the demons in question are commonly referred to as jinn.[3] The tendency to substitute the word *jinn* with *demons* is not uncommon among scholars. This creates a false sense of familiarity with the notion of jinn in classical Islam. Montgomery, however, noted that a feeling of familiarity and the seduction of recognition are the "Scylla and Charybdis of any journey into the past."[4] Whereas jinn were commonly referred to as devils (*shayāṭīn*) in writings of the elite, throughout the centuries, the word *jinn* has also served to denote polytheistic deities, angels, fire spirits, fairies, animals, spirits of nature, living humans, and souls of the departed. Ibn ʿArabī claimed that similar tendencies can also be observed in the Qur'an. For example, he pointed out that the word *jinn* was used in the surah *al-Dhāriyāt* for concealed beings in general—irrespective of whether they are satanic in nature or not.[5] This is not entirely surprising, for the Arabic root *j-n-n* conveys the meaning of being veiled, hidden in darkness, and unseen. A jinni hides itself from the world, Ibn Manẓūr (d. 1311) explained—and thus its name.[6]

Medieval lexicographers associated the word *jinn* with all that is mysterious and unseen: *al-janān*, "the heart hidden by the chest,"[7] the gardens of Eden (*janna*), and the darkness of the night. The Arabic language, Ibn Fāris (d. 969) noted, bears witness to how the invisible realm invades the main aspects of life. Each time the letters *jīm* and *nūn* are brought together in Arabic, as in jinn, they hint at hidden, unseen things. Ibn Fāris taught that paradise is referred to as *janna* since it is hidden from sight—and that a fetus in the womb is called *janīn* because we cannot see it.[8] Lawrence surmised that jinn were named after paradise (*janna* → *jinn*), since they are closer in nature to heaven than to Earth. A similar theory can be found in al-Ṭabarī's *History*, where he argued that the name "jinn" implies that these creatures have served as guardians of paradise (*khazana al-janna*).[9] Whereas most scholars agreed that the word *jinn* is of Arabic origin, several other possibilities were proposed. For instance, MacDonald surmised this word was incorporated into the Arabic language from the Latin *genius* (pl. *genii*).[10] Waardenburg, however, argued that the Arabic *jinn* was derived from the Aramaic word *ganya*. According to Waardenburg, this word originally served to denote pagan gods degraded to demons.[11] In contrast, Inayat Khan traced the origins of the word *jinn* back to the Sanskrit word *jñāna*, which stands for wisdom and "the realm of the muse and the source of poetry and music, where thought is unhindered in its movement and existence."[12] Inayat Khan consequently identified jinn as "the beings of knowledge, whose hunger is for knowledge, whose joy is in learning, in understanding, and whose work is in inspiring and bringing joy and light to others."[13]

The invisible nature of the jinn folk often served as the main criterion for distinguishing between humans and jinn. For whereas humans are visible, Ali argued that any invisible, hidden force or spirit can be identified as a jinni.[14] On his side, Sells defined jinn as "semi-spirits."[15] Carboni, however, believed that jinn are half-humans, half-animals.[16] Expanding the definition of jinn to include animals was not uncommon among medieval scholars either. For instance, Avicenna (d. 1037) defined jinn as "airy animals capable of changing themselves into different forms."[17] In light of the fact that jinn tend to disclose themselves in animal form, Wellhausen maintained that Islamic zoology cannot be distinguished from demonology. This opinion was also shared by Smith.[18] As the lines between jinn and animals were blurred, jinn were often discussed as a part of Afro-Eurasian fauna. Notable zoological compendiums by al-Damīrī (d. 1405) and al-Jāḥiẓ also contain entries on jinn. As a result, jinn still tend to be perceived as cryptids: the unrecognized animal species made of smoke and fire.[19] These and similar vague definitions of invisible beings were strongly condemned by Ibn Barrajān (d. 1144). It is not by coincidence, Ibn Barrajān maintained, that the surah *al-Jinn* describes God as *the Knower of the Unseen, who does not disclose to just anyone what is the Unseen* (Qur'an 72:26–27). Ibn Barrajān taught that the mutually inconsistent, imprecise definitions of invisible beings cannot be taken as a proof that all things are relative with regard to the Unseen. Such definitions only serve to demonstrate one's general lack of knowledge on the matter: "The Unseen is relative to some, but not others—like angels and their knowledge are unseen to us, but they are not invisible to themselves. Such is also the case with jinn. Everything that is hidden from our witnessing and our knowledge is the Unseen with regard to us."[20]

Ibn ʿArabī's knowledge of the Unseen was based on the Islamic normative tradition and the Divine inspirations, revelations, and unveilings he received. On the authority of the Qur'an, he acknowledged that the word *jinn* can be used for all spiritual beings. On the authority of the Divine revelations, he consequently identified jinn as one of the six species of the universe. Members of this species were thought to be different in nature than minerals, plants, animals, angels, and humans.[21] This is to be attributed to the fact that all jinn share a distinct anatomy and a single common ancestor. The following subchapter will examine the creation of jinn and the impact of jinn's anatomy on their character and behavior (§2.2). We will then attempt to uncover the identity of the forefather of doppelgangers (§2.3).

2.2. Anatomy of the Unseen

Ibn ʿArabī taught that the first jinni was created sixty thousand years before God made Adam of clay. He furthermore noted that most people presume this jinni was named Ḥārith, the Great Lion.[22] Some scholars, however, argued that the first jinni's name was Jānn, Mārij, Sūmiyyā, ʿAzāzīl, and/or Mahadeva. More pious than angels, the first jinni lived as a mountain hermit. Later on, this jinni became the Divine treasurer and one of the bearers of His throne. For 3,024,000 years, descendants of the first jinni ruled over the Earth. The Chishti Order of South Asia believed that the reign of jinn on Earth corresponds to Satya Yuga and Treta Yuga, which are the first two world ages in Hinduism. As the third age began, jinn slowly turned away from God. Nevertheless, they thought themselves more pious and better than humans.[23] Ibn ʿArabī, like the Brethren of Purity, believed that the act of genesis is the process of continuous refinement which culminated with the creation of mankind. Jinn were eventually forced to hand over the riches of Earth to Adam's descendants, as Adam was made in God's form.[24] Whereas al-Ghazālī taught that the true cause of enmity between human beings and jinn belongs to the realm of revelations, other scholars maintained that the first jinni's refusal to prostrate themselves before Adam was their declaration of war against humans.[25] On his side, Ibn ʿArabī believed that Ḥārith's jealousy was the initial cause of the conflict. Having seen how God made Adam in His form, Ḥārith's face twisted with loathing, and he refused to kneel before the human.[26] "Don't be misled by his piety!" noted al-Diyārbakrī (d. 1574) on the forefather of all jinn. "Evil lurks behind every pious deed."[27]

Al-Diyārbakrī was convinced that the first jinni in existence was the one who declined to bow before Adam. Ibn ʿArabī opposed this theory. He also denied that the first jinni was named Ḥārith. Ibn ʿArabī, however, admitted that "Ḥārith" was the name of the arrogant jinni who refused to prostrate himself before Adam. He believed that Ḥārith was the first jinni to turn evil, like Cain was the first sinner among humans. However, neither Cain nor Ḥārith were the first of their race.[28] Elsewhere, Ibn ʿArabī recorded that the first sinner was named Iblis. The latter name can also be found in the Qur'an. The surah *al-ʾAʿrāf* reads: *We ordered angels to prostrate before Adam. They all prostrated except for Iblis, who was not among them. God asked Iblis: "What prevented you from prostrating when I commanded you to do so?." Iblis said: "I am better than him. You created me from fire and he was created from clay."* (Q 7:11–12). The quoted ayahs from the surah *al-ʾAʿrāf* have led to speculations whether Iblis/Ḥārith is an angel or a jinni. On his side, Ibn ʿArabī argued that the fiftieth ayah of the surah *al-Kahf* (*except for Iblis, who was one of the jinn* (Q 18:50)) resolves the dilemma.[29] Iblis merely happened to grow up among angels after he was captured in a war between angels and jinn. Having spent a long time among angels, Iblis became one of their leaders. Whereas Teuma's research indicates that this was the predominant view among *ʿulamāʾ*,[30] there were also those who argued that jinn are a tribe of angels. Among the prominent supporters of this theory were the Prophet's companions Ibn Masʿud (d. 653) and Ibn ʿAbbās (d. 687), Ḥasan al-Baṣrī (d. 728), al-Ṭabarī (d. 923), al-Damīrī, and ʿAbd al-Karīm al-Jīlī (d. 1424).[31] Ibn ʿArabī, however, maintained that jinn differ from angels in character, anatomy, and behavior.

> Let it be known that jinn are strong spirits, that they are at the same time subtle and corporeal bodies. They are under the dominion of the essences of fire. We [i.e. humans] are under the dominion of earth and water. The elements of earth and water are heavy elements because of the strength of their spirits and the subtleness of the essences of their bodies. God gave jinn the power

> to appear in different forms and like the quick actions of angels, jinn are capable of actions transcending the abilities of humans. Only this much is different—that the spirits of the jinn are lower spirits and the angels are heavenly spirits.[32]

The main difference between the heavenly spirits and jinn is that the latter need food to survive. Jinn diet, according to the Islamic normative tradition, consists of rice, dung, bones, and leftovers from any human meal that was eaten without uttering a praise to God. A qarīn, however, feeds on evil deeds of humans. In the early modern period, the *ʿulamāʾ* began to speculate whether jinn are capable of consuming the souls of living beings.[33] Ibn ʿArabī, however, believed that the favorite foods of jinn are meat and bones. He was also informed by another Sufi, who learned of it by the means of Divine revelation, that jinn do not eat the actual human leftovers. They rather gather around the food and feast on its smell. This is sufficient to keep a jinni satiated. "One of the People of Revelation told me he saw the jinn approaching a bone, sniffing it like predators. Then they returned to whence they came from, having taken their daily sustenance. Their nourishment was from that sniffing."[34]

Citing Aisha, the favorite wife of the prophet Muhammad, Ibn ʿArabī pointed out another difference between angels and jinn. Aisha recalled to have heard the Prophet say that angels were made of light. In contrast, the first jinni was created from smokeless fire.[35] The Qur'an also contains the verses describing how God made jinn from smokeless fire (Q 55:15) and/or flames of a scorching desert wind (Q 15:27). Even though he was well aware of the references concerning the creation and anatomy of jinn from the Qur'an, Ibn ʿArabī also proposed a third possibility, suggesting that jinn were actually crated from the admixture of fire, water, air, and earth. Hence, the word *mārij* was used as a synonym for jinn.[36] Jinn bodies were sometimes referred to as *jasad* in Ibn ʿArabī's works. A *jasad* was understood to be an intangible form of existence—as opposed to the corporeal body of human beings (*jism*).[37] Intangible forms of existence are not restricted by accidental properties. Hence, whereas a human being would need to travel for 14,000 years to traverse the seven heavens, a jinni could reach the heavenly Throne in a matter of moments.[38] Having set out to create the first jinni, God mixed air with fire, heating the air "till it started burning like a lamp," reads

Chapter 9 of *al-Futūḥāt*.[39] However, in the second chapter of *al-Futūḥāt*, Ibn ʿArabī recorded that jinn were created as the Divine spirit mixed with whirlwinds.[40] Since a creature made of fire could never breathe on its own, God added water/humidity to the mixture—and thus He created jinn bodies. The most detailed description of how jinn were created was preserved in Ibn ʿArabī's *K. ʿAnqāʾ mughrib*. This work also contains Ibn ʿArabī's remarks concerning the role of earth in the creation of jinn bodies.

> When the Muhammadan Light shined towards the Earth, its lowlands and highlands were torn asunder and heat was generated between them. This heat then assumed a distinct form in plants. At that moment, a spark flashed from the heat. Through that spark, jinn were brought into existence in two classes: one class exalted and one class debased. This was due to the fact that the aforementioned heat was a product of the Muhammadan Light and the Earth. This is why Allah, the Exalted One, declared: "He created jinn from the mixture (*mārij*) of fire"—i.e. from the mixture of earth and light. Jinn in whom the light predominates are those who adhere to the Divine Light, whereas those in whom earth predominates are attached to perdition (*al-bawār*). This is due to the fact that the subtle rays descend upon those who are by nature disposed to be an infidel in the channels (*anābīb*) of that Satanic Fire—albeit their origin is from the Sovereign Light (*al-nūr al-sulṭānī*).[41]

Exalted and debased jinn were sometimes referred to in Ibn ʿArabī's works as the Jinn of Light and the Jinn of Fire. Jinn doppelgangers—and debased jinn in general—were also described as "devils" (*shayāṭīn*). Today, it is generally assumed that the word *shayṭān* was incorporated into the Arabic language from Geez. In contrast, medieval Arab philologists linked this word to the Arabic root *sh-y-ṭ* ("burning with anger") or *sh-ṭ-n* ("to be remote").[42] The quoted excerpt from Ibn ʿArabī's *K. ʿAnqāʾ mughrib* suggests that a jinni is bound for perdition if earth is the predominant element of its body. In contrast, *al-Futūḥāt al-Makkiyya*, Ibn ʿArabī's magnum opus, attests that earth *should* be the predominant element since devils become humbler when earth subdues the fire of their bodies.[43] Notwithstanding the fact that *K. ʿAnqāʾ mughrib* emphasized differences between the physiognomies of exalted and debased jinn, Ibn ʿArabī did not presume that devils are a subspecies of jinn. Each jinni—whether a ghoul, ifrit, or a qarīn—can be referred to as "devil" if it is arrogant and if it distances itself from God. In short, Ibn ʿArabī taught that a *shayṭān* is an infidel from among the jinn.[44] Even though the definite article (*al-*) is frequently used in the Arabic language, it is sometimes difficult to determine whether Ibn ʿArabī was referring to a common devil (i.e. a qarīn), the lower soul, or Iblis the Devil. The main embodiments of the Divine Name *al-Mudhill* were all referred to as "the Devil" (*al-shayṭān*) in Sufi literature.

A jinni's name can sometimes serve as an indicator whether a text is referring to a qarīn or Iblis. For example, whereas the prophet Muhammad was accompanied by a jinni named al-Rayy, Najm al-Dīn Kubrā (d. 1221) had a qarīn whose name was Qanṭarūn. Kubrā also recorded that one of his acquaintances was followed by a qarīn named Istaftīn. The second time Kubrā encountered his doppelganger, the jinni introduced itself as "Yūnāq" However, when pressured by Kubrā, his qarīn professed that its name is also ʿAzāzīl.[45] This could potentially make Yūnāq's identification as a qarīn problematic, since there are records indicating that ʿAzāzīl was the original, true name of Iblis before he was expelled from paradise. Sufi tendencies to refer to a qarīn as "one's own Iblis" make it even harder to distinguish between Iblis the Devil and the Devil Within—not in the least since Ibn ʿArabī hinted that Iblis *also* flows through the blood of Adam's children. Whether Ibn ʿArabī was referring to Iblis or "one's own Iblis" when speaking of the Devil in the blood is open to interpretations.[46] In general, the only way to determine whether the text is referring to a devil or the Devil is to rely on context. One major difference between the two is that a qarīn, unlike Iblis, will react positively to the proper moral conduct of its victim. And whereas few Sufis have aspired to murder Iblis or to have him converted to Islam, jinn doppelgangers were thought to be vulnerable to magic, soul work, and proselytism—though Ibn ʿArabī warned his readers that no creature is as remote to God as an evil jinni.[47] Exalted jinn—the so-called good spirits—were, however, ranked between human beings and angels in excellence. Ibn ʿArabī mentioned a jinni named Hāmah b. ʾAlhām b. Lāqīs b. Iblīs as the prime example of a believing, pious jinni.[48] In spite of the fact that the Muhammadan Light is the predominant component of their bodies, exalted jinn like Hāmah are not to be confused with angels. For whereas angelic bodies were made of pure light, the bodies of exalted jinn also consist of fire, water, air, and earth.

Ibn ʿArabī taught that bodily form and constitution determine the character and behavior of living beings. As a creature made of light, an angel is free from suffering and hatred, and its obedience to God is unwavering. Were they made of pure light, jinn would be the same.[49] However, the element of fire has a dominion over their character disposition. Ibn ʿArabī often compared jinn to fire in his works. Like fire, jinn are restless and brash, consumed with desire to outshine and subjugate everyone around them. Whereas fire was said to be a good servant and a bad master, jinn are neither. They are volatile and unpredictable, as likely to harm as to extend a helping hand. A summoned jinni will obey the summoner for a moment only so that it can defy them a moment later. Although jinn are endowed with free will and intelligence, their lack of focus can make them appear unintelligent. However, their cognitive abilities appear comparable to human cognitive abilities—and their skills in poetry, architecture, glasswork, linguistics, and magic were even said to surpass those of humans (see §2.6). Like humans, jinn possess self-consciousness and the inherent knowledge and awareness of their bodies. The meaning of life, God, and the nature of their inner spirits are nevertheless a mystery to both humans and jinn. This is why God endowed humans and jinn with rational faculties, so that they could seek knowledge, obey the Divine laws, and keep their passions in check. The overabundance of fire in jinn bodies, however, makes it difficult for them to maintain self-control. Jinn were thus thought to be more likely to break laws than humans. Ibn ʿArabī observed that jinn's hunger for glory exceeds that of humans. He also noted that their fiery nature induces them to meddle into human affairs. Since jinn are both arrogant and ambitious, they like to expose shameful deeds of others to make themselves look better. However, when affronted, they were known to exact revenge beyond what is reasonable and just.[50]

Some scholars suggested that jinn have a smaller variety of character traits than humans. Knowing a single jinni can thus help a Seeker to form a relatively accurate impression of the jinn folk. Hence, it can be presumed that the Forefather of Jinn was as arrogant as Iblis, for it is not in jinn's nature to be obedient. Although jinn can be humbled, Ibn ʿArabī noted they are never humble per se.[51]

Al-Azmeh, however, argued that doppelgangers differ from other jinn in this regard. For whereas the behavior of any other jinni is determined by the element of fire, a doppelganger's personality mirrors that of its human. If a human being is arrogant and wicked, their doppelganger will act accordingly. In contrast, humble human beings are accompanied by humble doppelgangers.[52] Whereas the element of fire dictates jinn's character and behavior, the element of air allows them to assume any shape they want.[53] Jinn's creativity is seemingly endless when it comes to shapeshifting.

> There is a species of jinn in the form of a dog with tails and their language is an incomprehensible growl. Other jinn species resembles men—except for the fact they have their mouths in their chests and speak by hissing. Some of them look like long snakes with wings, feet, and tails; others look like one half of a man, with one eye, one hand, and one foot. These jinn walk by leaps and jumps and their language resembles that of cranes. Other jinn have the faces of men and their backs are covered with scales, resembling the shell of a turtle. They have claws on their hands, long horns on their heads and their language resembles the howling of wolves. Some jinn have two heads and two faces like a lion's heads. These jinn are large and speak an incomprehensible language. Other jinn are round-faced, with white hair, tails like oxen and spit fire from their mouths. Some resemble women—with hair and breasts. There are no males in this race and these women are made pregnant by the wind and they give birth only to jinn which resemble them in appearance. They have ravishing voices and attract many individuals from other races by the charm of their voices. Other jinn assume the forms of reptiles and insects. Although they are large in size, they eat and drink like cattle. However, some other jinn resemble sea monsters—except for the fact they have tusks like a boar and long ears.[54]

Ibn ʿArabī argued that the great variety of jinn forms reflects poorly on their imagination. His argument was based on the fact that none of these forms is something they invented. Jinn rather tend to disclose themselves as something that already exists, resembling animals, humans or half-humans, and half-animals in appearance (figure 2.1). Ibn ʿArabī furthermore taught that jinn's shapeshifting

Figure 2.1. Ṭīṭān, the jinni with the head of a goat, the body of human, and legs of an elephant. *Source*: Ṭūsī, *ʿAjāʾib al-makhlūqāt* (MS Sam Fogg 14229), ff.265. Used with permission.

abilities emphasize their sense of belonging to the realm of the Unseen. Sometimes, a jinni can utilize this ability to help those in need.[55] Some who claimed to have seen "the jinn that whisper in the hearts of men" spoke of their tall frames and huge heads, with straight, spiky hair.[56] Whereas quranāʾ can be both male and female, it was mostly assumed that a male jinni will serve as a doppelganger to a human female and vice versa. However, there were also those who claimed that each doppelganger resembles its human in gender and appearance. When in doubt whether a person is a human or a jinni, people were advised to check whether that person has a cat-like eyes or legs resembling that of a goat or camel. Even so, when Ṣakhr usurped Solomon's throne, his queen was unable to tell the difference between her husband and his qarīn. The king was eventually forced to track down his lost magic ring, subdue the jinni, and resolve the confusion.[57]

The anonymous scribe who was working on the thirteenth-century copy of *Daqāʾiq al-Ḥaqāʾiq* (MS BnF Persian 174) depicted Ṣakhr with a multitude of faces—which were likely meant to emphasize his treacherous, duplicitous nature.[58] The Islamic normative tradition also contains records of jinn taking the form of snakes, stray dogs, and other vermin (*hawāmm*) in general. The lower soul and/or qarīn in the animal form were typically described as a black dog tailing its victim.[59] Whereas the demoness Qarīna preferred to disclose herself as a cat, the form of a dog appealed to quranāʾ the most, possibly due to the fact that dogs are almost as ambiguous as jinn in Islamic culture. Early modern and medieval scholars were never unanimous when making judgments on dogs. Whereas some have emphasized dogs' submissiveness and loyalty, other scholars dismissed them as creatures made of the Devil's saliva. Black dogs were said to be particularly cruel, ignorant, and depraved—and as likely to cast an evil eye on humans as jinn.[60] Since quranāʾ get their sustenance from lust, corruption, and evil deeds of humans, a doppelganger's victim has a certain impact on its appearance. The following story was recounted in al-Ghazālī's *ʾIḥyāʾ ʿulūm al-dīn:*

> ʾAbū Hurayra (d. 680) said that a devil of a believer and a devil of an infidel once came together. The infidel's devil was sleek, plump and attractive, whereas the believer's

> devil was emaciated, unkempt and naked. The devil of the infidel said to the devil of the believer: "What happened to you, Emaciated One?" The devil replied: "I am with a man who, when he eats, pronounces God's name, and I stay hungry; when he gets dressed, he pronounces God's name, and I stay naked and when he anoints himself, he pronounces God's name, and I remain unkempt." The other one said: "I am with a fellow who does nothing of the sort! Hence, I partake in his food, drink and clothes."[61]

Although doppelgangers can change their form at will, Ibn ʿArabī noted that no jinni will ever take the form of the Prophet. In his commentary of Ibn ʿArabī's *Fuṣūs al-ḥikam,* Bosnevi (d. 1644) surmised that this form is off limits to quranāʾ because the prophet Muhammad represents the embodiment of the Divine Name *al-Hādī,* the One Who Guides. Since doppelgangers are embodiments of the Name *al-Mudhill,* the One Who Leads Astray, their very nature prevents them from disclosing themselves as the Prophet.[62] Contrasting the beautiful, noble appearance of the prophet Muhammad, jinn were typically described as ugly creatures. When the archangel Gabriel forced them to assemble in front of Solomon, the king threw himself on the ground, shocked by the appearance of his servants. On his side, al-Ṭabarī surmised that jinn's ugliness is God's punishment for the sins they have committed. Once beautiful Iblis was thus made ugly by God for refusing to bow before Adam.[63] Such theories, accompanied by grotesque depictions of jinn in arts and literature, made no impression on Abū al-Ḥasan al-Ashʿarī (d. 936) and his followers. They pointed out that there are hadith indicating that not even the Prophet got to see a jinni with his own eyes. Hence, they argued, no person who claims to have seen a jinni can be taken as a legal witness.[64] Although they are ever-present among humans, jinn mostly pass unnoticed. This is why they were sometimes referred to as "the Concealed Ones" among Akbarians. Elusive jinn were furthermore associated with the Divine Name *al-Laṭīf,* the Sublimely Subtle, in Ibn ʿArabī's works. Ibn ʿArabī also compared jinn to silent, unpronounced letters in Arabic words and prepositions.[65] The following verses were composed by Ibn ʿArabī to describe the properties of the Divine Name *al-Laṭīf* with regard to jinn (doppelgangers):

> *Al-Laṭīf* is one of the well-known Names,
> With its graciousness obvious, apparent in the creation, marked.
> He is the Subtle—so he does not appear to our view.
> For how could the subtlety of the essence be perceived
> By the one who is void, empty?[66]

Whereas some scholars claimed that jinn are invisible since they are colorless, Ibn ʿArabī attributed jinn's ability to make themselves invisible to the element of fire. In spite of the fact that the element of air has a dominion over jinn bodies, it is fire that makes them insubstantial (*sakhīf*) and subtle (*laṭīf*). A sleeping human, Ibn ʿArabī noted, could easily spot a jinni in a dream, through the eye of imagination. Jinn bodies cannot be seen by the awake—except by the means of a revelation or when a jinni decides to condense its body so that humans can see it. To accidentally spot the jinn folk, even as they battle in the sky, was deemed unlikely among Akbarians.[67] This is due to the fact that most jinn feel as if the human eye confines them, forcing them to retain a certain form for an extended period of time. And, according to Ibn ʿArabī, this is less than appreciated by the jinn folk. Hence, were a human to catch a glimpse of a jinni, the spotted jinni would lean from side to side as if to move. Jinn use this tactic to make the human eye lose focus as it attempts to follow a moving target. Jinn will then use that person's temporary lack of focus to make themselves invisible again.[68] To see a jinni, Suhrawardī (d. 1191) advised lighting incense (figure 2.2) and removing noisy objects and anything made of iron from the house.[69] Other suggestions included extracting the brain of a fly and mixing it with eggs of an ant. This admixture was then to be dried, ground into powder, and applied on a human's eyelids to grant a person the ability to see jinn.[70] Ibn ʿArabī, however, believed that things are not as simple as that. For he argued that jinn's ability to make themselves invisible was the Divine blessing granted to descendants of the first jinni. Hence the warning from the surah *al-ʾAʿrāf: The Devil will watch you, with its tribe, from a place you aren't seeing* (Q 7:27). Ibn ʿArabī reasoned this devil hides in the human blood:

Figure 2.2. Conjuror burning incense to be able to see and summon jinn. *Source*: ʿĀdil Shah, *Nujūm al-ʿulūm* (MS Chester Beatty 02), ff.125. Used with permission.

God described them as *al-laṭāfa,* the Subtle Ones, and created them from the admixture of fire . . . The Devil was named *al-Laṭīf* since it flows through Adam's descendants with their blood and since one is unaware of its presence. If it weren't for the Lawgiver's warning of the incoming troops of devils and the whispers of the Devil from within the chest of humans, no one but the People of Revelation would know of these devils. One of the traits of the Name *al-Laṭīf* in satanic jinn pertains to His exalted words to Iblis: *Lead to the destruction of any human you can with your seductive voice. Make assaults on them with your cavalry and infantry. Share with them your wealth and children and make promises to them* (Q 17:64).[71]

When God ordered the Devil in Blood to share its children with mankind, the Devil was promised the same number of children as Adam. That way, each person can be born with a devil yoked to them.[72] God's pact with the Devil thus led to the birth of doppelgangers.

2.3. The Forefather of Doppelgangers

The identity of the Devil in Blood has been the subject of speculations. For instance, Winkel was convinced this Devil is none other than "Jānn," the forefather of all jinn.[73] This would make quranāʾ the direct descendants of the first jinni, for Ibn ʿArabī described this creature as a hermaphrodite (*khunthā*): "God created the first jinni with vulva and one part of him joined sexually with another part. As a result, something like the offspring of Adam was born of this jinni, male and female alike. Some of them then went on to mate with one another."[74]

Ibn ʿArabī rejected the theory that jinn stopped reproducing 4,000 years after the first jinni was created. He also dismissed Ibn Manẓūr's claim that all jinn were created through the metamorphoses of the forefather of all jinn. Ibn ʿArabī rather believed that male descendants of the first jinni reproduce by casting air into the womb of a female jinni. When two jinn come together for mating, they spiral together in mid-air like "a smoke exiting from an oven or from a potter's kiln; one part of a jinni interlacing with another part of the other jinni. Both jinn enjoy that interlacing—and what they cast is like the pollination of the date-palm, stripped off by the winds."[75] Whereas Winkel identified the forefather of all jinn as the Devil in Blood, we believe that Ibn ʿArabī was referring to Iblis when writing about this Devil and its children. Even though the first jinni is the single common ancestors of all jinn—including Iblis—jinn doppelgangers are likely the products of "standard" jinn reproduction. Not only does the name Iblis appear in the relevant paragraphs of *al-Futūḥāt* and in the surah *al-ʾIsrāʾ* (Q 17:61–64), which Ibn ʿArabī quoted to describe the Devil in Blood, but Iblis/Ḥārith was also identified as the father of all evil jinn (including quranāʾ) in Ibn ʿArabī's works.[76] Racius furthermore demonstrated that the name Jānn was equally used in Islamic culture for the forefather of all jinn (*ʾabū al-jinn*) and Iblis, the father of devils (*ʾabū al-shayāṭīn*).[77]

It should also be noted that Ibn ʿArabī used the term *jānn* as a synonym for the jinn folk in general. The forefather of all jinn thus was referred to as "the first of *al-jānn*" in his works.[78] A third option was proposed by Canaan, who argued that neither Iblis nor Jānn is the forefather of quranāʾ. Palestinians rather believe that jinn doppelgangers are the direct descendants of ʾAḥmar, the king of jinn. Canaan identified Lilith, the first wife of Adam, as the first qarīn(a) and the mother of devils.[79] In Syrian folklore, she was sometimes referred to as the Outcast (*maṭrūda*) for being repudiated by Adam. The reasons for repudiation were her disobedience and infertility. However, she later proved to be capable of bringing Iblis's children into the world.[80] Similar stories can also be found in writings of the elite. Al-Jīlānī thus spoke of al-Shayṭāna, the consort of Iblis, and the thirty-one eggs she laid. From each of these eggs, 10,000 devils were born, and these devils later reproduced among themselves.[81] Other scholars, however, surmised that Iblis is a hermaphrodite, like Ibn ʿArabī's forefather of all jinn. Among the prominent supporters of this theory was al-Ghazālī, who taught that Iblis lays eggs directly into the hearts of men. Al-Ghazālī believed that this is how evil jinn gain access to their victims.[82]

Another story explaining how doppelgangers first gained access to the human heart was recorded by ʿAṭṭār of Nishapur (d. 1221). According to ʿAṭṭār, the first qarīn was a child named al-Khannās, the son of Iblis. One day, taking advantage of Adam's absence, Iblis entrusted al-Khannās to Eve's care. When Adam found out, he murdered the child, had it chopped to pieces and hung each piece from the branch of a tree. When Iblis returned and asked of the child, Eve confessed the murder. Unperturbed, Iblis called out to the dead child, and al-Khannās came back to life. Some days later, the Devil came back and left al-Khannās with Eve once again. Enraged, Adam had it murdered, and he also burned the body to prevent it from coming back to life. Iblis, however, returned and revived al-Khannās for the second time. The third time Adam found al-Khannās in his house, he killed the jinni and forced Eve to eat one half of the corpse. The other half Adam ate himself. When Iblis returned, Eve tearfully recounted the whole story to him. To her shock, the Devil beamed with delight and said: "This is precisely what I wanted, to gain access to the human insides! Since the human breasts are now my abode, my goal is finally achieved!"[83] Ibn ʿArabī gave no credit to such stories, for the surah *al-ʾIsrāʾ* (Q 17:64) attests that God ordered Iblis to share his children with humans.[84] The Qur'an furthermore clarifies that *whereas God created mankind from dry clay like pottery, He created Jānn of the jinn from smokeless fire* (Q 55:14–15). Fire is used in pottery to give dryness and firmness to clay. Under the assumption that satanic fire was used to create humans, several scholars interpreted this ayah as a warning there is a little bit of Jānn in every human. This is the lower soul/qarīn: the essence of satanic flame that neither sleeps nor rests.[85]

2.4. Taxonomy of the Unseen

Al-Shiblī calculated that the ratio between devils and humans is 90:1. Assuming that each human has a qarīn of their own, this would mean that doppelgangers represent around 1.12% of the total number of evil jinn.[86] This subchapter aims to determine whether—and under which criteria—doppelgangers can be identified as a separate subspecies of jinn. Scholars were never unanimous when it comes to jinn taxonomy, and there is no decisive list of subspecies of jinn. Even so, there were several notable attempts to enumerate these subspecies and to pinpoint doppelgangers' place among them. For instance, ʾAbū Thaʿlaba maintained that the Prophet divided jinn into three categories. These are (1) the flying jinn; (2) jinn that take the zoomorphic forms of snakes, insects, and scorpions; and (3) the wandering jinn (*Ṣaḥīḥ Ibn Ḥibbān* #6156). In some variations of this narrative, jinn belonging to the third category were described as "jinn which are subjected to reward and punishment."[87] Jinn of the third category were identified by Philips as quranāʾ, whom Philips defined as the wandering, earth-bound jinn.[88] Disparate classifications of jinn in Islamic orthodoxy were assembled and analyzed in detail by al-Shiblī. Most classifications al-Shiblī tracked down are threefold. The first of these classifications, by ʾAbū al-Qāsim al-Suhaylī, divides the jinn folk into (1) jinn that take the form of snakes, (2) jinn that take the form of a black dog, and (3) jinn in the form of whirlwinds. The other classifications al-Shiblī listed are more in line with the previously quoted hadith.[89] Variations between al-Shiblī's classifications can be attributed to variations between the hadith dealing with the topic. Nünlist, however, argued, that all jinn al-Shiblī described fall in one of the following categories:

1. Jinn in the animal form
2. Jinn in the human form
3. Jinn in the form of whirlwinds

Nünlist's threefold division is a prime example of a classification of jinn based on their form. However, a classification of jinn based on their form would only make sense under the assumption that jinn cannot change their form at will. Among the notable proponents of this theory was al-Shiblī, who surmised that God instructed jinn on how to perform certain rituals. Once these rituals are properly executed by a jinni, God will change its form. Al-Shiblī, however, noted that no jinni is capable of shape-shifting on its own.[90] In contrast, Ibn ʿArabī maintained that jinn can assume any form they want (as long as they do not try to pass themselves off as the prophet Muhammad). Classifications of jinn on the basis of their form were thus rare among Akbarians. Apart from (1) classifications based on the form and appearance of jinn, there were also attempts to classify the jinn folk based on their (2) place of residence, (3) origins, and (4) behavior. Al-Jīlī's classification is one of the most elaborate classifications of jinn based on their place of residence. In accordance with the Islamic normative tradition, Ibn ʿArabī spoke of the seven Earths in his works. Al-Jīlī believed that the lower six of these seven Earths are the dwelling places of jinn. These are:

1. The Earth of Devotions (*ʿarḍ al-ʾibādāt*), where God-fearing jinn live. At nightfall, these jinn descend to the dwelling place of humans, where they would sometimes fall in love with the children of Adam. Albeit God-fearing, jinn from the Earth of Devotions envy spiritual Seekers. Hence, they become yoked to Sufis—presumably as their doppelgangers—and bring them to ruin. Their victims appear to be deaf, blind, mute, and unable to understand the word of God, unless this word was recited by a jinni.
2. The Earth of Nature (*ʿarḍ al-ṭabʿ*) is inhabited by the unbelieving jinn which tend to appear in human form.

3. The Earth of Lust (*ʿarḍ al-shahwa*), which is inhabited by the children of Iblis.

4. The Earth of Exorbitance (*ʿarḍ al-ṭaghyān*), which is the realm of ifrits and other powerful jinn.

5. The Earth of Impiety (*ʿarḍ al-ʾilḥād*) is the abode of evil *mārid*, which are counted among the most powerful among the jinn folk.

6. The Earth of Misery (*ʿarḍ al-shaqāwa*), which is the floor of hell, is inhabited by jinn in the form of snakes and scorpions.[91]

In contrast, Wahb b. Munabbih's (d. 737) classification is based on jinn's mating practices and diet. Wahb believed that the real jinn are like the wind: they neither drink, sleep, nor procreate. However, some jinn eat, drink, and mate with one another. Wahb listed ghouls, *saʿālī* (sg. *siʿlāh*) and the like as examples of these other subspecies.[92] Al-Masʿūdī believed that different subspecies of jinn like quranāʾ (to whom he referred to as *waswās,* for the way they whisper to people) originate from different eggs, which were laid by the forefather of all jinn.[93] Although the total number of subspecies varies from one work to another, the most commonly mentioned are:

- *Ḥinn,* which—like quranāʾ—tend to assume the form of a black dog. A jinni of this type can be distinguished from real animals by the faint, chirping sounds it makes. These jinn were said to be prone to casting an evil eye on those humans who would chase them away when they come begging for food.[94]

- *Shiqq* is a lower form of jinn. They are half-men which attack and devour travelers. These jinn are commonly used as riding animals by other, more powerful jinn.[95]

- *Siʿlāh* is a subspecies of forest jinn (figure 2.3). Humans who fall under their spell are forced to dance with *saʿālī,* which tend to disclose themselves in animal forms. Wolves are their natural enemies.[96]

Figure 2.3. Si'lāh, a forest jinni. *Source*: al-Qazwīnī, *'Ajā'ib al-makhlūqāt* (MS Garrett no. 82G), ff.392. Used with permission.

- *Nasnās* is the subspecies of jinn known for their beautiful orchards and gardens. Their gardens bloom in arid lands with no need of water. These jinn have one eye, one arm, and one leg each. Nevertheless, they can run faster than horses. Were a human to enter their realm, *nasnās* would retaliate by throwing sand at them. Persistent intruders could also be afflicted with madness.[97]

- *Dalhāth* is a sea jinni which devours the corpses of victims of shipwrecks (figure 2.4). A starved *dalhāth* will sometimes attack the ships approaching their islands. These jinn were thought to be capable of making their victims faint with their piercing cries, and they were said to prefer riding ostriches.[98]
- *Mārid* is the subspecies of powerful jinn which are proficient in stone masonry and capable of carrying heavy loads. These jinn were said to be prone to eavesdropping on angels and conveying Divine secrets to humans.[99]

Whereas contemporary biologists divide species into subspecies based on their place of residence and phenotypic differences, jinn were divided into *ḥinn, mārid,* and the like based on their character traits and abilities. A saying attributed to the prophet Muhammad reads:

Figure 2.4. Dalhāth attacking a ship. al-Qazwīnī, *Source*: *ʿAjāʾib al-makhlūqāt* (MS Garrett no. 82G), ff.392. Used with permission.

> People say that *ḥinn* are weak jinn, just like a jinni which does not believe and commits sin, attacks and corrupts is referred to as "shayṭān." If a jinni is strong enough to do building, carry heavy loads and eavesdrop, it is then referred to as "mārid." If a jinni is even stronger, we will refer to it as "ʿifrit" and if it is even stronger—"ʿabqarī," just like a man who fights in a war courageously, without hanging back, is said to be "courageous." An even braver man is referred to as "hero." If he is even braver, he is called "buhma" and beyond that—"alyas."[100]

A similar opinion can be found in *K. al-Ḥayawān*, where al-Jāḥiẓ attests that a wicked, strong *mārid* is commonly referred to as "ifrit."[101] "Particularly bestial, diabolic and hostile variety of the *mārid*s of the d̲jinn which allured men from their path by assuming different forms, then fell upon them unawares, destroyed and devoured them" was identified by MacDonald as a "ghoul."[102] Whether quranāʾ should be classified as a distinct subspecies was a matter of debate among scholars. Based on the fieldwork he conducted in Syria, Fatarcek listed qarīn(*a*) as a separate class of jinn—alongside ghouls, ifrits, and the like.[103] A similar classification, where quranāʾ were listed as a separate class of jinn, can also be found in Nünlist's "Demonology in Islam."[104] In contrast, Dols identified the jinn living in the human blood as ifrits. Padwick and Blackman, both of whom have been conducting field research in Egypt, also sided with this opinion.[105] Unlike ifrits, quranāʾ were not widely known for their physical strength. Even though the Islamic normative tradition and Ibn ʿArabī speak of a certain ifrit, which attempted to distract the Prophet while he was praying,[106] ifrits were rarely accused of leading believers astray. They were rather associated with natural disasters and epidemics. Deception, whispers, and flattery were thought to be the main weapons of a ghoul.

Al-Qazwīnī recorded that people compared ghouls to both humans and animals. He also noted that no other jinn are as famous as ghouls.[107] Throughout the centuries, legends spoke of the subspecies of desert jinn which prey on travelers. Whereas some ghoul stories spoke of the jinn appearing as beautiful women, lighting fires in the night and using their enchanting voices to lure travelers astray (figure 2.5), ghouls were also described as undead

Figure 2.5. A ghoul falls off a horse, allowing the man to escape. Three other jinn also lurk nearby. *Source*: Ṭūsī, *ʿAjāʾib al-makhlūqāt* (Walters MS. 593), ff.169. Courtesy of the Walters Art Museum, Baltimore.

monsters breaking into cemeteries to devour human corpses.[108] In poetry, a ghoul was a synonym for ugliness and bad character traits. Al-Qazwīnī, however, maintained that ghouls have no fixed body form. Transient things were often compared to ghouls in Islamic culture. Al-Qazwīnī illustrated this tendency with a poem attributed to Kaʿab b. Zuhayr (d. 662):

> She never remains in one state as she once was,
> Her garment changing like a ghoul.[109]

Since ghouls rely on seduction and deception to lead humans astray, Davidson identified them with the lower soul/mind, Iblis and *waswās*. Davidson maintained that such comparisons were common among Sufis, and he quoted Rūmī's verses to back his claim:

> The cry of ghouls is the cry of an acquaintance—
> An acquaintance who would lure you to perdition.
> The ghoul keeps on crying:
> Hark, ye caravan people!
> Come towards me, here is the track and landmarks.
> The ghoul mentions the name of each, saying:
> "O, so-and-so," in order that she may make
> That person the one of those who sink.
> When he reaches the spot, he sees wolves and lions,
> His way lost, the road far off and the day late.
> Pray tell me, what is the ghoul's cry like?
> It is: "I desire riches, position and renown."
> Bar these voices from the heart,
> So that mysteries may be revealed.[110]

Both ghouls and quranāʾ rely on seductive whispers to lead humans astray, but there are several differences between them. Whereas a qarīn is conceived at the same time as its human, ghouls are created when a jinni is hit by a shooting star. According to al-Qazwīnī, this usually occurs when a wayward jinni attempts to eavesdrop on angels. If an injured jinni falls into water, it will become a crocodile. If it falls to the ground, the jinni will be transformed into a ghoul. On his side, al-Jāḥiẓ maintained that ghoul is a general term for "any type of jinn which lures travelers and is a shape-shifter."[111] The malice of quranāʾ is, however, reserved for the humans they are yoked to. In conclusion, we believe that doppelgangers can be identified as a distinct subspecies of jinn based on their specific behavior, diet (human sins), and their place of residence (the bloodstream of humans). Whereas all evil jinn can trace their ancestry to Iblis the Devil, the bond between a qarīn and its victim is another major point of difference between a doppelganger and any other ghoul. That said, apart from doppelgangers, other jinn can also get attached to living beings, places, and objects. As a result, it is sometimes difficult to distinguish between a jinni companion (*tābiʿ*) and a doppelganger (qarīn).

2.5. Unseen Companions and Doppelgangers

This subchapter examines the nature of the bond between a qarīn and its human. We will not dwell here on a qarīn's influence on human behavior, as this is the topic for another subchapter (§3.3). Our present goal is to scrutinize the impact of the bond on a qarīn. We will also contrast the behavior of jinn doppelgangers and various jinn companions in this subchapter. Jinn doppelgangers, guardian spirits, and the spirit companions of humans and animals were all identified as one and the same type of demonic doubles by Nünlist. We will, however, seek to demonstrate that the aforementioned companion spirits cannot be universally identified with quranāʾ. Whereas Ibn ʿArabī associated quranāʾ with humans, Nünlist emphasized the proximity of jinn (doppelgangers) to animals. Not only were jinn identified with animals—but medieval scholars also documented their love for riding. Hence, Nünlist maintained that the belief in demons in Islam is closely connected with the riding metaphor. He furthermore suggested there are similarities between the human victims of quranāʾ and the riding animals of jinn.[112] These were said to include ostriches, gazelles, snakes, wolves, boars, and bears. Bedouins of old Arabia believed it is dangerous to hunt these animals after dark.[113]

The jinn folk were known for their love for fine horses and would reportedly surround and kiss the horse of the poet ʾAbū al-Najm.[114] Al-Suyūṭī claimed that camels also served as the mounts of jinn. Passing through a caravan of camels was thought to be dangerous since there are always jinn among them.[115] Camels were thought to be as obstinate and as unruly in nature as jinn—with Ibn ʿArabī going as far as describing them as "devils" (*shayāṭīn*). Ibn ʿArabī taught that eating the flesh of a camel would strengthen the power of one's qarīn and other devils in their heart. He furthermore noted that the Prophet ordered believers to pray as far away as possible from camels. This is due to the fact that prayer represents a state of closeness to God and, like any other devil, camels were thought to be distant from Him.[116] No two things, Ibn ʿArabī maintained, are drawn to one another without a reason, like the crow and the dove from a story who loved one another because each of them had a lame leg.[117] Whereas a shared disability brought the two birds together, Ibn ʿArabī did not explain why jinn are drawn to camels. Al-Shiblī later speculated that jinn feel affection for camels since a camel once helped Iblis to sneak into paradise. This is why God had the camel cursed. Its legs fell off and the camel became a snake, condemned to crawl on its belly and to seek nourishment in the dust.[118]

Writing on the proximity between jinn, snakes, and camels, Waardenburg noted that the Bedouins still believe that snakes, like doppelgangers, can "yoke" themselves to humans and inspire them to certain actions.[119] The Prophet was rumored to have said: "The one who kills a serpent kills an unbeliever and the one who leaves it alive out of fear does not belong with us."[120] Jinn, however, do not forget a favor. The early modern and medieval scholars believed that injuring a snake could have dire consequences. According to al-Damīrī, this is especially the case with *al-ʾarqām,* which he described as a snake that is either black and white or black and red in color. These snakes were said to be both malevolent and voracious. However, for one reason or another, jinn were thought to be especially protective of them. Punishments for injuring a snake under their protection were said to include broken bones, epileptic seizures, and death. When ordered to leave one such snake in peace, a man snapped at ʿUmar b. al-Khaṭṭāb: "Leave it alone and it shall eat you—but if you kill it, you will be killed for it!"[121] In contrast, being kind to snakes could induce jinn to benevolence. Jinn tend to appear in serpent form, with some scholars arguing that this is the real reason why they are protective of snakes. On his side, Ibn ʿArabī maintained that humans are entitled to kill any snake they want. Jinn have no right to claim revenge in such cases, "for whoever takes on a form other than their proper form and gets to be killed [for being mistaken for a snake], there is no blood price and no retaliation for them."[122] In conclusion, even though jinn love their riding animals, to the best of our knowledge, there are no records indicating that animals can have doppelgangers like humans.

In Palestine and Maghrib, victims of quranāʾ are referred to as *maqrūn.*[123] Nünlist made no distinction between *maqrūn* and protégés and mounts of jinn. These were all identified as victims of demonic possessions in his works, "for both animals and humans can serve as mounts of demons. The riding often happens externally. However, spirits can also penetrate the human body." According to

Nünlist, "this is often associated with the idea of disease. The role of a man serving as a mount of jinn and his function as a carrier of jinn within himself are identical."[124] Throughout the centuries, the passive participle *majnūn* has often served to denote a mentally unstable person—a suspected victim of demonic possession. Dols, however, noted that the early Muslims believed that a person targeted by jinn is as likely to become a seer or poet.[125] In the early years of his mission, the prophet Muhammad also was described as *majnūn* when he called for the destruction of old shrines and customs. Whereas the clouded mind of *majānīn* was traditionally blamed on jinn, Ibn ʿArabī used the passive participle *majnūn* for recipients of the Divine revelations. "The True (*al-Ḥaqq*) seizes their hearts instantly, suddenly. He keeps them busy with Himself and their minds are seized. They become blissful upon seeing Him, they give over wholly to His presence and stroll around, aloof in His beauty. They are intelligent people with no brains and they are known to the outside world as being insane, *majānīn*—i.e. those who have been veiled, concealed from the management of their intellects."[126]

Even though quranāʾ have many weapons at their disposal, insanity is not one of them. Jinn doppelgangers were, however, said to be prone to striking those who wronged them with epilepsy (*ṣarʿ*).[127] Ibn ʿArabī gave no credit to such tales—and we believe rabies might have inspired the popular narratives revolving around zoomorphic appearances of jinn and people whom doppelgangers have afflicted with seizures and madness. Wild animals display abnormal behavior when infected with rabies, including the absence of fear, aggression, and venturing into human settlements. As the virus spreads, infected animals become overwhelmed with lethargy. Such animals can appear friendly and allow themselves to be petted. The rabies is transmitted to humans when an infected animal bites or scratches its victim. As the brain deteriorates, seizures, hallucinations, paralysis, and a state of agitation resulting from the infection could be mistaken for demonic possession. Another possible explanation was offered by Avicenna, who noted that seers and magicians rely on hyperventilation and scrying to induce spiritual experiences comparable to those described by Ibn ʿArabī. Such simpletons, Avicenna remarked, claim to have suffered the influence of jinn (*al-īhām li-masīs al-jinn*) once their experiments go wrong. Ibn ʿArabī, however, argued that those who keep the company of jinn are more likely to be arrogant than insane. This is not to say that an average jinni strives to corrupt the human character by possessing them—but rather, Ibn ʿArabī believed that each person becomes like his friends in due time. Even though jinn can be and brisk and unfocused, Ibn ʿArabī found them to be of sound mind in general.[128] In conclusion, whereas other jinn strive to make the human soul and personality defunct by possessing them,[129] a qarīn seeks to corrupt first and foremost. This is a major point of difference between a demonic possession and a bond between a qarīn and its human. To the best of our knowledge, there are no extant records describing the attempts of doppelgangers to drive their humans to insanity. A qarīn would seek to make its human sick only under exceptional circumstances, for the reasons that will be explained in the concluding section of this subchapter.

It is, however, necessary to reexamine the relationship between jinn doppelgangers and jinn guardians before drawing our final conclusions on the differences between quranāʾ and other companion spirits. Not only were doppelgangers confused with demonic riders, but they were also identified with the guardians of natural resources and sacral places and objects. For instance, according to Schaffer, Mandinika people still believe that each place has its "spirit double or djinn."[130] The following paragraphs will analyze the purported behavior of jinn guardians, with the intention of demonstrating that these jinn cannot be collectively identified with *quranāʾ*. Having examined numerous records on the topic, we concluded that most, if not all, jinn guardians assumed their "duties" willingly, either because of their love of the object they guarded or because they wished to harm humans. The Qur'an emphasized the latter motive. For example, the surah *al-Anʿām* attests that jinn like to cause confusion and discord among humans (Q 6:71, 112). They were thus said to be prone to hide under statues of deities, haunting temples and deceiving seers, false prophets, and magicians. Jinn doppelgangers could also act in a similar manner when given an opportunity (i.e. when their human visits a temple). Jinn guardians, however, tend to reside at the place they are guarding, and they would defend it fiercely when challenged. For instance, when Khālid b. al-Walīd (d. 642) ordered the sacred trees around the sanctuary of al-ʿUzzā to be cut down, he was confronted by a jinni in the form of a black woman. Gnashing teeth, the female jinni threw herself at Khālid, but as he retaliated, splitting her skull, her body quickly turned to ashes. According to al-Alūsī, the female jinni lived under al-ʿUzzā's idol and unsuccessfully tried to defend it.[131]

In his book on satanic deceptions, al-Jawzī (d. 1201) reported there used to be a tree people worshipped instead of God. One day, a pious man decided to cut it down. An evil jinni appeared to him in human form and asked: "What do you want?" The man explained that he was setting off to cut down the tree which was being worshipped in God's place. To this the jinni replied that, since the man did not worship the tree himself, there was no harm for it to remain where it was. However, the man was adamant that he would cut the tree down. The jinni then offered him a deal: provided that he spared the tree, each morning the man would find two gold coins under his pillow. The man accepted the offer—and lo and behold, the following morning two gold coins appeared beneath the pillow. However, the miracle did not last, and the next day there was no gold to be found. Consumed with fury, the man grabbed his axe and dashed towards the tree. This time, the jinni appeared to him in its true, hideous form and asked mockingly: "What do you want?" The man retorted that he would now definitely cut down the tree that was being worshipped instead of God. However, the jinni shook its head and told him that it was not within his power to do so—not anymore. As the man charged towards the tree, the jinni threw itself on him, overpowering him with ease. Then it said: "Don't you know who I am? Why, I am the Devil! At first, you were angry for God's sake and I had no power over you. Thus, I tricked you with the promise of coins—and later, when you got angry because of money, I was able to overpower you!"[132]

The antagonist of al-Jawzī's story did not merely wish to cause discord and confusion. Evil jinn were commonly featured as defenders of polytheism and the enemies of God in poetry and literature. Al-Jawzī surmised that jinn were also responsible for the rise of polytheism in the Arabian Peninsula. On the authority of Ibn al-Kalbī (d. 819), he claimed that the first polytheistic cult in Arabia was established by the jinni named ʾAbū Thumāmah. This jinni liked to speak in verses. One day, ʾAbū Thumāmah instructed a man to dig at the shores of Jeddah, where ancient idols were buried:

> Make haste and leave Tihāmah,
> Accompanied by peace and luck.
> Make way to the shores of Jeddah;
> Idols in fine array there you will find.
> With thee to Tihāmah take them back,
> Let nothing alarm thee, fear no attack.
> Bid the Arabs to worship them, one and all,
> They will hear thy voice and heed thy call.[133]

Mani's demonic double was also credited with establishing a religious cult. However, this does not necessarily mean that Mani's doppelganger and/or ʾAbū Thumāmah wished to be worshiped as gods themselves. Due to the lack of primary sources, little can be ascertained of the nature and pervasiveness of the pre-Islamic jinn cults. There are also no records indicating that doppelgangers have been worshipped either before or after the advent of Islam.[134] Ibn Taymiyya claimed that polytheists and magicians worshipped the jinn folk inadvertently, by reciting "incantations, spells and formulae which are in general circulation among people and which contain unintelligible words in Arabic that are connected with jinn."[135] However, there are reports indicating that jinn were consciously worshipped in the tribes of Banu Mulayḥ and Banū Sāsān. Members of these tribes were said to be tricksters, magicians, and vagrants—not unlike the jinn they worshiped.[136] In the early years of Muhammad's mission, legends had been circulating that jinn were the offspring of polytheistic deities and Allah. These legends could serve to explain why jinn were protective of old shrines and statues. But in light of the fact that the Qur'an denies the existence of gods other than Allah, medieval scholars payed them no heed (Q 4:36, 5:76, 7:197). Olomi argued that the jinn folk spread and protected disbelief only so that they could harm humans.[137] In other words, Olomi surmised that jinn are not the enemies of God and that their feud is with humans alone. Knowing that God hates disbelief, jinn (doppelgangers) seek to draw a wedge between Him and humans by inspiring false prophets and protecting old temples and idols from Muslims when possible.

Even though Olomi's theory is plausible, we believe that the story of the foolish man and the evil jinni was likely based on an older Bedouin tale describing the conflict between a woodcutter and a nature spirit. The same might be true for the female jinni which was guarding the trees around al-ʿUzzā's temple.[138] In al-Jawzī's version of the story, the man survived the encounter. Most raiders and intruders into jinn territory were not as lucky. Abū al-Faraj al-Iṣfahānī (d. 967) thus reported an incident when jinn assumed the form of flying serpents to murder the men who set their trees on fire.[139] Among the Bedouins, old trees were often seen as dwelling places of jinn. Jinn's love for nature is well documented in poetry and literature, and Chellhod believed that jinn's love for shadowy groves inspired Bedouins to address them by saying: "You who find the darkness pleasant"! While shadows provided jinn with cover during the day, tree barks and tree crowns offered them protection from prying eyes during the night.[140] Al-Zamakhsharī's thesaurus thus linked the root *j-n-n* and jinn with the expression "the tall palm tree" (*nakhla majnūnah*).[141] Although jinn were known for their hatred for citruses, there are no other records indicating their love for arecaceae. Tall trees and shadowy groves were all seen as dwelling places of jinn. Werth reasoned jinn are attracted to trees and shrubs since their roots grant them access to the underworld.

> Muslims believe the jinn can exist in places with connections to the underworld, such as springs, wells, cisterns and all places linked to underground water. Jinn might also dwell in caves, rock chasms, dark valleys, gorges, graves, etc., because of their connection to the underworld. Even cracks in the ground caused by great heat, a scratch in the ground made with a plough or a space dug for a house foundation can be sufficient opening to allow the jinn access to the surface of the earth. Trees (and shrubs) reach into the underworld with their roots; consequently, jinn often inhabit them as well.[142]

The underworld was seen in many cultures as the abode of demons. However, the behavior of jinn with regard to trees has more in common with the fairy folk and other spirits of nature. The Brethren of Purity identified jinn as forces of nature rather than devils. In other words, jinn were defined by the Brethren as "the natural forms and forces operative in the world, like the minds that steer the celestial bodies, acting with steady invariance and understanding. . . . Their freedom is obedience to God's command."[143] Upton and Bylebyl explicitly identified jinn with fairies.[144] Like fairies, jinn were thought to be capable of transforming deserts into fertile soil. Bedouins once believed that the most beautiful and the most fertile lands in the Middle East belong to jinn (figure 2.6).

Figure 2.6. Jinn were thought to be capable of transforming arid lands into fertile soil. *Source*: al-Qazwīnī, *ʿAjāʾib al-makhlūqāt* (MS St Andrews 32(0)). Courtesy of the University of St Andrews Libraries and Museums.

Many springs and oases in the Middle East are associated with jinn to this day. Building a house or traveling near the dwelling place of jinn without offering them a tribute was thought to be dangerous, as jinn shared their resources only with a chosen few.[145] A jinni guardian would sometimes extend its protection to humans and animals on their land. A short and strange anecdote documenting this type of behavior survives in the writings of al-Tūnisī (d. 1857).

> One of the strangest things I heard when I was on Jabal Marrah was that the jinn there look after their livestock—the ones grazing in the pastures—and these do not have shepherds. Several men whose word one would normally trust told me that if anyone were to pass by their livestock and see there was no shepherd and perhaps give in to the temptation to take an ewe or a cow or anything else and then try to slaughter it, his hand would stick to the knife at the creature's throat, and he'd be unable to let go of it until its owners came. They would seize him and force him to pay the highest price for it, after reviling him and giving him a painful beating. I heard this so often it achieved the number of independent transmitters it would need, were it a prophetic hadith, to be accepted as authentic—but I still didn't believe it.[146]

Pre-Islamic, Bedouin legends of nature spirits likely served as an inspiration for the later-date notions of jinn guardians in writings of the elite. It is, however, debatable whether jinn guardians and Mandanika spirit doubles can be universally identified with quranāʾ. The root *q-r-n* in the Arabic language conveys the idea of a bond between two things. Hence, Ibn Manẓūr argued "a qarīn is any person who befriends you and qarīna of a man is his wife because he befriends her."[147] Jinn guardians fit this wider definition of quranāʾ. The same goes for the archangel Gabriel, who was sometimes figuratively described as the qarīn of the Prophet.[148] There are also instances where Ibn ʿArabī used the term qarīn for one's guardian angel.[149] However, when the term qarīn was used with regard to jinn in Ibn ʿArabī's works, it always served to denote (1) a descendant of Iblis (2) who lives in the blood and hearts of humans, (3) whose fate is tied to the fate of its victim. The third criterion is essential for making a distinction between jinn doppelgangers and the great variety of jinn companions and guardian spirits. A qarīn does not merely follow its human around: its looks, fate, and personality are all determined by its victim. Most written sources—with Ibn ʿArabī's works included—assumed this means that a doppelganger will profit from the proper moral conduct of its victim. However, there are also examples of more literal interpretations in poetry and literature. This is especially the case with the oral traditions from Upper Egypt, where people believed that any damage done to a qarīn would also affect its human. This also includes old age, sickness, and death. Were a doppelganger to drive its human to insanity, it would have likely suffered the same fate.

> This point was brought out clearly one day three years ago when a large number of women had come to see me and to have their eyes doctored. One of them was speaking about her *ḳarīneh,* so I said, "But your eyes are very bad now, what about those of your *ḳarīneh*"? "Oh," she replied, "her eyes also are bad." "Poor thing," I said. "But who is looking after her eyes"? "Why, your *ḳarīneh, gināb es-sitt* [honored lady]," the woman immediately answered.[150]

Blackman's patients believed her qarīn was busying itself with their doppelgangers while she was treating them, thus mimicking its human in conduct. Likewise, an evil person is accompanied by an evil doppelganger. Many jinn rely on seduction and deception to lead humans astray, but quranāʾ are the only subspecies that match the standard contemporary definition of a doppelganger. As of the eighteenth century, this term has served to denote a paranormal concept and a demonic twin of human beings in popular culture and literature. A qarīn fits this criterion. Not only are quranāʾ conceived and born at the same time as their humans, but they also resemble their victims in appearance. For instance, if a person is left-handed or one-eyed, their qarīn will look the same.[151] Bronfen, who studied how the term *doppelganger* has been used in the English language, identified a person's doppelganger as "mirror of the[ir] soul" and/or "embodiment of that part of the soul that inhabits the human psyche as a foreign body"; "harbouring both dangerous temptations and the promise of redemption."[152] Our decision to render the term qarīn into English as "doppelganger," rather than "double," was partially based on Bronfen's research, for the definition of a doppelganger she pinpointed matches the Akbarian notions of quranāʾ. Our decision was also influenced by the necessity to emphasize the differences between quranāʾ and Mandinika jinn doubles, spirits of nature and other jinn that haunt certain places, objects, and/or people by choice. A qarīn is the true spiritual twin of its human—a doppelganger rather than a companion spirit. We believe that jinn companions, guardian spirits, and Mandinika jinn doubles better fit the wider definition of a *tābiʿ*. The term *tābiʿ*, Ibn Manẓūr explained, was used in Islamic culture for any sort of companion jinni and/or a female jinni which follows a human being (*jinniyya tatbaʿu l-insān*). Ibn Manẓūr noted that the Prophet used to know a woman who had a companion from among the jinn (*tābiʿ min al-jinn*). This jinni is not to be confused with her doppelganger. Having fallen in love with the woman, the jinni merely kept close to her.[153] The besotted jinni was, however, free to leave the woman any time it wanted—which is not the case with a qarīn. A doppelganger does not come to its human by choice, and it is likewise not free to leave their bloodstream on a whim.

Whereas other jinn companions and guardian spirits often feel affection for their humans, shrines, and animals, it is debatable whether quranāʾ can fall in love with humans. For example, al-Safi noted that a confirmed bachelor is referred to in Sudan as *mujawiz*—i.e. the one married to their qarīn.[154] Similar beliefs, with people claiming themselves to be married to their qarīn, have also been encountered by al-Shamy in Egypt.[155] An Egyptian widow told Blackman how good her qarīn was to her; taking care of her children and providing them with money. A powerful qarīn might even help its human resist the attempts of other jinn to possess them. Egyptian doppelgangers would sometimes teach their "wives" how to prepare remedies for the sick, and they would share some of their knowledge of the Unseen with them—like the jinni lover of ʿUfayra and other sorceresses of the old.[156] Love stories describing the relationships between humans and jinn were especially popular during the reign of the caliph al-Muqtadir (d. 931). Some of these stories also speak of the children born to a human and a jinni. The most famous of these children was Bilquis, the queen of Sheba. Her father Hadhad was said to have married a daughter of the king of jinn.[157] Whereas the queen of Sheba was famous for her beauty, jinn-human hybrids were usually described as evil, deformed creatures. One such hybrid, the fortune-teller named Shiqq, had no bones apart from the skull, and his face was located in his chest.[158] Khawṣ b. Ḥuwayl—who is better known as Dajjāl the Antichrist—was also identified as the product of a liaison between a mortal man and a jinni.[159] Nevertheless, al-Ashqar noted there are still clans in the United Arab Emirates claiming descent from the jinn.[160] Ibn ʿArabī was also rumored to have married a jinni. According to al-Damīrī,

> A certain shaykh was asked about Ibn ʿArabī. He replied that he was an evil shaykh and a liar. "A liar as well?," someone asked. "Yes indeed," the shaykh said. "We were discussing the marriage with jinn and he said: 'Jinn are fine spirits and human beings are coarse bodies; how can the two come together?' " Then he was away from us for a time and came back with a bruise on his head. We asked about the bruise and he said: "I married a woman from among the jinn, we had some trouble and she afflicted me with this bruise!" The original storyteller added: "I do not think this was a deliberate lie on Ibn ʿArabī's part. It was rather one of the anecdotes circulating among the spiritual Seekers."[161]

In another version of the story, the female jinni gave birth to Ibn ʿArabī's children. But as soon as he made her angry, she scarred Ibn ʿArabī's face and disappeared, never to be seen again.[162] Krawietz surmised that claiming a love relationship with a female jinni has been used as a means to exculpate oneself from marriage in conservative religious societies.[163] There are, however, no records of Ibn ʿArabī using his demonic lover as an excuse to keep himself away from his marital bed. As a matter of fact, Akbarians were adamant that quranāʾ are the original source of rumors concerning Ibn ʿArabī's supposed marriage to a jinni. For example, Bosnevi recorded how one particularly evil jinni seduced ʾIbrahīm al-Buqa-

ʿiyy into writing "a warning for the feebleminded of Ibn ʿArabī's heresy," where he accused Ibn ʿArabī of consorting with a female jinni and having children with her.[164] It is also worth noting that Ibn ʿArabī opposed the idea that a child could be born to a human being and a jinni.[165] Ibn ʿArabī's opinion was also shared by Shibilī, who argued that no human will ever find peace and comfort in the embrace of a jinni. Most love stories between mortal men and jinn have no happy ending, with humans ending up abandoned, blinded, or worse. Even though not all jinn are as wicked as quranāʾ, female jinn reject moral codes and obligations imposed by human society.[166] Some people believed that jinn doppelgangers prefer to intermarry. Each time two humans are married their doppelgangers also say their vows. And each time a child is born to them, a qarīn of a wife gives birth as well. A similar opinion can also be found in al-Ghazālī's works. However, al-Ghazālī maintained that evil jinn reproduce at a faster rate than humans. Hence the greater number of inhabitants of the unseen society.[167]

2.6. Society of the Unseen

The concluding section of this chapter was envisioned as a general introduction to the little-known but widespread reports of the unseen society that doppelgangers also belong to. This subchapter is furthermore aiming to contribute to the better understanding of the character and intelligence of jinn (doppelgangers) by examining their cultural sensibilities and accomplishments, with the intention of setting the relationship of quranāʾ and their victims in a broader context of human-jinn relations.

Insofar as a qarīn has been feared as the shadow of the Self, the world of jinn has been perceived as a mirror of the human society.[168] Extant reports on jinn society mostly focus on its social stratifications. For example, like humans, jinn were said to have kings and prophets of their own. Folk tales from Upper Egypt depict the queen of quranāʾ as the fire-breathing woman with loosened hair. She was thought to be prone to targeting pregnant women and sending snakes and scorpions after children.[169] In Russia and Dagestan, the common folk identify the queen of doppelgangers as

ʾUmm al-Ṣibyān. In Russia, this queen was thought to be a witch rather than a demoness. When ʾUmm al-Ṣibyān gets jealous of a woman who has children, she instigates her children's quranāʾ to have them murdered.[170] However, most written sources identify ʾAbū Dibāj as the ruler of jinn doppelgangers. This jinni also features prominently in Palestinian folklore.[171] ʾAbū Dibāj was usually portrayed as a learned jinni, proficient in alchemy and sorcery. The cunning-folk would thus often try to compel him to disclose the locations of stolen items and hidden treasures. ʾAbū Dibāj's secretary, ʾIsmāʿīl, was said to be the most knowledgeable among the jinn.[172] Al-Tilimsānī, who claimed to have successfully summoned ʾIsmāʿīl, "the secretary of that most glorious king," was informed that the jinn society consists of seventy groups. Each of these groups contains seventy thousand tribes (*qabīla*), which are divided into seventy thousand clans each. "Were a needle to fall from the sky," ʾIsmāʿīl said, "it would fall on one of them."[173]

Jinn were described by Ibn Manẓūr as social, invisible beings. Each jinni will thus state the name of its tribe when introducing itself.[174] Most jinn tribes were unsurprisingly identified as the counterparts of Bedouin tribes.[175] To the best of our knowledge, there are no surviving records indicating that polytheistic nations have their counterparts in the world of jinn. There are, however, records of non-Arab, Muslim tribes of jinn. These include the Persian tribes Banū Sāsān, Tirān and Māhān, the Turkish tribe Khāḳān, and the jinn of Niṣībīn.[176] The total number of jinn tribes varies from one source to another. In his works, Ibn ʿArabī spoke of the twelve main clans and their sub-branches. He believed that the twelve clans are in the state of perpetual warfare. As a consequence of intra-jinn conflicts, dust devils and whirlwinds were said to appear in deserts.[177] Although Ibn ʿArabī did not provide us with the names of the twelve clans, *Mandal al-Sulaymanī*, the anonymous manuscript documenting the demise of Ṣakhr, the presumed doppelganger of king Solomon, lists their names as the following: Banū al-Zarqāʾ, Banū ʾArḥam, Banū Hawjil, Banū Khaṭfān, Banū Harhara, Banū ʾAraq, Banū al-Ḥabshā, Banū Saḥāb, Banū Shajīḥ, Banū Dalhash, Banū Ṣaḥābiyyūn, and Banū al-Qāwāʿid. Ṣakhr identified Banū al-Qāwāʿid as the only tribe "jinn that whisper into the hearts of men" come from (figure 2.7). Even though jinn live longer than

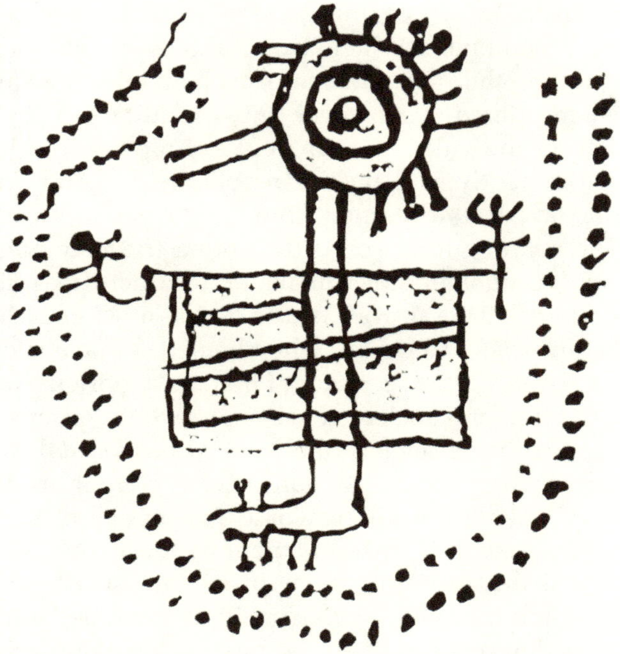

Figure 2.7. A sigil containing an image of a jinni from the Banū al-Qāwāʿid tribe. Drawing by the author based on *Kitāb al-Mandal al-Sulaymanī* (MS 2774), ff.6.

humans, these creatures are not immortal. The author of *Mandal al-Sulaymanī* thus emphasized the fact that the jinni named Bashīr is the current leader of Banū al-Qāwāʿid, with Ṭhalshīn being his second in command. A jinni named Sarīʿ was said to be another prominent member of this tribe.[178]

Throughout the centuries, the science of stars (*ʿilm al-nujūm*)[179] has been closely entwined with jinnealogy. As a result, the names of the twelve clans were sometimes substituted with the names of zodiac constellations. These are: Aries (*al-Ḥaml*), Taurus (*at-Thawr*), Gemini (*al-Jawzāʾ*), Cancer (*as-Saraṭān*), Leo (*al-ʾAsad*), Aquarius (*ad-Dalw*), Virgo (*al-ʾAdhrāʾ*), Libra (*al-Mīzān*), Scorpio (*al-ʾAqrab*), Sagittarius (*al-Qaws*), Capricorn (*al-Jadiy*), and Pisces (*al-Ḥūt*). Humans were thought to be more likely to suffer an assault from the clan corresponding to their zodiac sign—presumably due to the malign influence of their doppelgangers. Women born when

Mars was in Capricorn were said to be particularly vulnerable to the whispers of their doppelganger and the wrath of the jinn folk in general.[180] Not only were jinn clans associated with the zodiac constellation, but they were also linked with the heavenly spheres and planets. Ibn ʿArabī spoke of the nine spheres in his works, seven of which were said to contain planets. These are the Sphere of Saturn (*zuḥal*), Jupiter (*al-mushtarī*), Mars (*al-mirrīkh*), Sun (*al-shams*), Venus (*al-zuhra*), Mercury (*ʿuṭārid*), and the Moon (*al-qamar*). Ibn ʿArabī linked these planetary spheres with the seven Names of God—i.e. with the Creator who is Living, Knowing, Wanting, Powerful, Speaking, Generous, and Just—and with the seven prophets: Adam, Jesus/Yahya, Yusuf, Idris, Harun, Moses, and Ibrahim. There was also a strong tendency among Sufis to link the planetary spheres with the seven angels and the seven kings of jinn (Table 2.1).

Islamic notions of the seven angels guarding the seven planetary spheres and the seven jinn kings were in all likelihood inspired by Greco-Egyptian mysticism, where planets were perceived as manifestations of unseen gods (*theoi*). *Theoi* were served by the spirits known as *daimones*. Philo of Alexandria (d. 50) was among the first to identify *theoi* with angels. Muslim scholars later identified these angels as the guardians of the seven kings of jinn. *Daimones* were, however, perceived as guardian spirits and doubles

Table 2.1. Jinn Kings, Angels, Prophets, and their Planets

Planetary sphere	**Jinn king**	**Angel**	**Prophet**
Moon	Murrah	Jibrāʾīl	Adam
Mercury	Burqān	Mīkāʾīl	ʿĪsā /Yaḥyā
Venus	al-ʾAbyaḍ	ʿAnyāʾīl	Yūsuf
Sun	al-Mudhab	Rūqyāʾīl	Idrīs
Mars	al-ʾAḥmar	Samsamāʾīl	Hārūn
Jupiter	Shamhūresh	Ṣarfyāʾīl	Mūsā
Saturn	Maymūn	Kasfyāʾīl	Ibrāhīm

Based on the data provided in Ibn ʿArabī, *Kitāb ʿAnqāʾ al-Mughrib*, 52; Ibn ʿArabī, *The Seven Days of the Heart*, 10; FM.II:272, and Canaan, *Aberglaube und Volksmedizin*, 23.

of humans.[181] Noble was among the first to write about the impact of pseudo-Aristotelian hermeticism and the Platonic notions of *daimones* on the Islamic conception of the Perfect Nature that Ibn ʿArabī also professed.[182] Elmore furthermore identified Greco-Egyptian *daimones* with familiar spirits (quranāʾ) and other jinn in Ibn ʿArabī's works.[183] It is, however, worth noting that Ibn ʿArabī would have likely opposed the idea that the Greek *theoi* can be identified with angels, not in the least since he believed that the spirits of planets can be summoned by a magician and bound to their will. In contrast, the surah *Maryam* makes it clear that angels *descend only by the command of your Lord* (Q 19:64). Ibn ʿArabī, however, left open the possibility that the spirits of planets might be identical with jinn (doppelgangers).[184] Among the prominent supporters of this theory was Ibn Rushd, who surmised that the belief in jinn in Muslim cultures and societies was inspired by the emission of heat from heavenly bodies. Ibn Rushd insisted this heat is not to be mistaken with fire. The heat of heavenly bodies was thought to contain souls. These celestial souls would sometimes create organic bodies on Earth so that they could inhabit them for the time being, hence the legends of the presumed impact of the kings of jinn on the life on Earth. Following the decay of their bodies, celestial souls return to their heavenly spheres. Whether these souls are the same as human souls was identified by Ibn Rushd as one of the most difficult problems in Islamic philosophy.[185] On his side, al-Tahanāwī (d. 1745) was adamant that the spirits of the planets are neither human souls nor jinn.[186] The Brethren of Purity, however, believed there are two types of evil souls/devils. The first type clings to the bodies of planets and does not depart from them. These devils influence life on Earth in accordance with what is written in the stars. The devils belonging to the second group were identified as jinn by the Brethren.[187] Whereas the Brethren of Purity believed that Mercury is the planet in charge of jinn, Pseudo-Majriti noted that the most powerful devils have been associated with the planet Saturn, Dragon's Tail, and/or with the Fixed Stars. These creatures would sometimes help magicians in exchange for ritual offerings. Pseudo-Majriti believed that no other nation was as proficient at harnessing the power of these devils as Indians.[188] Each of these jinn falls under the jurisdiction of the four lords: Māzar, the Lord of the East; Kamṭam, the Lord of the West; Qasūra, the Lord of the South; and Ṭaykal, the Lord of the Sea. Each of these lords was thought to have a jinn-king as his deputy. For instance, the Lord of the East, was served by ʾAḥmar, the Red King. This jinni was identified by Canaan as the forefather of doppelgangers.[189]

ʾAḥmar is a malevolent creature. Illuminated manuscripts typically depict the Red King in the same posture as Mars. For instance, in the fourteenth century manuscript of *Kitāb al-Bulhān* (Ms. Bodl. Or. 133), both ʾAḥmar and Mars appear carrying a sword in one hand and a severed human head in another (figure 2.8). Like Mars, ʾAḥmar has been associated with war and bloodshed. In the attempt to curb its malevolent influence, the Ottoman owner of the Ms. Bodl. Or. 133 cut ʾAḥmar's neck, disfigured its face, and gouged out the eyes of its mount. According to Gruber, it was once a common practice among the Ottoman and Safavid audience to disfigure portraits of religious figures. Such treatment was usually reserved for enemies of the Prophet.[190] Curiously enough, other jinn from *Kitāb al-Bulhān* were spared from such treatment.

Figure 2.8. Mars and the jinn king of Mars. *Source*: al-Iṣfahānī, *Kitāb al-Bulhān* (MS. Bodl. Or. 133), ff.10, 31a.

Alongside Barqān, Maymūn, and Mudhab, ʾAḥmar was said to be the most powerful of the seven kings. The power of each king was thought to be connected to the days of the week, and it was once a common practice to call upon the ruler of each day, every day, in order to be safe from machinations of the six other kings. According to Canaan, the malevolent ʾAḥmar was usually asked for help on Tuesday. Hence, this jinni was sometimes referred to as the "Jinn King of Tuesday."[191] McGregor noted that the tendency to identify jinn kings with the seven planets and the seven days of the week can be traced to the ninth century AD, when *Epistles of the Brethren of Purity* identified the jinn family of Birjīs (Jupiter) and Nāhīd (Venus) as a part of the retinue of the jinn-king Bīwarāsp the Wise.[192] This epistle is a rare example of jinn being portrayed as sedentary, cultured nobility. Jinn were otherwise typically described as nomads in philosophy and literature. In all likelihood, this is to be attributed to the fact that most medieval works on jinnealogy have been distributed among city populations. The target audience of these works likely felt that jinn are something foreign and dangerous to the established order in Muslim cultures and societies. Another possible reason why jinn were associated with nomads is related to the fact that the earliest jinn narratives were transmitted among the Bedouins of old Arabia. Many of the purported traits of jinn culture—including their sense of honor, social structures, and their love of poetry, horsemanship, and camels—evoke the Bedouin society of old Arabia.

Jinn doppelgangers were not typically described as honorable creatures. Ṣakhr, in particular, took the first opportunity to betray Solomon's trust and usurp his throne. However, this is not to say that jinn have neither laws nor a sense of justice. Kings of jinn would sometimes deliver justice to humans who were wronged by other jinn. For instance, al-Damīrī reports of a man from Baghdad whose daughter was kidnapped by a jinni. A wise man advised the grieving father to travel to the ruin of al-Karkh and remain seated in a circle he drew on the floor, invoking the name of God until the jinn-king arrived. When the king appeared in front of him, the man sought justice. Having listened to his case, the king informed him that a jinni from China had fallen in love with his daughter and had her kidnapped. The king then ordered for the girl to be reunited with her father.[193] Muslim jurisprudents have also debated whether human beings owe the jinn folk a fair treatment. The Kairouanese judge ʾAbū Muḥammad al-Shabībī (d. 1380) thus issued a fatwa forbidding Muslims to kill a jinni who did them no harm.[194] Akbarians generally looked down on causing harm to living beings unless one was forced to execute a punishment prescribed by Sharia, and Ibn ʿArabī emphasized the fact that the Prophet refrained from enslaving jinn.[195] There was, however, no general consensus among scholars on the matter. Nasnās, a subspecies of jinn known for their intelligence and their love for nature, were thus purportedly killed for food in Yemen.[196] Enslaved jinn were also forced to build cities, temples, and dams in human service. According to legend, the jinn folk were involved in the building of Palmyra. In the old Arabia, this city was known as Tadmur. The building process was described by al-Nābighah al-Dhubiyānī (d. 604) in the following verses:

> Put the jinn in chains!
> Thus, I permitted them to build Tadmur,
> With stones and pillars.[197]

Other examples of jinn-made structures include the thermal baths of Tiberias (figure 2.9), the temple of Jerusalem, the city of Rome, and Solomon's City of Glass. Solomon's ability to control jinn was linked to his signet ring. This ring was entrusted to him by the archangel Gabriel. To enslave a jinni, all he needed to do was to imprint his signet seal on an iron surface.[198] Solomon's jinn were said to have despised their master. Having grown tired of their hateful glares, Solomon ordered Ṣakhr to make him a drinking cup made of glass so that he could keep an eye on his jinn when drinking. Al-Qazwīnī maintained that this is what had him inspired to build a city of glass.[199] The dying Solomon was aware that jinn would never willingly lend him their strength to see his projects to the end. Hence, he leaned on his staff so that he would remain seated in death. His goal was to trick his slaves into working for him for as long as possible. Not realizing that Solomon passed away, jinn toiled away at their construction sites for some time after his death. However, their servitude came to an end when they were informed of Solomon's death by *ʾashkāl*, the treacherous insect. In gratitude, jinn swore an oath to supply these insects with food to the end of days.[200]

Figure 2.9. Jinn slaves working at the bathhouse of Tiberias. *Source*: al-Iṣfahānī, *Kitāb al-Bulhān* (MS. Bodl. Or. 133), ff.35b.

The jinn folk tend to approach humans with alternating curiosity and hatred, in fear of their cooking pots and chains. "The children of Adam were evil to me," a jinni named ʾAbū Hadrāj said, "and I treated them likewise."[201] Jinn doppelgangers in particular have no more reason to love their humans than any other jinni. Their love for poetry was, however, said to exceed their hatred for mankind.[202] Evil doppelgangers would thus sometimes inspire their humans to become great poets. Rare examples of jinn hospitality were also usually reserved for poets. Zuhair b. Numair, the companion jinni of the poet Ibn Shuhaid, thus took him to the land of jinn, "luxuriantly overgrown with trees and sweet-scented because of its flowers."[203] The high level of Ibn Shuhaid's poetry led the vizier ʾAbū Bakr Yaḥyā b. Ḥazm to accuse him of consorting with jinn. A poet that young, reasoned Ibn Ḥazm, could never compose verses such as his. Ibn Shuhaid, however, replied that all poets are inspired by their jinn.[204] Among the most famous jinn muses were ʿAmr, the jinni companion of the poet al-Farazdaq (d. 728), Hawbar, Hajal, and the jinn chieftain Shiniqanaq. In most cases, it is not possible to determine which subspecies these jinn belonged to. A rare exception is the muse of Ḥasān b. Thābit (d. 674), which was clearly identified as a *siʿlāh*,[205] and there are also reports of quranāʾ turning their victims into poets. Such was the case of the Omayyad poet Kuthayyit ʿAzzah (d. 723). He composed the following verses to commemorate the first time he saw his doppelganger:

> He appeared strange to me, a man made of brass!
> He told me to recite some poetry.
> And recited some poetry himself.
> I said: "Who are you?"
> He said: "I am your qarīn from among the jinn!"
> This is how I began reciting poetry.

Kuthayyit had no gift for poetry before his qarīn decided to lend him its talent.[206] What reason the qarīn may have had to turn an untalented person into a poet remains unclear. On the one hand, jinn's love for poetry is well documented, and there are no surviving records indicating that quranāʾ are averse to fine verses. However, there is also a possibility the qarīn was attempting to corrupt Kuthayyit by getting him involved with poetry. For, as Ibn ʿArabī pointed out, the surah *Ya-Sin* reads God *did not teach Muhammad to versify, nor would that be worthy of him* (Q 36:69). A wicked doppelganger would have no such qualms, however.[207]

Poetic talent was both prized and reviled in Islamic culture—and the same goes for music and magic. These three talents have been closely associated with jinn (doppelgangers) in Islamic culture. On the authority of the Prophet's companion ʾAbū Umāma al-Bāhilī (d. 705), it was reported that God designated poetry as the Qur'an of the Devil. Iblis then demanded a messenger to spread his "book"—and God gave him flute.[208] Yāqūt was among the first to use the term *azif* for jinn music in general.[209] *Azif* was chiefly performed on flute, pipe, mandolin, and harp. Whereas flute, pipe, and mandolin were presumably invented by Iblis the Devil, al-Qazwīnī recorded that a jinni named Murra b. al-Hārith made the first harp. When Murra was summoned to appear in front of Solomon, the jinni took the form of a monkey. Although Murra was ugly, no human could match the beauty of its music. Unfortunately for the jinni, Solomon feared that Murra's music might corrupt believers, and thus he put him in chains.[210] As the inhabitants of human blood and hearts, jinn doppelgangers were not generally known for their music performances. If they were to sing, their voices would have likely resembled the clucking of a chicken, for this is how the prophet Muhammad described jinn voices in general (*Ṣaḥīḥ al-Bukhārī* #7561). Dhū al-Rummah (d. 715), however, compared jinn chants to the sound of "trees moaning in the wind."[211] Junayd (d. 910) furthermore recalled how his teacher used to admire the jinn singing in the mountains. Such was the beauty of their voices that he fell down unconscious. When the teacher woke up, he found that someone had laid flowers on his chest.[212] Music, even when performed by jinn, was not universally perceived as evil in Islam. This can be seen from Junayd's story. Another example can be found in al-Ghazālī's works, for he believed that music can be used to establish a relationship with angels and to cut off one's relationship with evil jinn.[213] The same goes for magic.

The term *siḥr*—which is the most common Arabic word for magic—has a wide scope of meaning, to the point where Savage-Smith noted there are nearly as many definitions of magic as there are people writing about it.[214] On his side, Burnett compared the Arabic *siḥr* to nigromancia. This is especially the case when jinn magic and image magic are concerned.

> Under this heading [i.e., of nigromancia] is another art, called the "notory" art, that enables one to learn all the

> sciences by means of all sorts of words, figures and characters. This art is not devoid of alliances with evil demons because the unknown words function to create a compact between humankind and the devil. Even if this method is associated with fasting, prayer and a pure, chaste life, it is forbidden anyway and a sin, because the evil demons are hidden by this beautiful appearance in order to seduce and lead men astray.[215]

Jinn doppelgangers were especially valued by those who wished to learn of hidden thoughts and intentions of others; since no other jinni is in a better position to consult with the other person's qarīn.[216] According to legend, the first human to dabble in jinn sorcery was ʿAnāq, the daughter of Adam. ʿAnāq gained power over jinn by learning their names, which were entrusted by God to Adam.[217] Other magicians were, however, forced to rely on ritual offerings and coaxing to appease the jinn folk. One of the most notorious magicians in Islamic culture was Ibn Hilāl of Kufa. According to legend, he was able to see the future and traverse great distances with the help of his jinn.[218] Like Pseudo-Majriti, Ibn ʿArabī associated magic with brahmins of India and the Egyptian sorcerers who stood up to Moses. He mostly referred to magic as the science of mystery (*ʿulūm al-sirr*) and *sīmīyāʾ*.[219] Ibn ʿArabī defined *sīmīyāʾ* as natural magic—i.e. as the knowledge of plants, stones, and the secret properties of names and letters. In general, Ibn ʿArabī's opinion of magicians was poor. Even though magic can be tempting and alluring, Ibn ʿArabī argued that it cannot bring long-lasting success to a spiritual Seeker. Magic was compared to a beautiful dream in his works, for whereas a dream might appear real to a sleeping human, they will discard it as an illusion the moment they wake up. Magic has limited power and limited use in spiritual wayfaring, irrespective of the fact whether a spiritual Seeker can coax their qarīn into helping them or not. Ibn ʿArabī said:

> Jinn are the most ignorant creatures in the world of nature when the knowledge of God is concerned. They inform their companions of certain events and of what has transpired in the universe. Jinn acquire this knowledge by eavesdropping in heaven. A magician then imagines things and believes God is honoring him. Such a man

> should be wary of his delusions, for you will never find a companion of jinn who has gained any knowledge of God whatsoever. The furthest limit that a man favored by the jinn can reach is the knowledge of plants, stones, names and letters granted to him by the jinn. This is the art of *sīmīyā'*. A man favored by jinn will only gain blameworthy knowledge from them. If someone claims to be a companion of jinn—provided that he speaks the truth—ask him of anything pertaining to the Divine knowledge (*al-ʿilm al-ʾilāhī*) and you will see that he never tasted it.[220]

Jinn were said to have learned the art of *sīmīyā'* from Hārut and Mārut. These evil angels were imprisoned at Mt. Damavand for the sins they committed, alongside the sorcerer al-Ḍaḥḥāk and Ṣakhr, the presumed qarīn of king Solomon.[221] Jinn's punishment was less severe, for God merely forbade them to ascend beyond the world of nature. It is therefore not surprising that all miracles jinn have performed pertain to the world of gross matter. These miracles were said to include bringing forth summer fruits in winter, walking through walls, and traversing great distances in an instant. Such things, al-Qayṣarī noted, are of no value to Sufis.[222] Even so, jinn pride themselves as the teachers of men. Upon being asked which language they prefer to use when speaking to humans, a jinni named ʾAbū Hadrāsh said: "We are the folk of clairvoyance and cleverness. We know all human languages and we have a language that humans do not know."[223] Jurists at the court of the jinn-king Bīwarāsp also boasted that jinn have taught humans how to build houses, grow crops, and differentiate between good and evil. In his commentary of Ibn ʿArabī's *Fuṣūs al-ḥikam*, al-Qayṣarī, however, argued that jinn have limited cognitive abilities. Whereas al-Qayṣarī maintained that no jinni can grasp abstract concepts,[224] Ibn ʿArabī believed them to be capable of analytical thinking (*naẓar*) and deduction (*ʾistidlāl*).[225] Although neither *naẓar* nor *ʾistidlāl* are harmful per se, excessive reasoning has alienated jinn from God. This was especially the case with Iblis, whom Ibn ʿArabī described as "the most obstinate denier of God."[226] No jinni has ever brought the tyranny of reason (*ʾistibdād bil-raʿy*) to such excess as Iblis the Devil.[227] Iblis felt no personal responsibility for his eviction from paradise. Ibn ʿArabī furthermore noted that he also refused to repent for not bowing before Adam. Instead, the Devil pointed out that God created jinn and not the other way around. Hence, Iblis reasoned, God is at fault for making them arrogant, brazen, and prone to sin.[228] The Devil said:

> Since God knew in advance what would become of me, what is the wisdom of His having created me? Since He created me according to His will and wish, why did He [then] command me to know and obey Him? And what was the wisdom of this command (*taklīf*) since He neither benefits from obedience nor is He harmed by disobedience? Since He created me and made me compelled [to act in the way I did], why did He curse me and drove me out of Eden? Why did He let me tempt Adam and his consort? It would have been better for them and more appropriate to His wisdom to create them with inborn knowledge of the right behavior (*ʿalā al-fiṭra*), without leading them into temptation. And lastly, why was I allowed to pester humanity? Would it not have been better to have a world free from evil?[229]

Mullā Ṣadrā (d. 1635) compared Iblis's arguments to the reasoning of "a fallacious sophist."[230] Ibn ʿArabī's opinion of rational thinkers was not as harsh. Even though the People of Reflection (*ʾahl al-naẓār*) often make mistakes when interpreting the Divine matters, Ibn ʿArabī pointed out that every intelligent human partakes in philosophy—provided that philosophy is properly identified as the love for wisdom.[231] Hence, Ibn ʿArabī did not condemn Iblis for valuing the power of the mind. He furthermore believed that no skeptic is in the wrong just for thinking things through. Ibn ʿArabī rather thought that the Devil made a mistake by applying reason to things which should have been left to faith.[232] The Divine command, Ibn ʿArabī noted, demands obedience. God endowed humans and jinn with rational faculties to subdue their passions, not "to acquire sciences" and/or relativize His orders. This is something that well-read men and jinn tend to forget.[233] Whereas jinn are curious, Ibn ʿArabī noted they are not naturally drawn towards God and the knowledge of God.[234] This is why they repeatedly turn down human preachers who wished to instruct them on how to act, think, and believe. Although humans have no knowledge of the jinn prophets, it would be safe to assume that the content of the revelations they received pertained to the jinn folk. For the Qur'an attests that the message of each prophet was tailored to serve the needs of his community (Q 10:47, 14:4). Even so, revelations received by a human prophet could also be relevant for jinn. This is especially the case with Muhammad's mission, and the surah *al-ʾAḥqāf* indicates that Muhammad also preached to jinn (Q 46:29–31). Since they were taught by the Prophet, Ibn ʿArabī believed that the jinn folk are also obliged to abide by Sharia.[235] Muhammad's jinn followers were described in Ibn ʿArabī's works as eloquent, assertive, and humble. Unlike their brethren, these jinn were always eager to learn more from the Prophet.[236] Apart from Muhammad, jinn were said to have respected the authority of al-Ḥusayn b. ʿAlī (d. 680), Ḥasan al-Baṣrī (d. 728), Wahb b. Muhabih (d. 738), and Ibn al-Jawzī (d. 1200)—at least when religious matters were concerned. According to al-Suyūṭī, such was the popularity of Ibn al-Jawzī's lectures among the jinn that they afflicted him with an eye infection to prevent him from leaving the city before he could finish his course. Jinn students proved to be more respectful towards Wahb b. Muhabih. As he was engaged in prayer in the mosque of al-Khayf, a bird landed close to him. Knowing that the bird was actually a jinni in disguise, Wahid had it greeted. The bird then asked for permission to attend his lectures. It said: "Do you forbid us from learning from you? Many of us attend your meetings and we always go back to our people to recite them what we heard from you. We attend your prayers, fight in your jihad, we visit your patients and walk with the mourners at your funerals. We accompany you as you engage in *ʿumrah* and hajj and we listen to the Qur'an when you recite it."[237]

Whereas Wahb graciously agreed to the jinni's request, other Sufis were reluctant to take jinn as apprentices. Some Sufi masters, al-Qushayrī (d. 1073) noted, would fall silent upon noticing there was a jinni sitting among their students, for many Sufis believed that jinn are unfit to hear their lectures.[238] On his side, Ibn ʿArabī believed that jinn, like humans, can become well-versed in Divine knowledge (*mutaḍalliʿ min al-ʿilm al-ilāhī*).[239] The possibility of a spiritual ascent is not denied to the jinn folk either. Apart from humans, jinn are the only species in the universe that can learn, develop, and, to a degree, dictate their fate.[240] Whereas some jinn choose to turn away from God, others are mindful of the true purpose of their existence. For the Qur'an makes it clear that God created humans and jinn only to worship Him (Q 51:56). To the best of our knowledge, there are no records of doppelgangers that converted to Islam of their own accord. This is likely related to the fact that jinn doppelgangers are the embodiments of the Divine Name *al-Mudhill,* the One Who Leads Astray. Hence, they fully depend on humans to set them a good example to follow. Like Muhammad preached Islam to his jinn, it is up to each Seeker to convert their doppelganger to Islam and help it ascend through the stations of spiritual wayfaring.

Chapter 3

The Devil Within

> It is as though our dreams were watching us and directing our lives with external vigor whilst we simply enact their pleasures passively in a swoon. Except that the jinn are more solid than dreams.
>
> —A. S. Byatt[1]

> You yourself are the cloud veiling your own Sun!
> So recognize the essential Reality of your being!
>
> —Ibn ʿArabī[2]

Ibn ʿArabī referred to the microcosm as the Great City (*al-madīna al-kubra*). A diagram depicting the Great City was preserved in the holograph of Ibn ʿArabī's *K. ʿAnqāʾ mughrib* (figure 3.1). Due to the ambiguous form of the original diagram, manuscript copyists were confused whether the Great City has seven or eight districts in total. Ibn ʿArabī's decision to omit the names of these districts from his diagram was another source of confusion among scholars. However, most interpreters agreed that the center of the diagram represents the human heart (*qalb*).[3] Whereas interpretations of the outer City districts varied from one manuscript to another, the body (*jism*), soul (*nafs*), and spirit (*rūh*) have been identified as the main parts of the microcosm. On the macrocosmic level, these correspond to Mulk, Jabarūt, and Malakūt.[4] Whereas the human body is visible, the soul and spirit belong to *jānn*, "which is the invisible and

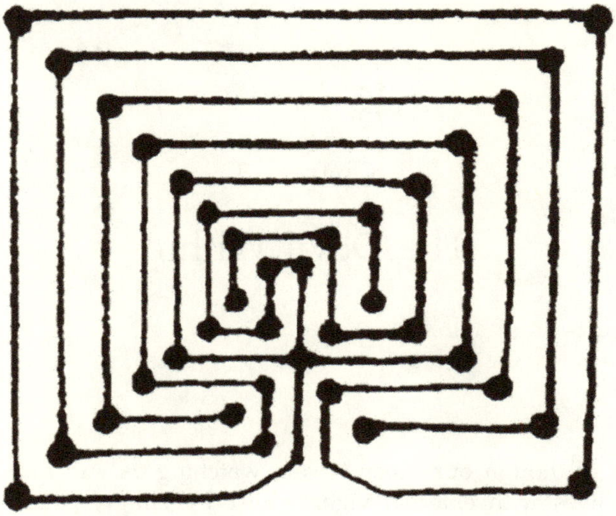

Figure 3.1. Ibn ʿArabī's diagram of the Great City. *Source*: Ibn ʿArabī, *Kitāb ʿAnqāʾ mughrib* (Ms. or. oct. 3266), ff.41. Used with permission.

true dimension of human beings."[5] Differences between *nafs*, *rūḥ*, and other aspects of *jānn* were never entirely clear in practice. Ibn ʿArabī's tendencies to refer to both jinn (doppelgangers) and the forefather of doppelgangers as *jānn* only made it more complicated to understand a qarīn at work. A qarīn was said to reside in the heart—together with the soul, spirit, and, possibly, God Himself. Ibn ʿArabī's notion of God residing in the heart was based on a *ḥadīth qudsī*, which reads: "Heaven and earth contain Me not, but the heart of my faithful servant contains Me."[6] This hadith led Ibn ʿArabī to believe that "the heart of a servant is the house of the True."[7] Ibn ʿArabī referred to a Seeker's efforts to tame the soul and purify their heart as the Conquest of the City (*fatḥ al-madīna*). A qarīn is a Seeker's enemy in this process. A doppelganger will cast itself as a veil over the human heart and stir up the soul which incites to evil (*al-nafs al-ʾammārah bi al-sūʾ*). To understand a qarīn at work, one must identify its tools and targets first. The definition of *nafs* is of particular importance since Ibn ʿArabī did not always make a distinction between *nafs* and the Devil Within. *Al-nafs* (*al-ʾammārah*) was concurrently identified in Sufi literature as the master, tool, helper, and the microcosmic counterpart of jinn doppelgangers. Our attempt to define the (lower) soul and its relation to the human body and spirit will be followed by an overview of the tactics used by quranāʾ in the siege of the Great City.

3.1. The Body, Soul, and Spirit

Human beings and jinn have inherent knowledge and awareness of their bodies. The bodies of both species were created from the admixture of fire, water, air, and earth. Whereas jinn are creatures of air and fire, water and earth were thought to be the predominant elements in human bodies. Ibn ʿArabī believed that the elements of water and earth provide humans with stability and superiority over jinn,[8] for the Qur'an attests that *God created man in the best of forms* (Qur'an 95:4). Ibn ʿArabī furthermore taught that the body is a vehicle of the soul. In return, the soul regulates the body's growth, food intake, nourishment, and digestion. When the body is in good condition, with its components and constitution in order, it can help a Seeker achieve their spiritual goals. However, bodily imbalances can equally obstruct a spiritual quest. Physical features were sometimes taken as an indicator of corrupt character traits among Akbarians. The more corrupt a person is, the more powerful will their qarīn be. Among the most troubling signs of inner corruption were excessive body hair, short neck, smooth, flat forehead, and turquoise-blue or reddish-brown eyes with yellow dots in the iris.[9] Whereas physical features vary from one human to another, the Divine spirit (*al-rūḥ al-ilāhī*) is always the same—and perfect. To create a human being, God breathes some of His spirit into their bodily form (Q 38:71). This occurs when the fetus is four months old. The heart of the fetus thus becomes the palace of the spirit, with the brain serving as its watchtower. Following the birth of a child, the five senses become the spirit's spies and henchmen. The front of the body will serve the spirit as its guardian, the middle part as a minister, and the back as a treasury and a treasurer alike.[10] The Divine spirit was described in the surah *al-ʾIsrāʾ* as *something from the command of my Lord and you are not to be given knowledge of it, except a little* (Q 17:85). Scholars were, however, in disagreement with regard to the human spirit (*rūḥ al-insān*). Whereas some scholars thought that the human spirit is the seed of personality, others believed that the spirit grants the power of reason to humans. Then there were those who argued that the Divine spirit is identical with the human spirit.[11] Ibn ʿArabī, however, suggested that the human spirit is a child of the Divine Breath and the four elements which make the human body (i.e. fire, water, air, and earth). As a result, the human spirit has a dual nature, and it can either succumb to the darkness of the gross matter or turn to the Divine light.[12] The term *rūḥ* was sometimes used as a synonym for *nafs* in Ibn ʿArabī's works. For example, in Chapter 178 of *al-Futūḥāt*, Ibn ʿArabī extended an ayah from the surah *al-Nisāʾ* to read: "*rūḥ* is from Him—and this is *nafs*."[13] The term *nafs* has a wide scope of meaning, which Ibn ʿArabī compared to an ocean without a shore. "Gazing upon it has no end in this world and the next."[14] Ibn ʿArabī emphasized the need to study *nafs* to the point where Chittick remarked that *nafs* was his only research topic.[15] *Nafs* was important to Ibn ʿArabī since he believed that it was created to serve as an allusion (*ʾishāra*) to God. In other words, he who knows his *nafs* knows His Lord.[16] The Arabic *nafs* is typically rendered into English as "soul." However, this term has equally served to denote the human breath, spirit, essence, the creative power of God, and the Devil Within. In other words, Ibn ʿArabī used *nafs* as a synonym for *jānn* and the human subtlety (*al-laṭīfa al-insāniyya*) in general.[17] *Nafs* can be used as a reflective pronoun in the Arabic language, and Ibn ʿArabī was well aware of this fact. Thus, he noted that the word *nafs* "is used to express what each of us hints at when he says 'I' (*ʾanā*)."[18] The allusive nature of *nafs* and the confusion this term has caused among scholars were famously captured in al-Jurjānī's verses:

> Everyone joins the self to "I" but to what does this "I" refer?
> Speak, do not just scratch your beard!
> Is it the body? Or the soul? The intellect? Or the spirit?
> Or is it like the amalgam of horse and man in the knight?
> Whoever holds this view is mistaken: there are
> Many knights who don't know how to fasten their trousers!
> There's many a man who considers himself a weighty "I"
> Who doesn't attain the measure of a mote when he's weighed.[19]

Hakim was among the scholars who gave up attempts to differentiate between Ibn ʿArabī's notions of *rūḥ* and *nafs* altogether.[20] Shazad took things one step further. He noted that the term *nafs* was used in the Qur'an to signify the human being as a whole—with their body and spirit included.[21] The Qur'an also speaks of the three souls. These are the serene soul (*al-nafs al-muṭmaʾinna*), the blaming soul (*al-nafs al-lawwāmah*), and the lower soul (*al-nafs al-ʾammārah*) (Q 12:53, 72:2, 89:27–28). This is not to say there are multiple souls inhabiting the human body. In his commentary on Ibn ʿArabī's *Fuṣūs al-ḥikam*, al-Qayṣarī clarified that these souls represent the states of manifestations and transformations of the spirit—and the same goes for the human heart and intellect (*ʿaql*).

> Know that the supreme spirit (*al-rūh al-ʾaʿẓam*), which is in reality the human spirit (*al-rūḥ al-insānī*), is a manifestation of the Divine essence from the aspect of Lordship. . . . This spirit is the heart (*qalb*) on the account of its fluctuation between the face which adjoins God, thus receiving lights from Him, and the face which adjoins the animal soul (*al-nafs al-ḥayawāniyya*); emanating what it receives from the Creator in accordance with its preparedness. . . . This spirit is the intellect (*ʿaql*) on the account of it conceiving its essence and origin and on the account of its delimitation and particular entification—and since it binds that which it perceives and apprehends and confines therein its objects of cognition. This spirit is the soul (*nafs*) on the account of its attachment to the body and its governance of the body. It is referred to as the vegetable soul (*al-nafs al-nabātiyya*) when a vegetal activity arises within it—and it is referred to as the animal soul when an animal activity arises within it. When the animal powers dominate over the spiritual powers, the spirit is being referred to as the lower soul (*al-nafs al-ʾammārah*). However, when a shimmer of the heart's light from the Unseen occurs within it, bringing forth perfection and awareness by the rational soul of its iniquitous end and the corruption of its states, it is called the reproachful soul (*lawwāma*), since it reproaches its actions.[22]

Chapter 70 of *al-Futūḥāt* offers another interpretation of the ambiguous relationship between the body, soul, and spirit. Here Ibn ʿArabī surmised that the soul is a child of the Divine spirit and the human body. Ibn ʿArabī also thought that the soul is higher in ranking than the body and lower in ranking than the Divine Spirit.[23] *Nafs* is ever-changing under the influence of external factors—to the point where Ibn ʿArabī identified it as "those attributes of a servant that are infirm and/or caused by something (*maʿlūl*)."[24] Sometimes, *nafs* can lead a Seeker to the presence of their Lord, "to the state of never-ending bliss."[25] However, it could also enable a qarīn to conquer the Great City. For this reason, *nafs* was concurrently described in the Islamic normative tradition as the worst enemy of humans—and the greatest masterpiece in God's creation.[26] Rūmī famously compared *nafs* to a hand extending the Qur'an to a Seeker while concurrently hiding a scimitar and a dagger in its sleeves. He also claimed that the Devil and *nafs* were once a single being; before God had it divided in two different forms.[27] Differences between jinn and *nafs* were porous and unclear in Islamic culture. Under the right circumstances, one could easily be transformed into another. Suhrawardī believed that such transformations occur after the death of an evil person. Several other philosophers were rumored to have shared this view, including ʾAbū Bakr al-Rāzī (d. 935) and Yaḥyā b. ʿAdī (d. 974).

> Al-Rāzī said in his *Kitāb al-ʿilm al-ilāhī* that the souls of wicked people who were transformed into jinn appear to some humans in form of angels and command them to go and tell people that an angel has appeared to them and told them: "God made you His messenger and I am an angel that was sent to you." This is the cause of the discord spreading and many people were killed as a result of machinations of these souls-turned-jinn.[28]
>
> Aristotle describes jinn as the creatures of air and fire. He also described them as "human beings." Likewise, Yaḥyā Grammarian and several other scholars acknowledged the existence of jinn and described them as impure parts of the erring souls which were separated from their

> bodies. These souls are prevented from reaching their primal origin since, rather than seeking knowledge of the True (i.e. God), they were living in confusion and stupefaction. Mani hints at something similar in his book—although his indications are expressed in subtle words and phrases.[29]

Some Akbarians used the soul's wickedness as the main criterion for distinguishing between *rūḥ* and *nafs*.[30] Al-Qushayrī took things one step further when arguing that *nafs* can be used as a synonym for "deficiencies of one's character traits as well as one's reprehensible morals and deeds."[31] That said, not all souls made jinn were evil in life.[32] Sometimes, a living human could also be transformed into a jinni. Such transformations were usually associated with Divine wrath and punishment. According to legend, this is how *nasnās* got to be created. "In the land of Wabār there are many creatures who have suffered the wrath of God. He changed their form into the *nasnās*, so men and women have only one half of their head and face, with one eye, one arm and one leg. They roam about, grazing in this forest all the way to the sea shore."[33]

A transformation of humans into devils could also be caused by magic. The following instructions can be found in Pseudo-Majriti's *Picatrix:*

> Take 2 oz. each of hawk, mouse, and black cat's brain; and 1/2 oz. each of sulfur and myrrh. Mix everything, and set it aside until it rots. When you wish to operate, take 8 oz. of it and an equal amount of crane excrement. Blend them together, and place it over a fire until smoke rises up. Whoever breathes in that smoke through the nostrils will be turned into a demon. They will lose both perception and memory and be unable to recognize where they are.[34]

With the possible exception of ʿAmr al-Jinnī, there are no surviving records of humans turned jinn in Ibn ʿArabī's works. Even so, a qarīn, or "what the devil in the human heart says" and "what *nafs* whispers of" were used as synonyms in *al-Futūḥāt*.[35] Ibn ʿArabī believed that a person becomes a qarīn of Iblis once they leave God's straight path. Pseudo-Majriti associated this transformation with the loss of perception and memory. Ibn ʿArabī, however, taught that greed, wrath, envy, arrogance, cowardice, and the lack of piety are the shared traits of evil souls and jinn.[36] An evil, debased soul was referred to in the Qur'an as *al-nafs al-ʾammārah.*

3.2. The Lower Soul

The form and nature of the lower soul were often compared to black dogs, snakes, and camels in Sufi literature. But most of all, the lower soul has been compared to jinn. The Akbarian school was not an exception in this regard. For instance, Ibn ʿArabī noted that the jinn folk know no peace: passionate and opinionated, they are in a state of constant movement. The (lower) soul was likewise thought to be in charge of the human bodily motions.[37] *Al-nafs al-ʾammārah* has been furthermore associated with lust (*shahwah*), anger (*ghaḍab*), capricious behavior (*hawā*), and the human self (*huwiyya*), and ego (*ʾanāniyya*). This is why Schimmel had it compared to "the flesh" in the biblical sense.[38] Whereas Schimmel spoke figuratively, ʾAbū Bakr al-Rāzī literally identified the lower soul with the flesh. Al-Rāzī believed that the lower soul consists of the heart, liver and other bodily organs—and Ibn ʿArabī noted this was a common opinion among physicians.[39] In contrast, Ibn ʿArabī held that the lower soul and the animal spirit (*al-rūḥ al-ḥayawānī*) are both subtle bodies (*ʾajsām laṭīfa*). The animal spirit was used as a synonym for the animal soul (*al-nafs al-ḥayawānyya*) in Ibn ʿArabī's works. Eating, drinking, sexual intercourses, fine music, clothes, fragrances, handsome boys, and women were listed in *al-Futūḥāt* as things the animal soul takes pleasure in. These are opposed to elated pleasures of the rational soul (*al-nafs-al-nāṭiqa*).[40]

Chapter 353 of *al-Futūḥāt* defines the rational soul as the admixture (*mizāj*) of the vegetable soul (*al-nafs al-nabātiyya*), the desiring soul (*al-nafs al-shahwaniyya*), and the wrathful soul (*al-nafs al-ghadabiyya*). Whereas the wrathful soul was simply described as a greedy, tyrannical soul consumed with wrath, the vegetable soul and the desiring soul were said to be in charge of the well-being and nourishment of the physical body.[41] Possible differences and the relationship between the wrathful soul, animal soul, and the lower soul are not entirely clear. For example, in his commentary of Ibn ʿArabī's *Fuṣūs*, al-Qayṣarī identified *al-nafs al-ḥayawānyya* as a soul that is prone to animal activities (*al-ʾafʿāl al-ḥayawāniyya*). These are likely the same carnal pleasures Ibn ʿArabī described in *al-Futūḥāt*; those that are coveted by the animal soul and the wrathful soul alike. *Al-nafs al-ʾammārah* was the term al-Qayṣarī used to indicate that animal powers have fully subdued the spiritual faculty (*al-quwwa al-rūḥiyya*) of a person. Evil and corruption thus become their permanent character traits.[42] An alternative interpretation was proposed by Leaman, who argued that the animal soul and demonic soul (*al-nafs al-ʾiblīsiyya*) are the two types of *al-nafs al-ʾammārah*. According to Leaman, these terms were used in philosophy and literature to indicate how far the corruption of the soul has spread.[43] Ibn ʿArabī notably identified the lower soul as each and every objectionable thought, inclination, and/or impulse of a person. These also include wrath.[44] When it comes to differentiating between the animal soul and the lower soul, it should be noted that Ibn ʿArabī did not view carnal pleasures as something negative per se. Depending on the circumstances, what the animal soul enjoys can be either commendable or blameworthy. The prophet Muhammad, Ibn ʿArabī's model of the Perfect Human, thus openly professed his love of women and perfumes (*al-Jāmiʿ al-ṣaghīr* #5435). The Prophet also enjoyed eating sweets, honey, and pumpkins (*Ṣaḥīḥ al-Bukhārī* #5431, *Mishkāt al-Maṣābīḥ* #4180). Ibn ʿArabī associated these and similar bodily cravings with the desiring soul and the animal soul. He did not disapprove of them per se, for he thought that God entrusted the soul with preserving the well-being of the physical body. Hence, Ibn ʿArabī argued, it is only natural that the soul would induce the body to crave good things in life. Wrath can also be praiseworthy when a person is angry for God's sake. Sometimes, however, the soul can develop a warped perception of what is good for humans.[45] In conclusion, we believe this warped perception can be taken as the main criterion for identifying *al-nafs al-ʾammārah*. Unlike a qarīn, the lower soul is not a separate entity within the body, for Ibn ʿArabī noted that "the soul is nonmanifest in entity but manifested in property."[46]

One must therefore look into the properties and behavior of *al-nafs al-ʾammārah* to define it. Whereas the lower soul, the wrathful soul, and the desiring soul all lust for carnal pleasures, the twisted perception of the lower soul makes the difference between them. This twisted perception leads to excessive, twisted desires. Fulfilling these desires then leads to the spiritual and physical demise of human beings. Inclinations of the lower soul were sometimes identified with the branches of Zaqqum (figure 3.2).

Zaqqum was described in the Qur'an as the tree growing at the bottom of hell. Its fruits are jinn heads, and wicked souls feast on them (Q 37:64–65, 44:43). Like the branches of Zaqqum yield demonic fruit, some Sufis believed that evil jinn are born of sins and desires of the soul:

Figure 3.2. The tree of Zaqqum, from al-Sarai's *Nahj al-Faradis* (The Paths of Paradise), c. 1465. *Source*: Public domain.

The coquetry of devil is due to thy cunning only.
Each desire in thee is itself thy own devil
When thou fulfil one desire of thine
A hundred devils are created in thee, that is all.[47]

In contrast, Ibn ʿArabī argued that the soul's vices originate from devils, "though not from the fire-based jinn, since these cast something good to the human heart from time to time."[48] These devils are likely identical with the evil jinn mentioned in *K. ʿAnqāʾ mughrib*, whose bodies are mostly made of earth.[49] Although the soul is not evil in essence, jinn are capable of corrupting it. In other words, God made a man upright, but then the Devil laid snares for him.[50] This would seem to suggest that Ibn ʿArabī believed that the fruits of Zaqqum came before the branches. Chapter 273 of *al-Futūḥāt*, however, left open the possibility that the chicken came before the egg. "I saw caprice (*hawā*) and lust (*shahwah*) whispering together. God gave this caprice the power over most rational faculties—that is, unless God protects them. Caprice stood in that place and said: 'I am the god being worshipped by all things in existence.' This is how caprice turns away from reason and everything that came from the Tradition *(naql)*. Evil jinn followed caprice and lust was in front of it."[51] Irrespective of the fact whether the chicken came before the egg, Ibn ʿArabī's works emphasized the strong, mutually dependent relationship between evil jinn and souls—not in the least since both of them induce humans to sin.[52] Ibn ʿArabī described temptations of the lower soul in *K. ʾMashāhid al-asrār*. Here he compared the lower soul and the doubting thoughts and temptations arising from his inner darkness to a desert filled with snakes, lions, and scorpions.[53] Another vision of Ibn ʿArabī's lower soul was described in *Rūḥ al-quds*. This vision made Ibn ʿArabī aware of the soul's attempts to refute the Divine revelations he received. Thus, he swore: "My soul, by the power of Him who gave you a nature inclined to rebellion and made you susceptible to all kinds of blameworthy traits, I swear I shall not leave you in peace until you live up to the teachings of the Book of God and the Way of the Prophet."[54]

Ibn ʿArabī emerged enlightened and purified from encounters with his inner darkness. Others, however, were not as lucky. In his commentary of Ibn ʿArabī's *al-Tadbīrāt al-Ilāhiya*, al-Halveti compared these lost souls to dervishes, whirling without purpose, like clowns in Satan's hands.[55] Their dance was famously captured in the art of Siyāh Qalam (figure 3.3). Parman and İpşiroğlu attributed the enduring popularity of Siyāh Qalam's works to the fact he chose demonic doubles and/or humans in the guise of demons as his models. Having abandoned themselves to the flow of instincts, these humans joined the world of spirits. "Demons are the side of ourselves we wish to see as being alien. Our drunken, frenzied double that we do not want to acknowledge."[56] Citing Freud, Parman associated demonic doubles with one's fear of death, castration, narcissism, and the excessive love for the Self. But most of all, quranā᾿ were compared by al-Zain, Corbin, Hadromi-Allouche, Klar, Nasser, Nünlist, and Parman to the shadow.[57]

The Jungian shadow can be broadly identified with inferior, unrecognized aspects of the human self. These include anger, jealousy, laziness, sexual urges, and the like. According to Hadromi-Allouche, who analyzed the Islamic Devil and jinn from the Jungian

Figure 3.3. The Dancing Dervishes, Siyah Qalam (the Black Pen), 14th century. *Source*: Public domain.

point of view, the integration of the shadow marks the first stage of self-realization. Throughout this process, one becomes aware that the human self transcends the ego.[58] Whereas the Jungian notion of the shadow is comparable to the descriptions of the lower soul and quranāʾ in Ibn ʿArabī's works, the devil is in the details. For the lower soul cannot be seen as a single part or aspect of *nafs al-ʾinsān*. The term *al-nafs al-ʾammārah* was rather used to indicate the state of the soul caused by evil jinn. A Seeker is required to elevate—not integrate!—their qarīn and/or *al-nafs al-ʾammārah*. The station of the soul that is slowly turning away from darkness towards God was referred to as *al-nafs al-lawwāmah* in the Qur'an (Q 75:2). At this stage, *nafs* begins to differentiate between good and evil and opens up to receive the influx of Divine inspiration and revelations. It is also at this point that the soul is the most vulnerable to whispers of jinn.[59] Ibn ʿArabī thus emphasized the need to familiarize ourselves with spiritual inrushes, so as to be able to determine what is it that inspires us to certain actions. To defeat a qarīn, one must familiarize themselves with its tactics.

3.3. The Sneaking Whispers

Akbarians used *ʾilhām* as a general term for passing thoughts and inrushes (*khawāṭir*) reaching the heart.[60] These thoughts and inrushes can be divine (*ilāhī*), spiritual (*rūḥānī*), psychical (*nafsānī*), or satanic (*shaytānī*) in origin. Ibn ʿArabī believed that the heart owes its name to the fact that these mutually opposing inrushes make it fluctuate incessantly between one state and another (*taqallaba* → *qalb*).[61] Each evil doppelganger hopes that (their) satanic inrushes will prevail. But a devil will already be pleased with itself if it manages to confuse a Seeker with regard to whether a spiritual inrush came from God or not. The heart and the soul are both vulnerable to the whispers of quranāʾ. Even though satanic inrushes can be pleasing to the soul, they invariably lead to dreadful outcomes. Ibn ʿArabī thus advised the reader to pray for a sign from God which will help them identify thoughts and inrushes that are satanic in origin.[62] The reader was furthermore advised to pay close attention to their inner thoughts and inrushes at each moment, so that their heart would be filled with shame. If a Seeker feels shamed before God,

He will prevent their heart from experiencing evil thoughts and inrushes.[63] That being said, Ibn ʿArabī's works also contain several methods for identifying satanic inrushes without direct help from God. For example, a Seeker was advised to check whether their thoughts and inrushes oppose Sharia, for Ibn ʿArabī believed that the Islamic religious laws set out the path to "the ultimate felicity when followed—and you will also obtain Divine love and the True becomes your hearing and seeing."[64] Sharia is thus comparable to the straight path (*al-ṣirāṭ al-mustaqīm*) leading to God. When a law is broken, a gap opens in the path and makes a pathway for the Devil to strike.[65] Without the guidance of the Law, human beings *sink to the lowest of the low* (Q 95:5). A qarīn would like nothing better than that—to the point where Ibn ʿArabī suggested that the children born to infidels have no spiritual companions whatsoever! This is likely related to the fact that children born to believers can refer to Sharia from early youth. This might be the reason why doppelgangers attempt to separate Muslim children from God early on. Quranāʾ are, however, reluctant to waste their time on the children of infidels, who do not know better than to sin and cannot be held accountable for their actions until they reach adulthood.[66] Neither angel, soul, nor spirit can make licit what God has made illicit. Apart from humans, jinn are the only beings God endowed with free will to break His laws. So when their passing thoughts and/or inrushes contradict Sharia, one can be certain that an evil jinni is their source. Seemingly convenient, this method is of limited use in practice. This is due to the fact that most jinn are smart enough not to contradict Sharia directly.

A qarīn will target a Seeker's understanding of the religious law instead. In other words, rather than pushing a Seeker to break the law, evil jinn seek to obstruct their victims when putting religious laws into practice. When a suspicious inrush appears to be in harmony with Sharia, Ibn ʿArabī advised a person to check the content of that inrush. For he noted that satanic inrushes mostly revolve around the things that are recommended by Sharia. Satanic inrushes also tend to focus on gray areas of the Islamic religious law, like whether a man is allowed to marry his stepdaughter or drink a fermented fruit juice.[67] The reader was furthermore advised to check whether their passing thoughts and inrushes are lacking in consistency.

No satanic inrush, Ibn ʿArabī maintained, can be subjected to close scrutiny. If one were to attempt to analyze the whispers of their doppelganger, their mind would constantly shift from one thought to another. This is due to the fact that jinn are the creatures of fire, constantly shifting and moving from one state to another. Such is the nature of their whispers as well. Hence, one can be certain they are dealing with satanic *khawāṭir* if they find themselves unable to pin their thoughts down. In contrast, Divine revelations are distinguished by the lasting sense of security and the increase of happiness and faith they bring.[68] That being the case, even the Prophet found himself unable to determine whether the revelations Gabriel brought him were divine in origin or not. He reportedly felt that Gabriel was pressing the words out of him, "as though he were a jinni accompanying a poet."[69] This made the Prophet suspicious of Gabriel. His wife Khadija thus came up with another method to distinguish between the Divine inrushes and a trick of a jinni. She first asked the Prophet to move around the room to see whether his movements will cause the vision of the angel to disappear, for jinn can only be seen with a fixed, unmoving gaze. Once she determined that the Prophet was able to see Gabriel no matter where he sat or stood, Khadija disrobed in front of the angel. Khadija's reasoning was based on the assumption that jinn are shameless creatures. When the archangel withdrew in silence, the spouses felt assured that Gabriel was an angel sent by God.[70] Having provided the reader with general instructions for identifying satanic thoughts and inrushes, Ibn ʿArabī concurrently maintained that it is next to impossible for an average person to determine whether an inrush is from a devil: it is not by coincidence that satanic inrushes were referred to as the "sneaking whispers" (*al-waswās al-khannās*) in the Qur'an (Q 114:4). Being aware of satanic tricks and machinations is among the greatest honors God bestows on his servants.

> Such a person is the one who gains understanding from God of what they are ordered to do and of what is prohibited, and what God gives to them in their innermost being. Such a person is the one who is able to differentiate between the inner promptings of their heart and [knows] what comes from God, what comes from their

> *nafs*, what comes from the touch of an angel and what comes from or the touch of a devil—such a person is the true human![71]

Ibn ʿArabī explicitly referred to a qarīn as the devil *in* the heart. When a devil is barred from entering the heart—as is the case with the Divine messengers and prophets—a person becomes immune to its whispering.[72] Nonetheless, the later-date Akbarians raised doubts whether a jinni can touch the heart directly. For example, al-Qayṣarī argued that the power of jinn over humans is limited to the breast and below. The same argument was previously made by al-Ḥakīm al-Tirmidhī (d. 869). Their reasoning was based on the fact that the Qur'an speaks of *the sneaking whispers* (al-waswās al-khannās) *echoing in the breasts of men* (Q 114:5). The quoted ayah led al-Tirmidhī and al-Qayṣarī to the conclusion that no jinni has power over the human heart. Hence, they taught that a devil is forced to rely on *nafs* to corrupt the heart. According to al-Tirmidhī, the Devil Within will first stir the blood with smoke and fire. This causes *nafs* to rise up from the stomach, filling the chest with evil promptings and desires. Both al-Tirmidhī and al-Qayṣarī believed that *waswās* only ever occurs in the chest.[73] Al-Makkī, however, argued that a devil whispers from the heart and eyes of men. When it comes to women, their doppelgangers operate from their eyes and buttocks.[74] The first thing to be affected by *waswās* is human nature (*tabʿ*). Whispers of a devil are then picked up by the lower soul, where they are transformed into evil promptings and desires.[75] Evil promptings sometimes lead to evil deeds. And each time a sin is committed, a black spot appears on the heart. If a human seeks forgiveness and repents, their heart will be polished clean. The Prophet, however, warned that repeated sins may cause the whole heart to rust (*Sunan Ibn Mājah* #4244). Surah *al-Muṭaffifīn* also speaks of sins causing the heart to rust (Q 83:14). Ibn ʿArabī's students and interpreters feared the impact of the lower soul and jinn on the heart, for the Prophet said: "Beware! There is a piece of flesh in the body. If this piece of flesh turns to good, the whole body becomes good. If it gets to be corrupted, the whole body will get to be corrupted and what I am referring to is the heart."[76]

On the authority of the Qur'an, Ibn ʿArabī acknowledged that the Devil pushes humans towards turpitude (Q 2:169, 24:21). Even so, he maintained that humans are, for the most part, protected from the machinations of devils. Evil jinn are thus not particularly interested in inciting humans to sin. A qarīn will rather seek to have a human accustomed to its presence. Its victim "sheds their religion gradually, like a snake discards its skin."[77] The Devil aims to throw the veil (*al-sitr*) between its human and the Creator by causing them to associate other things with God. This can lead to the eternal unhappiness to a Seeker since God does not look kindly on idolatry.[78] Inducing a person to idolatry constitutes a full-frontal attack of a jinni. However, Ibn ʿArabī taught that evil jinn could also attack a human from their left, right, and from behind. Like Iblis said to God: *I will sit in wait for them on your straight path. Then I shall come upon them from before them and from behind them and from their right and left* (Q 7:16–17). Ibn ʿArabī believed that the four jinn letters (*ʿayn, ghayn, sīn,* and *shīn*) symbolize the four directions jinn could attack from. "These [four directions] conclude their realities. They have no fifth reality from which they could seek an additional letter—so beware"![79] A comparative analysis of Ibn ʿArabī's and Sahl al-Tustarī's (d. 896) writings on the directions of satanic attacks on humans was conducted by Akkach.[80] What follows are the results of his findings, supplemented with concrete examples of satanic attacks from Ibn ʿArabī's works.

Akkach argued that the directions of satanic attacks cannot be studied independently of the symbolic interpretations of the human figure in Islamic philosophy and literature. For instance, in Ibn ʿArabī's works the front of the body was associated with clear vision and confidence. Ibn ʿArabī thus noted that the victims of frontal attacks tend to be skeptical and insecure in general. Apart from polytheism, jinn's frontal attacks could also inspire a Seeker to indulge in worldly pleasures.[81] Sensual pleasures and desires are among the most feared weapons of evil jinn. That being said, jinn doppelgangers have many other tactics at their disposal. For instance, Ibn ʿArabī noted that jinn are adept in scrutinizing the human character and intelligence. This enables them to adapt their tactics to target weak points of a specific person. Some jinn thus choose to sneak up on their victims from behind.

In contrast to the front of the body, in Ibn ʿArabī's works the human back was associated with ignorance, fear, and the Unseen. A jinni attacking a human from the back thus attempts to cause its victim to doubt the reality of the Hereafter. If a person was cowardly to begin with, their qarīn might try to convince them their spiritual endeavors are hopeless by saying: "You have no hope of attaining the level of benevolence of those who are born with good character and obedience."[82] If a person is ignorant, a jinni will try to exploit their ignorance by encouraging them to become an atheist or *muʿaṭṭil* (i.e. the one who denies the existence of analogies between the Creator and the created). But if a Seeker is curious by nature, their jinni will push them to embark on their quest for knowledge with haste, for there is always a chance a hasty Seeker will drown in the sea of knowledge, like Pharaoh chasing Moses perished in the Red Sea. If a person is prone to making pledges to God, the Devil will induce them to break their resolution by inspiring them to make another, more interesting pledge.[83]

Ibn ʿArabī associated the right side of the human body with piety, strength, and virtue.[84] When these are the predominant character traits of a victim, their qarīn might resort to its knowledge of Sharia to corrupt them. Whereas jinn have limited knowledge of God, Ibn ʿArabī noted they are well versed in religious laws. "Who created this? Who created that?'—these are some of the questions echoing in the heart when a jinni attacks from the right. Finally, the Devil whispers: '. . . and who created God?' "[85] These questions are meant to raise suspicion and doubt in the heart of a victim, for the Devil reasons it is sufficient to add a speck of dirt into water to make it undrinkable. Likewise, once the seed of doubt is sown within the heart, it can destroy piety in its roots.[86] A qarīn attacking from the right might also inspire a Seeker to make false interpretations of religious laws. Impassionate, dry nit-picking about religious laws were strongly condemned in Ibn ʿArabī's works. He also noted that theologians (*mutakallimūn*) have the tendency to mistake their interpretations of religious laws for the gospel truth. Victims of satanic attacks from the right tend to be overly confident and arrogant (*mutakabbir*) in general. Such theologians were no better than idolaters in Ibn ʿArabī's eyes, for he believed them to be prone to mistaking their scribblings for the True.

> A victim then starts reasoning "if this hadith were authentic"—or when the hadith is clearly authentic: "If there were another hadith that contradicted or abrogated

> this one—Imam al-Shāfiʿī would have kept this solution [but since he didn't do so, there is no reason to take the authentic hadith into account." This is the way it is if the man is Shāfiʿite. If he is a Ḥanafite, he will say: "Abū Ḥanīfa would have kept the solution." And so on and so forth, for the disciples of the imams. They claim that the hadith and its use are a source of error and that what is imperative is blindly following the imam's opinion and their example in the judgements they hand down.[87]

Shia Muslims were used in Ibn ʿArabī's works as the prime example of theological interpretations gone wrong. Their "errors" could also be seen as an example of a successful satanic attack from the right, for Ibn ʿArabī believed that evil jinn managed to corrupt the Shia by targeting their excessive love for Muhammad's family. According to him, the Shia merely admired the Prophet, his son-in-law, and his descendants at first. The Shia also realized that loving the Prophet and his family is one of the smartest ways to get closer to God. Ibn ʿArabī approved of their reasoning and conduct so far. God, however, warned believers: *People of the Book, do not be extreme in your religion without truth and follow not the prejudices of those who have already gone astray, misled many and lost the right path* (Q 5:77). Ibn ʿArabī felt that the Shia did not heed this warning. Under the influence of evil jinn, the Shia were first led to believe that Ali's descendants should be the first among men. This is why they refused to follow the Prophet's companions. Later on, they also grew to hate and curse the companions. Ibn ʿArabī furthermore accused the Shia of slandering the archangel Gabriel and the Prophet himself. In other words, he believed that the excessive love they felt made the Shia an easy target of evil jinn.[88] Since most people do not harbor emotions of comparable strength, a devil will slightly change its tactics when approaching a pious man contemplating whether to join a jihad by saying: "How can you abandon the lands you know so well, or leave your women and property unprotected, vulnerable, ripe for rape and pillage?"[89]

Whereas Ibn ʿArabī associated the right side of the human body with strength and virtue, he believed that the left is the direction of weaknesses, pretenses, and dependence. A jinni attacking from the left will thus seek to exploit human weaknesses. For example, if a person was miserly to begin with, their jinni assures them that they will live a long life in a hostile environment and that they will die dishonored, destitute, and alone if they were to share some of their money with others instead of saving it for the future. If a person is rich, their jinni might warn them not to be fooled by the plenitude they have—for who could say what tomorrow brings? If a miser is poor, evil jinn will seek to assure them that their financial situation is about to get worse. It will furthermore insist that the world is a hostile place and that no one will come to the miser's aid if they were to stumble and fall. Hence, a qarīn might say, each person must look out for themselves and set as much money as possible aside as life insurance. Ibn ʿArabī taught that God gave jinn power over imagination. Evil jinn are thus capable of painting vivid pictures of misery, cruelty, and poverty to their victims. Ibn ʿArabī, however, warned the reader that fretting over these imagined dangers would lead them to the brink of hell.[90] That said, it would be difficult, even for a jinni, to have a shallow, self-indulgent person concerned about the future. So when a qarīn senses that its human is lewd and greedy, it will stimulate their imagination to help them come up with lenient interpretation of religious laws, thus providing them with an excuse to do what they wanted to do from the start. A jinni might say: "The men of the first generation [of Prophet's Companions] absolved themselves of their religious duties by using their personal judgement (*raʾy*), the scholars used reasoning by analogy in the matter of legal statuses. They clarified causes (*al-ʿilal*) and made statutes on issues about which Law says nothing as they also did on things about which the Law is explicit, basing their opinions on the fact that these things have a single, same cause."[91]

A victim of a successful attack from the left tends to act as a hypocrite (*munāfiq*). However, a qarīn attacking from the left might also seek to make a person jealous and/or angry. Ibn ʿArabī noted that proneness to anger is a sure sign that one's heart is closed to God.[92] His teachings were likely inspired by the Islamic normative tradition in this regard. For not only did the Prophet confirm that anger is from the Devil (*Ṣaḥīḥ al-Bukhārī* #3282), but he also taught Aisha how a qarīn exploits the jealousy of wives to orchestrate their demise:

> Aisha reported that the Messenger of Allah, peace be upon him, left her one night and she became jealous. Then the Prophet returned and saw how upset she was. The Prophet said: "Aisha, what's wrong? Do you feel jealous"? Aisha said: "How can a woman not feel jealous with a husband like you"? The Prophet said, "Did your devil come to you"? Aisha said: "Messenger of Allah, is there a devil with me"? The Prophet said: "Yes." Aisha said: "Is there a devil with each person?" The Prophet said yes. Aisha said: "Then what about you, the Messenger of Allah"? The Prophet said: "Yes, with me as well. But my Lord has helped me against him 'til it embraced Islam as well" (*Ṣaḥīḥ Muslim* #2815).

Jinn doppelganger and the lower soul pester a Seeker—because they can. Ibn ʿArabī noted that the Islamic normative tradition is quite explicit on the matter: "Your soul (*nafs*) has the right over you, your essence (*ʿayn*) has the right over you and your guest (*zawr*) has the right over you. How can a person faced with rights ever be free? Whichever created thing has the right upon a man, he is a slave to that right."[93] A human being was not made to be a slave, but the Divine vice-regent on Earth with angels and devils prostrating themselves before them. This is why each person must train their soul in virtues. *Having fashioned the soul, God had it inspired as to what is its deprivation and what is its preservation* (Q 91:7–8). What each Seeker owes to God is to worship Him alone. What they owe to the world is not to harm any living being lest they are ordered to carry out justice in accordance with Sharia. Finally, a Seeker owes it to their soul not to take any path in life which does not lead to the happiness and salvation of the soul.[94] Attempting to carry out their duty to God, world, and the soul will bring each Seeker into the direct conflict with their qarīn.

Chapter Four

The Red Death

> Make me the master of the forelock of every obstinate tyrant and rebellious devil, whose forelocks are in Your hand.
>
> —Ibn ʿArabī[1]

> I ascended! I threw myself into the sea of perplexity and He left me swimming in it.
>
> —Ibn ʿArabī[2]

Surah *al-ʾAnbiyāʾ* attests that *every soul must taste of death* (Qur'an 21:35). There are People of God seeking no less than four deaths. The first is the White Death by hunger, which was linked to light and illumination (*ḍiyāʾ*) among Akbarians. Then there is the Black Death by sadness, which has been associated with patience and humility when facing insults and assaults from people. The Green Death has been associated with patched clothes and poverty in Ibn ʿArabī's works. The last is the Red Death of the soul. Red, Ibn ʿArabī explained, is the color of blood—and the Red Death owes its name to the belief that one could kill their *nafs*.[3] The Red Death has been closely associated with the Greater Jihad and jinn doppelgangers in Sufi literature. "To convert one's own Iblis to Islam," al-Maʿarrī and ʿAṭṭār noted, "means to effect the destruction of the lower soul."[4] Whether a qarīn can be converted to Islam was a matter of debate among scholars. Some scholars were adamant that it cannot be done. Undaunted by the reports that the qarīn of the Prophet embraced Islam, they argued that God simply ordered the qarīn to leave Muhammad in peace. Ibn ʿArabī rejected this hypothesis on the ground that no creature is beyond redemption. He argued that it is only fair to assume that a qarīn too can be brought to light.[5] Not all people were in favor of this option, with some Seekers proposing a more radical solution to the problem of doppelgangers. For there are hadith reporting that, when the Prophet was still a child, Gabriel came to him and cut out the heart from his chest to remove a blood clot (*ʿalaqa*) from it. The onlookers ran away screaming: "Muhammad was murdered! Muhammad was murdered"! The angel then washed the Prophet's heart in the Zamzam Well, returned it to his chest, and explained: "This clot of blood is the part of the Devil that was in you" (*Ṣaḥīḥ Muslim* #162). There are several other versions of this narrative, each of them reporting that the Prophet walked away unscathed from the encounter, save for the scar on his chest. However, different hadith contain different descriptions of the part of the Devil within Muhammad. Whereas some transmitters reported that two blood clots were found in the Prophet's chest, others claimed there was a black spot in his heart. Transmitters were also locked in disagreement on the identity of the one who removed the Devil's part. Whereas *Ṣaḥīḥ Muslim* accredited this feat to Gabriel, other transmitters reported that angels, humans, and/or birds had to work together against the Devil.[6] Whereas the hadith divulged that the Prophet's heart was cleansed in the Zamzam Well, the surah *al-ʾAnfāl* describes how God sent down rain *to cleanse and remove the Devil's filth* (Q 8:11). The archangel Gabriel still gained a reputation of being the sworn enemy of jinn and magicians.[7] It is therefore ironic that some people resorted to magic squares and spells to compel Gabriel to help them settle scores with their jinn (figure 4.1). Magic squares of this type were popular among expectant mothers, Muslim and Christians alike. The Coptic magic square Blackman purchased in the 1920s came with an accompanying spell: "Make it your charge, Jibrāʾīl, make it your charge, Mīkāʾīl, make it your charge, Rūfāʾīl, make it your charge, Surīyāl, make it your charge, Māniyāl! By the power and might of God, the Almighty, His broad Throne and dazzling Light—burn the accursed qarīneh and cast it to fire!"[8]

Figure 4.1. Blackman's magic square. Drawing by the author based on Blackman, *The Fellahin of the Upper Egypt*, 74.

The hadith report that Gabriel cut out part of the Devil from Muhammad's heart, rather than tossing it into fire. It is also worth noting that no hadith explicitly identified the Devil's part as a qarīn (or al-Khannās b. Iblis). Some Seekers thus placed their hope on another blade: Zulfiqar, the sword of ʿAlī, the bringer of the Red Death. The Prophet presumably referred to Zulfiqar when advising believers to slay their *nafs* with the sword of self-mortification and austerities.[9] Protective talismans against quranāʾ and Qarīna were often decorated with this sword. This is hardly surprising as many Sufis believed that it would suffice to cleanse one's soul to make their devils go away. Some even thought that the lower soul is "a sort of parasite"[10] that can be cut out and banished alongside qarīn with spells and talismans.

Ibn ʿArabī rather resorted to prayer than magic. He prayed for the clot of blood to be removed from his heart, so that he too could stand among the Cleansed.[11] Neither Ibn ʿArabī nor the hadith delineated the nature of this clot. Thus, it remains unclear whether Ibn ʿArabī was praying for his heart to be cleansed of sin, blameworthy character traits, and/or the qarīn's presence. We believe that Ibn ʿArabī's prayer was likely referring to the sins he committed. For whereas the hadith attest that the heart can be cleansed of sin (*Jāmiʿ al Tirmidhī* #3334, *Sunan Ibn Mājah* #4244), Ibn ʿArabī maintained that greed, avarice, anger, envy, gluttony, cowardice, and miserliness are the innate character traits of humans. "Whatever is in the innate character cannot be removed—except if one were to destroy the core being of the creature in question. . . . The entirety of what is innately created in the soul will not disappear through ego-struggles and spiritual exercises."[12] The evil ego and vices both serve to remind humans of their Lord. If it weren't for them, the human spirit would fancy itself the ruler and sustainer of the soul.[13] A qarīn's presence is another reminder that humans have limited control over their minds and bodies. Evil jinn were identified as the direct cause of human vices in Ibn ʿArabī's works. Human beings are thus easily tempted into casting spells to eliminate their doppelgangers. There are, however, no records of Ibn ʿArabī attempting this feat himself. As a matter of fact, he noted that even accomplished Sufis fail to realize that God loves all His creatures—including those He described as "evil." God created both Adam and Iblis and set their children against one another. "And even if the entirety of created beings, all of them, were to agree . . . they wished to annihilate what God wished to exist, they would fail."[14] Although it is lawful to oppose the Devil, there are no clauses in the Islamic religious law calling for the death of quranāʾ, for God's mercy also embraces the jinn folk. This is something that Iblis was well aware of as he stood up to Sahl al-Tustarī.

> The last thing Iblis said to Sahl is this: "God said *my mercy embraces all things* (Q 7:156) and this is a universally applicable affirmation. You must have noticed that I am one of the things He mentioned. For the word 'all' hints at the totality of things and the word 'things' hints at creation in general. Hence, His mercy also embraces me." "I didn't think you would be this ignorant," Sahl scolded. Iblis replied: "I didn't think *you* would say that. Don't you see, Sahl, that limitation (*taqyīd*) is your attribute, not His?" . . . This is when I realized Iblis possesses indisputable knowledge. Iblis was Sahl's teacher in this case [and not the other way around].[15]

When people reach a certain stage of spiritual development, they begin seeing good in everything. The prophet Muhammad thus prevented his followers from killing snakes, while Jesus worried for the well-being of a pig.[16] Ibn ʿArabī had less compassion for Iblis and his kin. He even professed his hesitancy to write on the problem of evil and the Devil, lest Iblis also profits from it. He was, however, aware that jinn rely on misconceptions about evil, sin, and justice to lead humans astray. All the while hoping that Iblis was too ignorant and too bloodthirsty to comprehend his teachings, Ibn ʿArabī put his thoughts on paper, for he was convinced that human happiness depends on whether one can be reconciled to the Divine order of things.[17] This also means responding to the problem of evil.

4.1. The Problem of Evil

This subchapter was envisioned as a discussion on the problem of evil represented by Iblis the Devil and his kin in Ibn ʿArabī's works.[18] Ibn ʿArabī was adamant that no human can go against the will of God, whether they are meaning to rid themselves of their doppelganger, change their fate, or disrupt the structure and nature of the universe. Nasr identified Iblis the Devil as the representation of Adam's desire not to accept the status accorded to him.[19] Iblis questioned God's decision to make Adam His viceregent, and his disobedience made him wretched. When God expelled Iblis from paradise and ordered him to share his wealth and children with humans, Iblis warned Him: *Most humans will not thank you for it* (Q 7:17). This is yet another case when the Devil's words rang true. Although most humans are averse to doppelgangers, their presence and behavior are in accordance with God's wishes. When jinn get in His way—like when He fears they might disrupt a faithful transmission of Divine revelations—He simply closes the heart of a prophet to prevent their qarīn from reaching them. Since the happiness and salvation of humans depend on their submission to God, Ibn ʿArabī understood why God would seek to ensure that His revelations are transmitted accurately. The fact that God did not stop humans from corrupting holy books once they were safely brought to them, however, left him astonished. Ibn ʿArabī was further astonished by the realization that no human is ever safe from the Devil Within.

> What is even more astonishing than [God's decision not to protect Torah from being corrupted by humans] is the fact that He created Adam with His two hands and that He did not protect him from disobedience and heedlessness. How does the rank of a single hand compare to that of two hands? How astonishing! The two hands of God are turned only towards Adam's clay and Adam's nature. Since the Devil whispered to him, this whispering came only from within Adam, from the direction of his own nature. This Devil was created from the same part that Adam was created from. Hence, it is by his own nature that Adam became heedless and yielded to the whispering of the Devil—and so the two hands of God turned upon his nature. This is why God did not protect Adam's offspring from disobedience either, which they carry within their own clay.[20]

The part of Adam the quoted excerpt is referring to is likely the element of fire, which is the cause of vices in jinn. Whereas the quoted passage may be interpreted figuratively—so as to read that fire has the same impact on the character of jinn and humans—it could also literally mean that fiery doppelgangers are an integral part of human nature. Human vices make them vulnerable to the Devil Within. Since one can never be free from vices, the threat of jinn can only be eliminated by converting a qarīn to Islam. Whereas God may silence one's qarīn for the time being, He will never separate it from its victim, nor will He ever stop jinn from attacking altogether. When a jinni senses that God has closed the human heart to it, it may assume a visible form and attempt a full-frontal assault instead.[21] In theory, one could be reconciled to the fact that evil jinn were yoked to humans out of obedience and respect for God. This would mean following the example of angels who, in spite of their reservations, recognized Adam as the Divine viceregent when God ordered them to do so.[22] On the one hand, Ibn ʿArabī backed the necessity of bowing to the will of God. But he also wished to convince his readers that humans benefit from the existence of evil jinn. In other words, Ibn ʿArabī argued that the world would *not* be a better place without quranāʾ. The world, as God's creation, was already made perfect as it is. Contrasting the sheer good of existence, Ibn ʿArabī identified the absolute evil with nonexistence (*ʿadam*).[23] On a more human level, evil can be seen as a failure to fulfill one's desire and/or anything that is disagreeable to humans. Unpleasant, painful experiences were commonly associated with the lower soul and the Devil in Islamic culture. Ibn ʿArabī partially agreed with this interpretation. Assuming there is evil in the world, it could only come from the creation, not from the Creator—for God is never evil.[24] "Hence," Ibn ʿArabī noted, "the angels spoke the truth and this is why God said *whatever evil visits you is from your* nafs (Q 4:79)."[25] Chapter 57 of *al-Futūḥāt,* however, argued that people misinterpreted the quoted ayah.

> It would be wrong to say that God is the One inspiring us to do good whereas the Devil inspires us to evil, for this would be both ignorant and discourteous. This is due to the fact that these incoming thoughts are not equal and evil is superior to good [here]. Again, take a look at His words: *Whatever good visits you is from God and whatever evil visits you is from your nafs* (Q 4:79). In this ayah, the noun *God* and the noun *nafs* are evident. The "evil" mentioned in this ayah is not something you did which goes against Sharia, which would then constitute a wrongdoing. No, what is meant here is a calamity and something that did not go in accordance with your wishes. This is the literal reading of the ayah. For it is an ill omen when infidels say He is to blame [for evil]. Thus, He said: *Everything is from God. What is the matter with these people? They can hardly comprehend anything!* (Q 4:78). In other words, when something happens to people in the created world, God said, based on what people were saying: *When something good visits them, they say: "This is from God." But when something evil visits them, they say: "This is from you* (min ʿindika). *You should rather say that everything is from God"* (Q 7:78). These are His words and we consider it an ill omen.[26]

Chapter 57 of *al-Futūḥāt* thus makes a distinction between evil and the wrongdoing associated with breaking a law. This is in contrast to the so-called "theology of submission," where evil was identified with going against Sharia. Proponents of this theology identified Iblis as the originator of evil in Islam.[27] The quoted paragraph, however, indicates that what humans consider to be "evil" is also from God. In another place, Ibn ʿArabī asserted that this world, by its very essence, requires the existence of evil.[28] However, he concurrently maintained that God does not wish for human suffering.[29] This leaves us with the question of why He created jinn to begin with, as He must have known they would attack humans. Ibn ʿArabī attempted to clarify the matter in Chapter 68 of *al-Futūḥāt:*

> What life is greater and more complete than the life of the hearts filled with God, no matter the circumstances? The presence of faith at the moment when opposition [to God] occurs repels the opposition and reverts it to something alive in His presence, seeking forgiveness until the Day of Reckoning. This is one of the mercies of the Name *al-Raḥman,* which is associated with God's two fingers.[30] The Devil aims to weaken what is good in humans, not realizing—because he is greedy and blind—that the curse and offence for this disobedience will come back to haunt him. This is one of the tricks God plays on Iblis. Had the Devil known that God, as a special favour to humans, was helping them with these satanic attacks, Iblis would not try to pull such tricks on humans. This is the trick God fooled Iblis with. Never have I seen anyone who was aware of this matter [before me]. If it were not for my knowledge of Iblis—and if it were not for my knowledge of his ignorance and bloodlust, I would not bring this up, lest Iblis stops attacking. I decided to bring this matter up since the Devil never learns, blinded by his greed for causing misfortune and his ignorance of how God favors humans.[31]

Chapter 208 of *al-Futūḥāt* further clarifies why jinn and the lower soul were set against humans:

> There are incoming thoughts that are Divine, angelic, satanic and psychical in nature. This Friend of God

> (*walī*) reached an understanding that psychical and satanic inrushes only ever come as a sustaining grace from God. These are not [manifestations] of the Devil's power over him. No, the Devil is in God's service even though he fails to realize it. The Devil is the messenger bringing something to be cast to the inner secret so that the Friend of God may ascend in a way the Devil does not understand. This is a part of God's trickery that is hidden from Iblis, who is rushing to assist sages (*ʿarifīn*) in ascending the stairs while imagining he is dragging them down instead.[32]

In other words, Ibn ʿArabī believed that jinn help humans by tempting them, for the nobility of human nature comes from successfully overcoming temptations. "Strike me with vanity," ʿAbd al-Salām b. Mashīh (d. 1227) prayed, "so that I may bring it to naught."[33] Ibn ʿArabī used the word *jihād* to describe one's struggles against temptation. If a Seeker manages to overcome temptations, they will be rewarded with the status of *mujāhid*. This is how Ibn ʿArabī interpreted the seventh ayah of the surah *Hūd*: *He might test which of you is best in deeds* (Q 11:7). However, the Devil's triumph is not guaranteed even when a person succumbs to temptation. This is due to the fact that sins lead to remorse. Ibn ʿArabī identified this remorse with repentance. Repentance leads to the transformation of the lower soul into the blaming soul, which can then be transformed into the tranquil soul. Such is the power of remorse that a sinner may be awarded the status of God's martyr (*shahīd*) while still being alive. Irrespective of the fact if a Seeker is successful in overcoming the temptations of a qarīn, they are likely to profit from self-disclosures of the Divine Name *al-Mudhill*. This is something that doppelgangers are well aware of. Hence, a jinni may try to convince its victim it will do them good to sin since this gives God a chance to disclose Himself as the Merciful (*al-Raḥmān*), the Compassionate (*al-Raḥīm*). Ibn ʿArabī strongly opposed this interpretation: "Is it that you are fooled by what a devil whispers in your ear, saying: 'If it were not for your sins and your revolt, how would Allah manifest His infinite mercy, compassion, and generosity?' Don't you see how irrational that evil teaching is?"[34]

No sinner can be certain whether they will be forgiven, cast to hell, or awarded the rank of *shahīd* once they repent for their sins. Ibn ʿArabī thus advised his readers against testing God's patience with repeated, calculated transgressions.[35] He nevertheless conceded that the occurrences of evil in this world also serve to enable the manifestation of certain Divine Names and attributes.[36] *I only created jinn and men to serve me,* said God in the Qur'an (Q 51:56). Ibn ʿArabī interpreted this ayah to read that God created jinn and humans "so that they would be humbled before Me. And they won't be humbled 'til they recognize Me in all things."[37] In other words, Ibn ʿArabī maintained that each Seeker was tasked with recognizing God's wisdom, mercy, and goodness in the twisted face of their qarīn. Ibn ʿArabī's insistence that jinn are doing humans a favor by tempting them to sin should be read in this context. Since God is never evil, neither are His self-disclosures, although this is something that each Seeker must verify for themselves. Seekers who accept some of His self-disclosures but not the others were strongly condemned in *al-Futūḥāt.*

> Were one of them to say that he is worshipping Me, his statement would be false since he is misinterpreting Me. How could it be true that he is worshipping Me when he denies Me when I give him a *tajallī*? The one who binds Me and defines Me in one form but not in another—this is but an image that he formed in his imagination and this is what he worships, all the while hiding the truth deeply in his heart, sheltered by one veil after another. Such a man fancies that he is worshipping Me, even though he is actually renouncing Me. Sages (*ʿārifūn*), however, recognize Me and I am not hidden from their sight in the world of created beings when they withdraw and hide from the creation and from their Selves.[38]

All Divine Names and attributes were manifested in the human form. As a result, human beings were exposed to the influences of each of these Names. Rather than shunning disclosures of His Names on the horizons and within themselves, a Seeker should strive to achieve the perfect balance and harmony of God's Names in their heart. Adam, the first Divine viceregent, knew Divine Names, all of them—and this gave him the perfect knowledge of

God and the world.[39] The prophet Muhammad, however, noted that God preferred him over Adam by two gifts: whereas Adam's wife abetted him in transgression, the Prophet's wives urged him to obey God. And whereas Adam's doppelganger was blasphemous, Muhammad's qarīn was a pious Muslim. Muhammad, unlike Adam, profited from the existence and advice of his qarīn.[40] The behavior of this qarīn illustrates Sufi teachings that each living being, form, and object can lead a Seeker to their salvation or doom. Schimmel's attempt to clarify these teachings centered on Rūmī's verses: "For God hides His grace in wrath and His wrath in grace. And everything created shows this double face:

> The cold wind became a murderer for the people of 'Ād,
> But for Solomon it served as a porter."[41]

Although he was not particularly compassionate towards jinn, Ibn ʿArabī was aware that one cannot embark on a spiritual journey without taking their qarīn with them. Unknowingly, quranāʾ help humans ascend as they attempt to harm them. (Un)willingly, enlightened humans then convert their doppelgangers to Islam. Sometimes, a jinni's conversion occurs without an active involvement from a Seeker, for each qarīn profits from the soul work of its human. A brave, compassionate Seeker might even try to help their qarīn by engaging with it directly. Ibn ʿArabī's works contain instructions on both indirect and direct ways to confront the jinn.

4.2. Confronting the Unseen

There are no tales of heroes killing their doppelgangers with swords the way *shiqq* and ghouls have been dealt with.[42] A qarīn is an elusive, sly creature. It relies on underhand tactics and subterfuge to achieve its goals. Some Seekers believed they would gain an upper hand over quranāʾ by making them fight in the open. They have thus sought for a way to conjure up their qarīn so that they could confront it directly. Jinn conjurors were known as Men of the Limit (*rijāl al-ḥadd*) in Ibn ʿArabī's works. Men of the Limit were named for their tendency to operate in the World of Jabarūt, "at the boundary limit (*ḥadd*) between the land of felicity and wretchedness."[43] They were said to be happiest when contemplating the dividing lines between antipodes. Men of the Limit also developed interest in the jinn living at these borders. Whereas other Seekers would burn incense and chant the Names of God to summon a spirit of their choice, Men of the Limit looked up to angels in their work. They claimed to have seen "jinn circling in groups among the meteors of piercing light"[44] and angels fighting them with comets. Their visions led them to the conclusion that jinn can only be subdued with fire.[45] Ibn ʿArabī did not necessarily agree with their conclusion, for he taught that the jinn folk are the creatures of fire who fear and loathe cold. If they were to be thrown into hellfire, jinn would only make the flames burn brighter. A Seeker wishing to subjugate a jinni would thus be wiser to expose it to low temperatures, wind, and water.[46] Humiliating an evil jinni strengthens the element of earth in its body, and Ibn ʿArabī taught that the strength of earth makes jinn predisposed to virtue. He furthermore thought that the Prophet's jinn were unwavering in their obedience to God due to the predominance of earth and water in their bodies. Even though the Prophet converted at least seven jinn with his sermons, Ibn ʿArabī maintained that, under normal circumstances, earth and water will never subdue the jinn's fire. "If a jinni is humble," Ibn ʿArabī noted, "this is due to the fact that something happened to it and made the element of earth predominant in its nature due to humiliation."[47] A brave Seeker thus seeks to confront and humiliate their qarīn—for its own good. That said, different scholars pinned different hopes on their doppelgangers. "As qareen or companion," Nasser noted, "the jinn provide a powerful means of communication with the realm of imagination, the fountain of all our hopes, aspirations, and creative desires."[48] On his side, Ibn ʿArabī advised against seeking jinn's friendship.[49] King Solomon made this mistake with Ṣakhr. Solomon treated the jinni in friendly manner, sought his advice (*shawarahu*), took long walks with him, and had him honored (*akramahu*). Ṣakhr, however, returned Solomon's kindness by plotting against him.[50] Ṣakhr's ruthlessness was an essential part of its nature, for Ibn ʿArabī believed that God purposefully removed all mercy from evil jinn and the Devil.[51] The Devil's ruthlessness was vividly described in the story of the imam Nakhjawanī.

> The imam said: "After I reached old age and decrepitude I saw Satan as the two of us stood at the top of a

> mountain. Putting my hand on my beard I said to him, 'I have reached old age and become decrepit. Spare me, if it is possible.' Satan said to me, 'Look over this side.' When' I looked, I saw a very deep ravine. It was a dizzying sight and I was seized with an intense fright and terror Satan said, 'I don't have any mercy or compassion in my heart. Should I get my hands on you, your place will be at the bottom of this pit that you see!' "[52]

Not even Solomon could force evil jinn to keep their ruthlessness in check. The best he could do was to keep them busy to prevent them from harming others. Evil jinn were thus ordered to cut down trees, move boulders, build dams and fortresses, dig wells, and dive into depths of the sea for precious stones and pearls. Solomon's jinn returned to their evil ways the moment they learned of his death.[53] Men of the Limit were fully aware of their malevolence. Summoning a qarīn to appear before a Seeker is not a task to be taken lightly. Preparations to summon an evil jinni included protective invocations, fasting, and extended periods of spiritual retreats. Ibn ʿArabī described one such retreat in his *K. al-Khalwa*.

> On the Doppelganger Retreat (*khalwa al-qarīn*): A group of my reliable brothers mentioned [this method] to me and confirmed its authenticity—although I have not practiced it myself because of the names used in this method. The people who told me about it said that new clothes (*thawb*) are put on each day for forty days, and the food is bread with olive oil at one meal and bread with raisins at another meal. These names are continuously repeated following the blessing-prayers (*ṣalawāt*) and, in most circumstances, the names are: bahluṭf[in], salayṭiyiʿ[in], ashmāṭūt[in], aṭūn[in], bahakshin, tahakkashin, yūqashin.[54]

Ibn ʿArabī's report on the Doppelganger Retreat suggests that he was not entirely opposed to confronting his qarīn head-on. He did not doubt the effectiveness of the Doppelganger Retreat either. Ibn ʿArabī was, however, repelled by the accompanying invocations, for he likely shared Ibn Taymiyya's fear that such invocations might cause him to inadvertently worship his qarīn.[55] Although he claimed never to have practiced the Doppelganger Retreat, the quoted invocation lingered in Ibn ʿArabī's mind for decades. Thus he had it inscribed on the title page of his *K. Maḥajja al-bayḍāʾ*. This work was composed in 600 AH; predating the earliest copies of *K. al-Khalwa* by three to five decades.[56] Neither *K. al-Khalwa* nor *K. Maḥajja al-bayḍāʾ* elaborate on the meaning and provenance of the names chanted during the Doppelganger Retreat. Possible connections of these names to the content of *K. Maḥajja al-bayḍāʾ* also remain unclear. A similar invocation can be found in the early but undated alchemical text *Dāʾirat al-aḥruf al-abjadiyya,* where it was used to invoke the spirits of the letters such as *dāl*. Protective amulets and talismans often contained this letter as well.[57] On his side, Ibn ʿArabī, however, noted that the angelic letters *kāf, qāf, jīm,* and *wāw* have dominion over jinn.[58] Apart from the letters, talismans against qarīn(a) typically contain the Throne Verse (Q 2:225), the surah *Yā Sīn,* the sword of ʿAlī, and figures of snakes and scorpions. Occult practitioners have long thought that knowing the names of spiritual entities makes it possible to control them. Amulets, sigils, and talismans were thus often inscribed with the names of jinn-kings and chieftains. ʾAbū Dibāj, the ruler of quranāʾ, and his secretary ʾIsmāʿīl were both commonly featured on Palestinian talismans (figure 4.2). Such talismans were of special interest to Tawfiq Canaan.

Whereas some thaumaturges and conjurors advised drawing jinn sigils on the palm of a young boy, Canaan's collection also contains talismans made of seeds, shells, blue beads, porcupine fur and palate, cat tails, donkey ears, and cooked, carved bones.[59] ʾAḥmad al-Dirbī suggested that a talisman against quranāʾ should only be made in the first hour of the first day of the week, all the while chanting appropriate invocations.[60] Ibn ʿArabī, however, argued that an invocation in itself would protect a Seeker from the Devil. The terms invocation (*manājāt*) and amulet (*tamīma*) were sometimes used as synonyms in Ibn ʿArabī's works. This is hardly surprising as written invocations and supplications have been widely distributed as protection against jinn.[61] One such invocation can be found in Ibn ʿArabī's *K. Manzil al-qutb*.

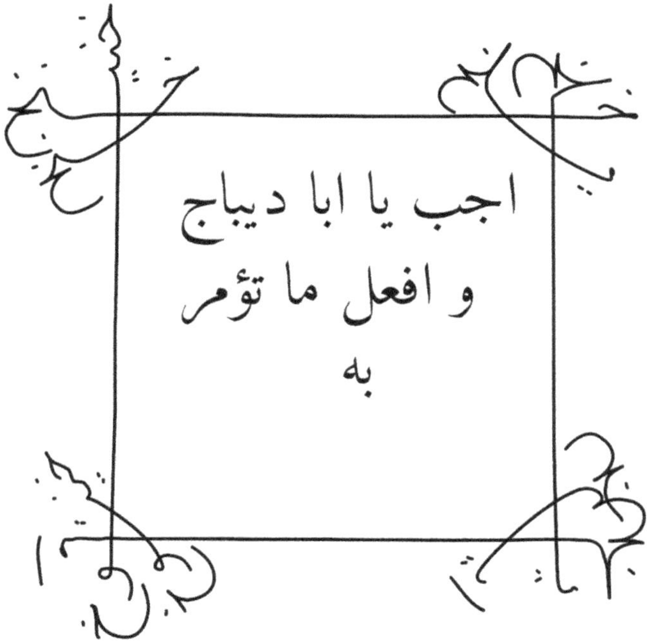

Figure 4.2. The sigil of ʾAbū Dibāj. Drawing by the author based on al-Ḥalwatī, *Kitāb mafātīḥ al-kabīr*, 50.

Invocation of the Muhammadan Station

This is the amulet against the Devil (*al-walhān*),[62] by the nightly star (*tāriq*)[63] of men and jinn. Say: I take refuge in God, (*al-malik*), the Lord (*al-rabb*), from the evil tempting the heart, fomenting the confounding words in the breast!

The hearts in pursuit of the mysteries (*al-qhuyūb*) are marked by the bestowed secret: this was the judgement of God that judges between you.

O, humans! In three strata (*ʾaṭbāq*) you've been placed: the double-layered crescent of the waning Moon and the Sun for the reminder of its rising.

Verily, your Lord is the Supreme Creator (*al-khallāq*), the knowing, His knowledge securing the wellbeing of

> the world, giving one's due through His judgement. The central point (i.e. *waṣaṭ,* the heart of the supplication) is incomparable, though the secrecy of the structure brings it up later in writing.
>
> He is wise and knowing, the secret and witness of the Unseen. Blazing fire is a sign upon His head, and the inner vision (*baṣāʾir*) enlivening the gaze. God is aware of all the creatures conceal and of what they reveal. Whoever has come [into existence] remains imprisoned in it, still in the clothing of a new creation.
>
> Surely, God is a witness over everything! O, God! I sealed (*khatamtu*) by right of Abraham, Ishmael and Isaac, by the right of Muḥammad, Ḥasan and Ḥusayn—may God's blessing be upon them all—except You heal the one who bears and possesses these names from every sickness and preserve him from all evil that arises in *nafs* or from the winds blowing through it.
>
> May God's blessings be upon our master Muhammad, his family and companions.[64]

"Invocation of the Muhammadan Station" does not contain unintelligible names like the Doppelganger Retreat. This would already make it the preferable option for Ibn ʿArabī—even though, in theory, one does not need to understand the words of an invocation to be able to use it. One such example can be seen in Chapter 177 of *al-Futūḥāt,* where Balʿām b. Bāʿūr used one special name (*al-ʾism al-khāṣṣ*) to curse Moses. Balʿām did not know the meaning of this name, "he had nothing of it but its letters and he pronounced them. . . . The letters were just an outward form, like a cloak on top of his clothes, like a snake discarding its skin. The insides (i.e. the meaning of the special name) would make Balʿām freeze of embarrassment for using it against one of the prophets."[65] Ignorant Balʿām also suffered the effects of his curse; as it made his tongue grow until it reached his chest. Balʿām's misfortune served as a warning no invocation can be used lightly. This is all the more true when summoning jinn. As well as using proper invocations, Men of the Limit taught that a summoned jinni must be met in the state of purity, lest it turns against a Seeker. Ibn ʿArabī differentiated between several types of purity in his works. These include the sensory purity of the physical body, the purity of mind from evil thoughts and suspicions, the purity of the soul from blameworthy traits, and the purity from desiring what is other than God.[66]

Sufis Ibn ʿArabī consulted with changed their clothes daily to ensure the sensory purity of their bodies during the Doppelganger Retreat. Ibn Manẓūr further recommended that a conjurer should wash themselves with pure water and use frankincense for perfume. Taking ritualistic ablutions was another common method to prepare oneself for thaumaturgical rituals.[67] Men of the Limit also laid great emphasis on their diet. For instance, Ibn ʿArabī thought that eating camel meat would strengthen the Devil Within—though jinn conjurors avoided eating meat in general. Al-Suyūṭī recommended eating pomegranates instead, as this would silence the Devil for forty days. Several talismans against qarīn(a) from Canaan's collections were also made of citrus fruit peel.[68] Bedouins once believed an evil jinni will die when hit by a date fruit—with the hadith reporting that eating dates saddens the Devil. "A man who eats seven dates each morning would also be protected from poison and magic on the day he eats them" (*Ṣaḥīḥ al-Bukhārī* #5445). Seekers aiming to summon their doppelgangers consumed different food than those who wished to weaken them. Ibn ʿArabī thus noted that those who practiced the Doppelganger Retreat would limit their food intake to two meals per day, consisting of bread with olive oil at one meal and bread with raisins at another. Some Men of the Limit thought that conjuration rituals must be done on empty stomach. Ibn Manẓūr surmised that this would help diminish one's engrossment in material reality. Extended periods of fasting—with the Doppelganger Retreat lasting for forty days—would cause a person to feel light, pure, and empty. Ibn Manẓūr believed that this would cause a conjuror to be closer in nature to jinn than humans. Jinn were presumably hesitant to harm such a person, and they were thought to be more likely to answer their calls.[69] Ibn ʿArabī had a different explanation than Ibn Manẓūr. He argued that fasting makes humans closer to God, not jinn. A qarīn flows in the blood—and Ibn ʿArabī noted that one could obstruct its flow with thirst and hunger. The goal of fasting is not to make humans feel thinner and lighter. Ibn ʿArabī rather taught that fasting weakens the body, so that one has less energy to waste on qarīn's suggestions. In other words, Ibn ʿArabī reasoned that a weak, emaciated person is more likely to be passive—and thus less likely to sin.[70] Contemporary Sufis also used this approach against their doppelgangers. "The way I overcome my qarīnu," said the shaykh Ahmed Muharram to Zwemer, "is by prayer and fasting. It is when a man is overcome with sleep that his qarīna gets the better of him."[71] Some scholars believed that dreams occur when the human soul is touched by immaterial traces from celestial souls. Jinn were especially known to appear in the dreams of poets—and the Prophet said "whereas the good vision is from God, a bad dream (*ḥulm*) is from *shayṭān*."[72] The hadith recommended seeking refugee with God from the Devil to cleanse the mind from effects of a jinn-inspired dream. Believers were furthermore advised to spit three times to the left, change their sleeping position, and never tell a soul what they dreamt of (*Ṣaḥīḥ al-Bukhārī* #704, *Sunan Ibn Mājah* #3908). Eating little, speaking little, and keeping away from people were among common methods to secure the purity of the mind and soul among Sufis.

> If you seek protection from the Devil of the carnal soul
> Go and hide from people like angels.
> Unless you abandon people of falsehood
> The doors of the truth shall not be opened before you.[73]

A clever man, Ibn ʿArabī noted, runs away from the company of both men and jinn.[74] In *Risāla rūḥ al-quds*, Ibn ʿArabī described how he hid from the world as he sought for the Divine visions and guidance. He hoped that solitude would help him cleanse his mind of fear and doubts. He was furthermore hoping to purify his soul but did not know where to start. In response to his prayers, Ibn ʿArabī was ordered to end his self-imposed isolation. This made him realize that it is his "inevitable office and religious duty" to provide spiritual guidance to people.[75] He furthermore maintained that the Muslim community and society serve as the best protection from the Devil.[76] For the hadith report a devil is closer to a single person than to a group of two (*Ibn Abī ʿAsim* #81). Spiritual Seekers also emphasized the purity of character—not in the least since jinn doppelgangers depend on human sins for sustenance. This led to the attempts to regulate jinn's diet. Comparable teachings can also be found in the Yundrung Bön tradition, as well as in the Nyingma and Kagyu schools of Tibetan Buddhism, where *chöd* has been practiced. To practice *chöd,* Jamgön Kongtrül (d. 1899) noted, means "accepting willingly what is undesirable, throwing oneself defiantly into unpleasant circumstances, realising that gods and demons are one's own mind, and ruthlessly severing self-centred arrogance through an understanding of the sameness of self and others."[77] *Chöd* practitioners identified their inner demons with anything standing between a spiritual Seeker and their goal—like jinn were said to be a veil between the Creator and the created. Buddhists, however, thought that a hungry demon is more powerful and more dangerous than the one that was fed to its satisfaction. The Red Feast *Chöd* was a spiritual practice performed to feed one's inner demon. The food offered at this feast were the body and soul of a Seeker. Deep in meditation, a Seeker visualizes their head being chopped off, their dismembered body and blood scattered on the ground to feed the demons. Nurturing the enemy was the preferred Buddhist method of unleashing the positive potential of one's inner demon and transforming the relationship between a demon and a Seeker.[78] Sufi practitioners were working towards the same goal by denying their doppelgangers food instead.

The lower soul and a qarīn were both compared to stubborn beasts of burden in Sufi literature. Such animals must be trained and broken before they can be useful to humans. Self-restraint was the main method used to achieve this feat. Murata interpreted the story of Solomon and Ṣakhr as an allegory of the spiritual practices which were used to tame the lower soul. In this story, Solomon lost his throne to Ṣakhr for being overindulgent towards his wives and qarīn. The moral of the story is that a Seeker falls prey to the lower soul without self-restraint, piety, and prudence.[79] Ibn ʿArabī also emphasized the importance of self-restraint. Although he believed that blameworthy character traits cannot be eliminated, Ibn ʿArabī thought it possible to redirect dark impulses and cravings of the lower soul. This was another common method to weaken a doppelganger. Chapter 114 of *al-Futūḥāt* contains several practical instructions for transforming blameworthy character traits into praiseworthy traits. For example, since each human is greedy by nature, Ibn ʿArabī advised the reader to be greedy for knowledge. Angry Seekers were likewise advised to try being angry for God's sake.[80] In other words, a Seeker should familiarize themselves with the Islamic normative tradition and learn what kind of actions and/or emotions are expected of them in given situations. "For humans are but slaves, constrained and compelled in their actions and destinies by the hand of the One that moves them. . . . In each situation you failed to get angry when the revelation told you to get angry—well, this is not a praiseworthy at all! Being angry for God's sake is among the most noble virtues of character."[81] Ibn ʿArabī also said: "You must restrain your anger since self-restraint is the sign that one's heart is open. If you were to restrain your anger, you would please the All-merciful and anger the Devil. If you were to tame and subdue your *nafs,* the Devil won't be able to conquer it."[82]

Apart from restraining their anger, Ibn ʿArabī advised his readers to refrain from taking vengeance against anyone (or anything!) who did them harm and to act in accordance with Sharia.[83] Bust most of all, Seekers were advised to be chaste:

> Chastity is the foundation of religion and the path to truth. If you are chaste, all your deeds will be pure and sincere; all you do will end well; you will be in harmony with the Divine order. You will be the recipient of divine generosity; all will turn to you. You will be under divine protection. If you are chaste and pious, avoiding the wrong and the doubtful, there is no doubt that you will receive all these blessings. But if you turn your back to chastity and piety, the Absolute Judge will place you in a shameful state—helpless, terrified. He will leave you by yourself in the hands of your ego. Then you will be a toy for the Devil, who will find no resistance, no opposition to his tempting you, to his taking you away from truth.[84]

The lower soul and vices were identified by Ibn ʿArabī as the greatest enemy of humans.[85] He taught that turning away from vices disperses the worries of a Seeker. Such a person will then be able to polish their heart through the recitation of the Qur'an and *dhikr*.[86] Najm al-Dīn Kubrā believed that *dhikr* burns the veil a qarīn threw over the human heart. When the veil is burnt, a qarīn gets to be converted to Islam.[87] Subduing jinn through self-work and *dhikr* is a long and arduous process. Ibn ʿArabī provides the example of ʾAbū Yazīd al-Bistāmī (d. 874), who worked "as the blacksmith of his soul for twelve years and the fuller of his soul for fifty years more; then he needed eight more years to cut the belt surrounding his outer being, and one more year to cut the one surrounding his inner being, and he still had to overcome even more obstacles."[88] Presumed victims of evil jinn were sometimes forced to undergo treatments resembling the spiritual practices Ibn ʿArabī described. Their caretakers denied them food and comfort under the assumption that jinn are attracted to decadence. They were also whipped with lemonwood since jinn were known for their hatred for citruses. Kept in solitude, under poor conditions, mental health patients were expected to entrust the rest of their treatment to God.[89] Such "treatments" were not exclusively reserved for the presumed victims of quranāʾ. The ability to entrust oneself to God—wholly, entirely—was thought to be crucial when fighting against evil. For example, Najm al-Dīn Kubrā noted that a playful, chattering qarīn would think nothing of slapping and cursing a Seeker. However, when fighting back, a Seeker risks *becoming like a dog himself* (Qur'an 7:175–76). Rather than returning the slap, the reader was advised to abandon themselves to God.[90] Having absolute faith and trust in God was greatly endorsed in Sufi literature. Al-Qushayrī noted that some jinn are also capable of it:

> Ibrahim al-Khawwas said: "I was on my way to Mecca, when I met a wild-looking person. I said to myself: 'Is this a man or a jinni?' He answered: 'I am a jinni'. 'Where are you headed?' I asked him. He said that he was going to Mecca. I asked him: 'Do you travel without any provisions?' He said: 'Yes! Among us, too, are those who travel putting their trust in God.' I asked him: 'What, then, is trust in God?' He answered: 'Taking [your provisions] from God Most High.' "[91]

There are no records of Ibn ʿArabī's students being forced to engage in self-destructive, irresponsible practices and behavior to demonstrate their trust in God. Ibn ʿArabī taught that being aware of God is already enough to keep one safe from both the Divine wrath *and* the Devil.[92] He furthermore noted that God's servants (*ʿibād*) will never fall victim to the machinations of jinn. Slightly edited ayahs from the surah *al-ʾIsrāʾ* and *Ṣāḍ* were quoted in *al-Futūḥāt* to back his claims: "Some properties of the Name *al-Laṭīf* with regard to devils from among the jinn are His exalted words to Iblis: 'Lead those you can to destruction with your seductive voice. Make assaults on them with your cavalry and infantry, share your wealth and children with them and make promises to them'. Iblis replied: 'By your Majesty, I will entice them astray, all of them, except for your servants (*ʿibād*) among them, those who are sincerely devoted.' "[93] God-fearing humans have the advantage when fighting against jinn *since God gives strength to those who believe through a firm word in this world and the next but He leaves the evildoers astray* (Q 14:27). Thus, the Devil said to the Prophet:

> Iblis the Liar told the truth to the Messenger of God, peace be upon him, when they met. The Liar was asked whether he had anything to say. Iblis answered: "Know, O Messenger of God, that God created you to serve as a guide. Even so, the success of guidance does not depend on you. God created me to mislead but the success of misleading does not depend on me either." Without another word, Iblis turned around and angels came between him and the Prophet.[94]

Prophetic narratives also emphasized the importance of religious devotion and piety. For instance, the Prophet reportedly said that the Devil Within stops whispering whenever a human speaks of God (*Mishkāt al-Maṣābīḥ* #2281). The Prophet also advised believers to recite Basmala during intercourse, so that a conceived child is protected from the Devil (*Riyāḍ al-Ṣālihīn* #1445). Some scholars interpreted this hadith as a warning that a child is assigned with a qarīn at the moment of conception. When the child is born, Basmala is once again whispered in the child's ear to protect it against qarīn. Failing to do so would presumably put the child at risk of becoming a depraved person or infidel.[95] Sincere, regular prayer was deemed to be essential for ensuring the safety of humans from their doppelgangers. Ibn ʿArabī taught that angels, humans, plants, and minerals were entrusted with the duty to pray to God. Thus, every night, the Prophet prayed for a protection against his qarīn. Ibn ʿArabī noted the Devil leaves the heart at the exact moment of *sujūd*, provided that a prayer is sincere.[96] The heart of a disbeliever was compared by Ibn ʿArabī to a puddle of water. Being small, a puddle is easy to pollute with satanic inrushes. But sincere faith and devotion can turn copper to gold—or transform a puddle into the ocean the Devil cannot touch. Ibn ʿArabī illustrated his teachings with the story of the shaykh ʾAbū Madyan and Iblis.

> One of the Friends from among the family of God—ʿAbdullāh al-Mawrūrī perhaps—informed me how he once saw Iblis and asked him whether he made any progress with the shaykh ʾAbū Madyan. . . . Iblis said: "How can I be compared to him while tossing satanic inrushes at him, at his heart. This is like a person urinating in the Mediterranean Sea. If one were to ask such a person why is he urinating in the sea, he would say: 'In order to pollute it, so that it would never be clean!' Did you ever see anyone who is more ignorant than that? Such is also the case with me and the heart of ʾAbū Madyan. The more I toss things at him, the more he alters (*qalaba*) his core being."[97]

Chapter 69 of *al-Futūḥāt* explains that turning one's core means changing oneself in a way that is pleasing to God. Ibn ʿArabī associated the ability to change one's core in the face of adversity with the high stations of spiritual development. Advanced spiritual practitioners were referred to as God's Guarded Friends in *al-Futūḥāt*. The Guarded Friends owe their name to the fact that some of them have a heart no jinni can reach. This makes them akin to God's prophets. Ibn ʿArabī believed that the Qur'an is referring to the Guarded Friends in the surah *al-Ṣāffāt*, which speaks of God providing *protection from every rebellious devil* (Q 37:7). Evil jinn are helpless against the Guarded Friends since their hearts prostrate with their bodies in prayer.[98] Iblis the Devil is well aware of this fact. His greed for disobedience still pushes him to attack God's friends, for he is the most foolish among the jinn (Q 72:4). Jinn doppelgangers are smarter than Iblis in this regard. Rather than attacking in vain, a qarīn submits to its human instead. A Guarded Friend's qarīn will do no evil from that moment on. This is how

Ibn ʿArabī interpreted the Prophet's words: "God supported me against my qarīn and he submitted."[99]

4.3. Beyond Marvels, in Death

The Zara people of the Bobo-Dyula tribe believe that those who tame their jinn will be blessed with peace and prosperity in life. Dignitaries and elders of this tribe were thought to have strong, viable relationships with their jinn. To this they (partially) owed their success in life. All human-jinn relationships normally end with the death of the person. The public funerals of Zara dignitaries were thus accompanied by *Lo Gue,* the Dance of the White Masks. The central figure of the dance was *Gyinna-Gyinna:* the embodied form of a personal jinni. Tightly leashed and bound, jinn are made to dance at the funeral processions of their deceased human masters. Bravmann, who studied and photographed several Lo Gue dances (figure 4.3), claimed that this was done to ensure

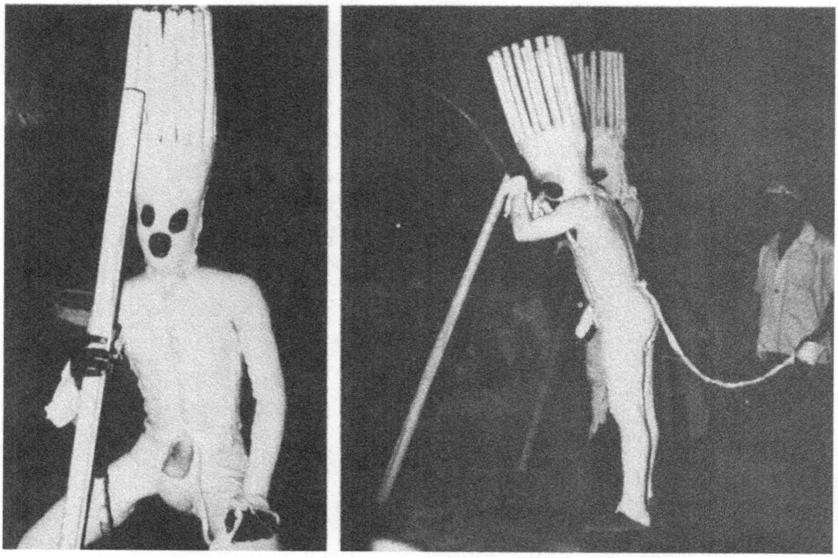

Figure 4.3. Lo Gue dance. *Source*: Rene Bravmann, "Gyinna-Gyinna: Making the Djinn Manifest," *African Arts* 10, no. 3 (Apr. 1977), 46–52, 87. Photo by Rene Bravmann.

that the spirits of the deceased would be reunited with their jinn in the world beyond.[100]

Akbarians believe that dead jinn and humans ascend to the world of *barzakh*. Most humans have no way of knowing what will happen to them from that moment on. Ibn ʿArabī was, however, fortunate in this regard, as God granted him the vision of him entering the heavenly gardens.[101] Ibn ʿArabī's account of this vision does not reveal whether his qarīn was fated to accompany him. On the assumption that god-fearing humans have god-fearing doppelgangers, Ibn ʿArabī's vision can be taken as an indicator that his qarīn was also bound for heaven, for there are several hadith indicating that pious jinn are not barred from paradise.[102] Nevertheless, some scholars argued that no jinni will enter the heavenly gardens. Among the prominent supporters of this theory were ʾAbū Ḥanīfa and Layth b. ʾAbī Salīm. Both these scholars claimed that pious jinn might be spared from hellfire at best. These jinn will dwell at al-ʿArāf in death, at the borderline between heaven and hell. However, most scholars rejected this theory, claiming that pious jinn are bound for heaven like humans.[103] Scholars were also in disagreement whether a pious jinni can fall back to sin. Whereas Ibn ʿArabī described jinn as fickle beings, Ibn Barrajān maintained that no Muslim qarīn would turn its back on God. God-fearing doppelgangers are not affected by evil deeds of their humans either. In the case when a human companion of a Muslim jinni turns to evil, their qarīn is released from their bond and replaced by another corrupt jinni. Parting ways with its human, a qarīn ascends to heaven.[104] Ibn Barrajān had a higher opinion of jinn than humans. Ibn ʿArabī, however, thought that jinn are creatures of the worldly abode; with little or no inclination to seek God and enlightenment. Whereas jinn have little interest in spiritual wayfaring, they categorically refuse to cede the Earth to humans. At the edges of the known world, the jinn folk are biding their time in exile, waiting to reclaim what they think is rightfully theirs. When God's wrath turned against the people of ʿImlāq, Thamūd, and ʿĀd, jinn used the first chance to take over their lands and cities, killing any human who dared to approach them. The fallen ʿAbqar was likewise overrun by jinn.[105] As late as the twentieth century, the jinn folk were still perceived among Bedouins as virtual owners of the ground. ʿAṭṭār's verses indicate this is certainly the way jinn see things:

Jesus, son of Mary, had fallen asleep
And had put half a brick under his head
When Jesus opened his eyes after his restful sleep
He saw the accursed Iblis above his head
He cried: "O accursed one, why stand you here?"
He replied: "because you placed my brick under your head.
The world is my domain, and it is clear that this brick belongs to me.
You are appropriating goods in my kingdom,
You have trespassed in my territory!"[106]

Iblis was powerless to retrieve the brick by force since Jesus's piety kept him safe from evil. But rather than arguing with Iblis, Jesus threw the brick away and went back to sleep with his face on the ground. The Devil said approvingly:

I shall now leave your presence,
Sleep well![107]

Jesus's disregard for the world of nature has been widely shared among Akbarians. For example, Halveti's commentary of *al-Tadbīrāt al-Ilāhiya* compared the visible world to "a stinking, dried up corpse, its bowels rotten, lying on a garbage heap."[108] Halveti's remark is seemingly at odds with Ibn ʿArabī's admiration for the beauty of nature. Ibn ʿArabī, on the one hand, professed there is nothing more beautiful than the world. However, he was also aware that Iblis is actively striving to make the Earth look beautiful to humans. In Chapter 198 of *al-Futūḥāt,* Ibn ʿArabī cited the thirty-ninth ayah of the surah *al-Ḥijr*, reading: *I will make things on the Earth look beautiful to them and lead all of them astray* (Q 15:39).[109] The hateful Iblis is also in God's service, whether he realizes it or not. Out of malice, the Devil tries to redirect the human gaze away from heaven, towards earth. Ibn ʿArabī, however, taught that humans are enamored with the beauty of nature since they instinctively recognize the beauty of the Creator that is reflected in it.[110] Marvels of nature lead a Seeker to God—not the other way around. The spiritual realizations and knowledge appear as a Seeker contemplates the visible world. Upon reaching a certain level of spiritual development, marvels of the unseen world unfold before a Seeker. It is at this point that some Seekers turn away from the world of nature. Once it has served its purpose, the beauty of nature becomes but a distraction and enemy, on par with the lower soul and Iblis. Ibn ʿArabī expressed these sentiments in verses:

I am tested by four darts,
By arrows from the bow drawn tight:
Iblis, the world, my *nafs* and my Self (*huwiyya*).
Lord, you are the Almighty over what is wholly apart.
Another one said:
Iblis and the world, my *nafs* and my Self,
How can I be holy—apart—with them being my enemy?[111]

The material world is in a state of ceaseless change and movement. It is thus not surprising that it holds sway over jinn. Jinn are fixated on the world of gross matter, and their desire to reclaim it and have it all for themselves makes them heedless of the things transcending the world of change and corruption. Human beings who sit in their company are likewise arrogant and heedless of what is eternal, transcendent, and immutable. Laws, God, universal meanings, and principles are of little interest to such humans and jinn. In contrast, God's saints and prophets care not for the world of gross matter. This world was famously described by the prophet Muhammad as the prison for a believer and a paradise for a nonbeliever (*Ṣaḥīḥ Muslim* #2956). *Humans were created in the finest of statures and then brought down to the lowest of low* (Q 95:4–5) to learn and advance in knowledge and virtue. A spiritual Seeker tastes the beauty of the world and faces its temptations, pain, and suffering. They will use that pain and beauty to ascend through the stations of spiritual wayfaring—taking a qarīn they subdued with them. Spiritual Seekers subdue their doppelgangers by turning away from the world, towards God. ʿAṭṭār's verses furthermore suggest that turning away from the world is also an opportunity to make peace with exiled jinn and the Devil. Callous as he was towards the Devil, Ibn ʿArabī would likely consider this a fair trade. For he noted that a person refusing to turn away from the seen world towards the Unseen is a beast and should be regarded as a beast.[112] God's friends and prophets are everything but. Thus, sometimes, the Devil may also be allowed to get his due.

Dear friend, these are the words of wisdom!

All that is, all that was and all that will be must not and cannot be but the way it is. Whiteness could never be without blackness, heaven cannot be without earth, substance cannot be without accident and Muhammad cannot be without Iblis. Obedience without disobedience and unbelief without faith are inconceivable. Such is the case with each and every opposite and this is the meaning of it, for it is only through their opposites that things get to be distinguished from one another.

—ʿAyn al-Quḍāt[113]

Notes

Chapter 1

1. Ibn ʿArabī, *Mashāhid al-ʾasrār al-qudsiyya*, 64–65. Cf. Ibn ʿArabī, *Contemplations of the Holy Mysteries*, 50.

2. Ibn ʿArabī, *al-Futūḥāt al-Makkiyya*, I:45. Hereafter referred to as FM. The terms "Akbarian school," "Akbarian Sufism," and "Akbariyya" are commonly used today to denote the teachings of Ibn ʿArabī and his students and followers. This is mostly justified by the fact that Ibn ʿArabī referred to individual religious beliefs and practices as "schools" (*madhāhib*). Ibn ʿArabī, *The Meccan Revelations*, vol. 1, 251. It is, however, debatable whether Ibn ʿArabī founded an independent school of thought (*madhab*) in his lifetime. An interesting take on the debate can consulted in Dajani, *Sufis and Sharia*, 5, 129–57.

3. This quote is typically attributed to ʿAlī al-Jurjānī (d. 1413). Papas, "Dog of God: Animality and Wildness among Dervishes," 127.

4. See Chodkiewicz's introduction to Ibn ʿArabī's *Prayer for Spiritual Elevation and Protection* (ar. *Ḥizb al-wiqāya*). Ibn Arabī, *Prayer for Spiritual Elevation and Protection*, 9.

5. "Ibn ʿArabī," Chittick noted, "can be considered the greatest of all Muslim philosophers, provided we understand philosophy in the broad, modern sense and not simply as the discipline of *falsafa*." Chittick, "Ibn ʿArabī." https://plato.stanford.edu/entries/ibn-arabi/. Accessed online October 30, 2021. See also Almond, *Sufism and Deconstruction*, 12.

6. Takeshita, "Ibn ʿArabi's Theory of the Perfect Man," 1. The list of Ibn ʿArabī's surviving works can be consulted at Clark-Hirtenstein, "Establishing Ibn ʿArabī's Heritage," 1–32.

7. al-ʿAjmī, *Ibn ʿArabī, ʿaqīdatuhu wa mawqif ʿulamāʾ minhu*, 204. Ibn ʿArabī, however, believed that fighting against the lower soul and the Devil is also a form of jihad. See FM I:467 and §1.4 of the present study.

8. al-Sīnūbī, *Ḥayāt al-qulūb fī al-maw ʿiza*, ff.63–65. Cf. Zildic, "Friend and Foe," 143.

9. Knyush, *Ibn Arabi in the Later Islamic Tradition*, 32, 59–60.

10. FM II:167, 399.

11. FM II:399.

12. Quoted according to Hirtenstein (ed.), *Muhyiddin Ibn ʿArabī: A Commemorative Volume*, 1. Cf. FM III:449–50.

13. al-Ghazālī, *al-Ḥikma fī al-makhlūqāt Allāh*, 11–15. See also Nasr, "God Is the Absolute Reality," 4 and Nasr, *The Need for a Sacred Science*, 8.

14. According to Plato, Socrates used to say that "wonder is the feeling of a philosopher and that philosophy begins in wonder." Plato, *The Dialogues of Plato*, vol. 3, 155. See also Aristotle, *Metaphysics*, 98.

15. See Descartes, *The Passions of the Soul*, 56 and al-Qazwīnī, *ʿAjāʾib al-makhlūqāt*, 25–26.

16. Quoted according to Hassig, *Medieval Bestiaries*, 15. See also Morisson (ed.), *The Book of Beasts*, 4–6.

17. Bakar, "The Unity of Science and Spiritual Knowledge," 10.

18. FM III:210.

19. FM I:51. Beautiful, ever-changing and terrible all at once—the visible world in Ibn ʿArabī's works was compared by M. Sells to jinn. Sells, "Bewildered Tongue," 93.

20. Quoted according to Beneito, "On the Divine Love for Beauty," 9.

21. FM I:756, FM II:244, 276, 342, FM III:36, FM IV:214.

22. al-Bīrūnī, *al-ʾĀthār al-bāqiyya ʿan al-qurūn al-khāliyya*, 284–85.

23. al-Masʿūdī, *Murūj al-dhahab wa-maʿādin al-jawhar*, vol. 2, 208. See also Daston and Park, *Wonders and the Order of Nature*, 14.

24. God is a hundred times more merciful towards humans than towards jinn. Al-Ghazālī, *Mukhtaṣar ʾiḥyāʾ ʿulūm al-dīn*, 462. For the reports concerning the banishment of jinn and jinn eavesdropping at the heaven's door, see *Ṣaḥīḥ Muslim* #5538; al-Qazwīnī, *ʿAjāʾib al-makhlūqāt*, 171–72; al-Jayyānī, *al-Baḥr al-muḥīṭ*, vol. 1, 141; Kabbani, *Angels Unveiled*, 171 and Kister, "Adam: A Study of Some Legends in Tafsīr and Ḥadīth Literature," 121.

25. FM II:106. Murata noted that jinn possess heavenly qualities even though they pertain to Earth. Murata, *Tao of Islam*, 137. This is in accordance with Ibn ʿArabī's teachings. It is, however, worth noting there are also records of Ibn ʿArabī saying that jinn are closer in nature to the visible than to the invisible world. FM II:106. Since jinn were condemned to live in the world of nature, they were once described by Ibn ʿArabī as the creatures of the worldly abode. FM I:423. In spite of this fact, Laughlin identified jinn as inhabitants of the World of Malakūt. Laughlin, "A

Brief Overview of Jinn within Islamic Cosmology and Religiosity," 69. Ibn ʿArabī, however, taught that no jinn can ascend beyond Jabarūt. The world of Jabarūt was described in his works as the imaginal realm and "the middle world of jinn and [other] spirit-beings." FM II:68.

26. Lory, "Sexual Intercourse between Humans and Demons in the Islamic Tradition," 49. See also Elmore, *The Fabulous Gryphon*, 178.

27. FM I:304. See also Nünlist, "Demonology in Islam," 533.

28. Nathan, *Nous ne sommes pas seuls au monde*, 213–14.

29. Daston and Park, *Wonders and the Order of Nature*, 14.

30. Bynum, "Wonder," 24.

31. al-Jāḥiẓ, *Kitāb al-Ḥayawān*, vol. 6, 250–51.

32. See Ibn Qutayba, *Ta'wīl mushkil al-Qur'ān*, 36–37 and Ibn Rushd, *Incoherence of the Incoherence*, 323.

33. One such case, where a skeptical philosopher and a theologian went to the mountains in search for a jinni, was documented in *ʿAjāyib-nāma*. See Ṭūsī, *ʿAjāyib-nāma*, 214.

34. Ibn Ḥazm, *Kitāb al-fiṣal fī l-milal wal-ahwā' wal-niḥal*, 12.

35. According to Dols, the existence of jinn was affirmed in the Meccan period of Muhammad's mission. The jinn folk were then gradually demoted from all-powerful beings to mischievous, insignificant spirits. Dols believed that this is to be attributed to the fact that the Prophet's attention later shifted on Iblis the Devil. This presumably made him lose interest in jinn. Dols, *The Madman in Medieval Islamic Society*, 214. See also Welch, "Allah and Other Supernatural Beings," 745.

36. al-Zain, *Islam, Arabs and the Intelligible World of Jinn*, 149.

37. Ibid., ix.

38. al-Ashqar, *The World of Jinn and Devils*, 21.

39. The term *jinnealogy* was used in this book for jinn studies in general. Taneja, however, used this term for "superseding of human chains of genealogy and memory by the other-temporality of the jinn" and "theological orientation that encompasses the registers of ironic commentary, counter-memory, and apotropaic magic." Taneja, *Jinneology*, 25.

40. Badeen and Krawietz, "Eheschließung mit Dschinnen nach Badr al-Dīn al-Shiblī," 36.

41. Zwemer, *The Influence of Animism*, 142.

42. Nawfal, *ʿĀlam al-jinn wal-malā'ik*, 16.

43. Schöller, "His Master's Voice," 44.

44. Padwick, "Notes on the Jinn and the Ghoul in the Peasant Mind of Lower Egypt," 445. In the light of the fact that Padwick conducted her research in 1924, further studies might be required to determine whether her observations are valid still. Dols also made similar observations in his

more recent publication. Dols, *The Madman in Medieval Islamic Society*, 214. Coulon's overview of medieval and the early modern fatwas furthermore demonstrates the extent to which jinn have played a role in the daily lives, medicine, and commercial transactions in the Middle East. Coulon, "La magie islamique," 643. See also Zadeh, "Magic, Marvel and Miracle in Early Islamic Thought," 235.

45. The most successful attempt to produce an all-embracing study on the topic to date was conducted by Fritz Meier. Unfortunately, Meier passed away before he could finish his book. A portion of Meier's notes on jinn was subsequently published by Tobias Nünlist under the title *Dämonenglaube im Islam* (De Gruyter, 2015).

46. Zwemer, "The Familiar Spirit or Qarina," 360.

47. These include: Blackman, "The Karīn and Karīneh" (1926); Winkler, *Salomo und die Ḳarīna* (1931); Parman, "The Demon as Human Double" (2004); and Perdigon, "Bleeding Dreams" (2015).

48. According to Nünlist, this is to be attributed to the fact that the Qur'an and sunnah have inspired writings of the Muslim elite and folk narratives alike. Nünlist, *Dämonenglaube im Islam*, 3–6.

49. Al-Ghazālī, *ʾIḥyāʾ ʿulūm al-dīn*, vol. 4, 74. There is a prophetic narrative attributing the first cry of an infant to a jab from this jinni. *Mishkāt al-Maṣābiḥ* #70.

50. See Gallorini, "The Symbolic Functions of Angels," 68; Hoyland, *Arabia and the Arabs*, 145; Moreman, "Rehabilitating the Spirituality of Pre-Islamic Arabia," 137–57; Basharin, "Образ джиннов в мусульманской магии," 135; Nasser, "The Jinn: Companion in the Realm of Dreams and Imagination," 144 and Fahd, "S̲h̲ayṭān." http://dx.doi.org/10.1163/1573-3912_islam_COM_1054. Accessed January 7, 2021.

51. Van Vloten, "Dämonen, Geister und Zauber bei den alten Arabern," 182.

52. Zādih, *Miftāḥ as-saʿāda wa-miṣbāḥ al-siyāda*, vol. 1, 364.

53. Wellhausen, *Reste arabischen Heidentums*, 156.

54. Zwemer, "The Familiar Spirit or Qarina," 360.

55. Smith, *Lectures on the Religion of the Semites*, 538–41. See also Gaudefroy-Demombynes, *Mahomet*, 29, 32–33 and Fahd, *Anges, démons et djinns en Islam*, 190.

56. Henninger's and Westermarck's criticism of Smith's theory can be consulted at: Henninger, "Beliefs in Spirits among the Pre-Islamic Arabs," 6 and Westermarck, "The Nature of the Arab Ginn," 264–68. However, not all scholars were convinced of Henninger's and Westermarck's analyses. Among the notable proponents of Smith's theory were Aloiane and Pinault. See Aloiane, "Anthropomorphic Representations of Evil in Islam," 423 and Pinault, *The Shiites*, 11–12.

57. Zwemer, "The Familiar Spirit or Qarina," 362.

58. See Hornblower, "Traces of a Ka-Belief in Modern Egypt and Old Arabia," 426–30; Blackman, "The Karin and Karineh," 168–9 and al-Shamy, "Twins / Zwillinge: A Broader View," 17. Ridgeway's arguments can be consulted at Tremearne, *Ban of Bori*, 138.

59. al-Safi, *Traditional Sudanese Medicine*, 205–6.

60. Meier's remarks can be consulted in the introduction he wrote to Kubrā, *Fawāʾiḥ al-jamāl wa-fawātiḥ al-jalāl*, 182–86, 194. See also Elsby, "Socrates's Demonic Sign (*Daimonion Sēmeion*)," 95–108.

61. al-Suyūṭī, *al-Ṭibb al-nabī*, 156. Al-Shamy documented the existence of similar beliefs among the contemporary spiritual healers in Egypt. One healer al-Shamy interviewed even went as far as saying that, were it really possible for an evil jinni to enter a human body, he would refuse to treat such a person since they would be better off dead than alive. Al-Shamy, "Belief Characters as Anthropomorphic Psychosocial Realities," 14.

62. Fahd, "Shayṭān." http://dx.doi.org/10.1163/1573-3912_islam_COM_1054. Accessed January 7, 2021.

63. Padwick, "Notes on the Jinn and the Ghoul in the Peasant Mind of Lower Egypt," 445.

64. Canaan, *Aberglaube und Volksmedizin*, 26. Byzantine legends of the purpureal demoness Gello might have served as another (in)direct source of inspiration for the tales of Qarīna. Wójcik-Owczarek, "A Few Words on the Sisinnios-type of Gello Story," 73–82. Another similar demoness has been referred to in Turkish folklore as "Albasty." Dallos explicitly linked this demoness to both Lilith and Gello. Dallos, "Albasty: A Female Demon of Turkic Peoples," 419.

65. There is a possibility that ʾUmm al-Ṣibyān, Tābiʿa and Qarīna were once perceived as different demonesses in their own right, each of whom was prone to causing miscarriages, seducing men, and targeting pregnant women and children. All three demonesses were often compared to Lilith. Several scholars have examined how these demonesses got to be mixed up and merged with one another in popular culture. Their analyses can be consulted at Westermarck, *Ritual and Belief in Morocco*, vol. 1, 401–2; Doutté, *Magie et religion*, 111–17 and Desparmet, *Le mal magique*, 170–84. Basharin believed that ʾUmm al-Ṣibyān and Tābiʿa were first identified with Qarīna in the early Middle Ages. Basharin, "Образ джиннов в мусульманской магии," 135. See also Coulon, "ʿAnāq bt. Adam," 152.

66. Westermarck, *Ritual and Belief in Morocco*, vol. 1, 400–2; Winkler, *Salomo und die Ḳarīna*, 37. A famous depiction of the demoness Tābiʿa as a dark-skinned woman cradling a human can be consulted in the fourteenth-century manuscript copy of *Kitāb al-Bulhān*, which is currently kept in the Bodleian Library in Oxford. al-Iṣfahānī, *Kitāb al-Bulhān* (MS Bodl.

Or. 133), ff.29. Another depiction of ʾUmm al-Ṣibyān/Tābiʿa in the form of a dark-skinned woman was preserved in *Kitāb al-Mandal al-Sulaymānī*, which is in the possession of the Institute of Ethiopian Studies in Addis Ababa. *Kitāb al-Mandal al-Sulaymānī* (MS Ar.286), ff.7.

67. See Canova, "Uno sheykh-serpente dell'Alto Egitto," 36; Hentschel, *Geister, Magier und Muslime*, 35; and Canaan, *Aberglaube und Volksmedizin*, 26.

68. "Menstruation," Ibn ʿArabī recorded, "is the pulse of Satan." FM I:362. Bedouins of old Arabia believed that even evil jinn flee from menstruating women to avoid being contaminated. This is why jinn cannot stand hares, for "they say that it menstruates like a woman, that it eats meat and such and that it ruminates and defecates globular dung." Ibn ʾAbī al-Ḥawāfīr, *Badāʾiʿ al-akwān*, ff.16. Quoted according to Kurk, "Elusive Giraffes," 54. Similar beliefs could also be found among ancient Romans. For example, Pliny worried that crops would wither, wine would turn sour, dogs would run mad, and knives would become dull if a menstruating woman were to approach them. Hence, Pliny concluded, "hardly can there be found a thing more monstrous than that flux." Mollenauer, *Strange Revelations*, 57.

69. Zwermer, "The Familiar Spirit of Qarina," 366.

70. In Dagestani folklore, jinn doppelgangers were thought to be the servants of the demoness ʾUmm al-Ṣibyān. Zwemer, "The Familiar Spirit of Qarina," 367–68. Fartacek's research on Qarīna in Syrian folklore can be consulted at Fartacek, *Unheil durch Dämonen*, 68. The Palestinian refugees from Southern Lebanon described Qarīna to Perdigon as "mush jinn, bas men al-jinn" (i.e. "not a jinni, but from the jinn"). Perdigon, "Bleeding Dreams," 145. Zwemer's interview with an unnamed shaykh in Caliub is another telling example of how the notions of doppelgangers have evolved in popular culture. Zwemer writes: "A learned Sheikh at Caliub, a Moslem village near Cairo, was also consulted on the subject. At first he tried to explain away the idea of popular Islam by saying that the qarina only referred to the evil conscience or a man's evil nature, but after a few questions he became quite garrulous and gave the following particulars: the expectant mother, in fear of the qarina, visits the sheikha (learned woman) three months before the birth of the child and does whatever she indicates as a remedy. These sheikh exercise great influence over the women, and batten on their superstitious beliefs, often impersonating the qarina and frightening the ignorant. The Moslem mother often denies the real sex of her babe for seven days after it is born in order to protect its life from the patina. During these seven days she must not strike a cat or she and the child will both die. Candles are lighted on the seventh day and placed in a jug of water near the head of the child, to guard it

against the qarina. Before the child is born a special amulet is prepared, consisting of seven grains each of seven different kinds of cereals. These are sewn up in a bag, and when the infant is born it is made to wear it. The mother also has certain verses of the Koran written with musk water or ink on the inside of the white dish. This is then filled with water and the ink washed off and the content taken as a potion." Zwemer, "The Familiar Spirit or Qarina," 368.

71. Winkler, *Salomo und die Ḳarīna*, 58–59, 64–70.

72. FM I:31–33, 134, 604. It should be noted that Taji-Faroukhi suggested that one prayer from Ibn ʿArabī's *Ḥizb al-wiqāya* might be referring to "umm al-ṣibyān." Taji-Faroukhi was, however, personally inclined to believe that the prayer in question is actually referring to baby colic or epilepsy. Ibn ʿArabī, *A Prayer for Spiritual Elevation and Protection*, 105.

73. FM I:134. Contemporary Akbarians still follow this approach. In his commentary of Ibn ʿArabī's *al-Tadbīrāt al-Ilāhiya*, Halveti noted how "today, as always, the Sufis aim to understand the real meaning of things, beyond their appearances. Whenever your eye rests upon any existent entity in this world of matter around you, seek its original attribute, its essential meaning, which will explain it or transform it. When you thus find the proof of its existence, you will have found its true reality." Ibn ʿArabī, *Divine Governance of the Human Kingdoms*, 13.

74. Bosnevi, *Sharḥ Fuṣūṣ al-ḥikam*, vol. 1, 176.

75. Scholastic notions of moral evil were chiefly based on the teachings of Augustine, who divided evil into two exclusive categories: sin (*peccatum*) and punishment for sin (*poena peccati*). Van der Lught, *Dark Matters*, 30. Whereas jinn's behavior has been commonly associated with sin, al-Shamy and Dols argued that these creatures were not generally associated with punishment for sin in Islam. al-Shamy, "Mental Health in Traditional Culture," 13–28; Dols, *Majnūn*, 215. Whereas al-Shamy and Dols documented the general tendencies in Islamic culture with regard to jinn, Ibn ʿArabī proved to be an exception to the rule. This can be seen from his reports on al-ʿUraybī. Al-ʿUraybī was an illiterate farmer and one of Ibn ʿArabī's teachers. When al-ʿUraybī was exiled from the city of Kutāmah, God sent an evil jinni to haunt houses of the city lords. The brazen creature exposed their sins to the public—and it did this in such a way that the lords begged al-ʿUraybī to have mercy on them and return to Kutāmah at once. As soon as he entered the city, the jinni disappeared, never to be seen again. Ibn ʿArabī's scattered notes on al-ʿUraybī have been assembled and analyzed by Abrahamov. See Abrahamov, *Ibn ʿArabī and the Sufis*, 166.

76. *Sunan Ibn Mājah* #3266. Iblis the Devil and other evil jinn eat with their left hand only. This is why the Prophet ordered believers to only

ever use their right hand when eating so as not to follow the example of evil jinn. *Ṣaḥīḥ Muslim* #2019.

77. One such jinni is al-Muṣrif. This jinni was described in the manuscript Rührdanz named "Dīwnāma." The facsimile of this manuscript was published in Shadrach's *The Book of the Deadly Names*. See Rührdanz, "Ein Illustrierter iatromagischer Text als bestanteil von ʿAjāʾib al-makhlūqāt-Handschriften," 183–93 and Shadrach, *The Book of the Deadly Names*, 48.

78. Shadrach, *The Book of the Deadly Names*, 164. The church al-Qalīs in Sanaa was a famous dwelling place of jinn. Jinn took over this church when the Ethiopians who built it were expelled from Sanaa. From that moment on, these jinn would either curse or possess treasure hunters who dared to venture into "their" church. Bauden (ed.), *al-Maqrīzī's al-Khabar ʿan al-bashar*, vol. 8, 275.

79. ʿUmar b. al-Khaṭṭāb (d. 644) was rumored to have said: "Women are demons which were created for us and we seek refuge in God against the evil of these demons." al-Qurṭubī, *Tafsīr al-Qurṭubī*, vol. 7, 68. See also al-Qazwīnī, *ʿAjāʾib al-makhlūqāt*, 172–73; Cornell, "Soul of a Woman Was Created Below," 257 and Saniotis, *Sacred Worlds*, 113–15.

80. Yāqūt, *Muaʿjam al-buldān*, vol. 2, 153. See also Lyons's introduction to *Tales of the Marvelous, News of the Strange*, 26.

81. The perceived behavior of jinn corresponds to the scholastic notion of natural evil in this regard. Common examples of natural evil include earthquakes, bodily pains, and deformations. In other words, natural evil is any sort of evil that is unconnected with moral responsibility. An overview of the scholastic notions of natural evil can be consulted at Van der Lught, *Dark Matters*, 30–31.

82. Brethren of Purity, *The Case of Animals Versus Man in Front of the King of the Jinn*, 240–41. Rather than emphasizing the hypocrisy of human nature, Krawietz advocated for a more compassionate, contemporary interpretation of jinn narratives. According to Krawietz, these narratives should be read as "a coping strategy for traumatized Muslims, to come to terms with unbearable strokes of fate and shocks: blind violence, unexpected losses, frightful events, various kinds of onslaughts, mental cruelty, the erratic behaviour of others, and ruptures within themselves can be translated into a large theatre of familiar categories of Jinn and an established grammar of action." Krawietz, "Ten Theses on Working with Demons (Jinn) in Islamic Studies," 332. Whereas Ibn ʿArabī's works do not support this interpretation, Taneja demonstrated the usefulness of Krawietz's approach in ethnography. Taneja, *Jinneology*, 19–55. Krawietz furthermore emphasized the importance of (reinterpreted) jinn narratives

in gender studies, surveillance studies, in transnational trance tourism, etc. Krawietz, "Ten Theses on Working with Demons (Jinn) in Islamic Studies," 331–36.

83. Brethren of Purity, The Case of Animals Versus Man in Front of the King of the Jinn, 126. Hence, Ibn Kathīr reasoned that jinn are more afraid of humans than the other way around. Basharin, "Образ джиннов в мусульманской магии," 117.

84. Ibn ʿArabī said: "Take a look at the respectful attitude of the Prophet! When God helped him prevail over an ifrit that assaulted him, the Prophet wanted to tie that ifrit to one of the columns of the mosque for people to see. Then he remembered the dua of his brother Solomon and he released the ifrit and allowed it to return to God in defeat. Solomon's state of power over jinn was granted to Muhammad as well . . . but he abstained from using it out of respect for Solomon." FM I:585.

85. FM I:273–74.

86. Ibn ʿArabī, *Divine Governance of the Human Kingdom*, 16. Najm al-Dīn Kubrā once described fear as the garment binding a person to their qarīn. Kubrā, *Fawāʾiḥ al-jamāl wa-fawātiḥ al-jalāl*, 80–81, 162.

87. FM III:132, 300. "Up until recent times," Chittick noted, "Islamic thought was characterized by a tendency toward unity, harmony, integration, and synthesis. The great Muslim thinkers were masters of many disciplines, but they looked upon them as branches of the single tree of 'Tawhid.' There was never any contradiction between astronomy and zoology, or physics and ethics, or mathematics and law, or mysticism and logic. Everything was governed by the same principles, because everything fell under God's all-encompassing reality." Chittick, *Science of the Cosmos*, 13.

88. All living beings other than humans and jinn have inherent knowledge of God. This is why they live in the state of perpetual felicity. FM IV:319. See also Chittick, "The Wisdom of Animals," 27–37.

89. *Musnad ʾAḥmad* #2/353. See also Q 6:112, 114:15.

90. FM IV:214. Cf. Chittick, *Self-Disclosure of God*, 104.

91. This is a shared trait of all embodiments of the Divine name *al-Mudhill*. Embodiments of this Name were collectively referred to as *mudhillūn* in Ibn ʿArabī's works. Chodkiewicz, *Ocean without Shore*, 52.

92. FM I:37, 40, 283–85; FM II:688.

93. As Chittick pointed out, the Devil and the lower soul are embodiments of God's deception (*makr*). Hence, Chittick argued that it would not be wrong to associate them with the Divine Name al-Mākir. Chittick, *Sufi Path of Knowledge*, 267. See also Harendrachandra, *Jalāluʾd-dīn Rūmī and his Taṣawwuf*, 308–9.

94. FM I:362, 939.

95. Awn, *Satan's Tragedy and Redemption*, 16.

96. FM II:30. Writing on the highest station of spiritual development—the so-called station of no station—Chittick noted that a person "passes from station to station, never losing a positive attribute after having gained it. One by one, in perfect harmony, he assumes the traits of the Divine Names. Having reached the highest station, he owns all stations." Chittick, *Sufi Path of Knowledge*, 375.

97. Ibn ʿArabī's definitions of "jihad" and "Jihad of the Soul" (*jihād al-nafs*) can be consulted at FM I:467. We will examine Ibn ʿArabī's notions of the Great City and the Red Death in the third and the fourth chapter of the present study.

98. Quoted according to Chittick, "Ibn ʿArabī's own Summary of the Fuṣūṣ," 10–11. See also: See FM I:124–25. Due to the prominence of microcosm-macrocosm analogies in Ibn ʿArabī's works, Nokso-Koivito argued that "it would not be an exaggeration to say that in them [i.e. in Ibn ʿArabī's works] Islamic microcosmism took one of its most elaborate forms." Nokso-Koivito, "Microcosm-Macrocosm Analogy in Rasāʾil," 63. Al-Halveti's commentary on Ibn ʿArabī's treatise *al-Tadbīrāt al-Ilāhiya* offers another curious interpretation of the relationship between microcosm and macrocosm. He explained that "when the eye of the heart recognizes the divine attribute manifested in a thing, it also recognizes the equivalent manifestation existing inside us. Then that thing is no longer outside and separate from us but is known as a part of human being. Therefore, we assign it its name from among our own names." Ibn ʿArabī, *Divine Governance of the Human Kingdoms*, 13–14.

99. FM II:119; Chittick, "Death and the World of Imagination," 51–52.

100. Yazaki, *Islamic Mysticism and Abu Talib Al-Makki*, 21.

101. Ibn al-Jawzī, *al-Muntaẓam fī tārīkh al-mulūk wal-ʾumam*, vol. 17, 239. Cf. Schimmel, *Mystical Dimensions of Islam*, 195.

102. See FM I:167 and Rašić, *The Written World of God*, 49–51.

103. Chittick, *In Search for the Lost Heart*, 41.

104. FM I:134.

105. Ali, *Philosophical Sufism*, 22.

106. As three of these publications are dated before 1931; future studies will be required to determine whether the described beliefs and practices are still as widespread in Muslim cultures and societies as before.

107. FM I:85; Brethren of Purity, *On God and the World*, 75.

108. al-Ghazālī, *Revival of Religion's Sciences*, vol. 3, 50.

109. *Mathnawī* II:2665–2751. See also Anushiravani, *The Image of Satan*, 101.

Chapter 2

1. Ibn ʿArabī, *Divine Governance of the Human Kingdoms*, 6.

2. Ibn ʿArabī, *al-Futūḥāt al-Makkiyya*,I:279. Hereafter referred to as FM.

3. Lory, "Sexual Intercourse between Humans and Demons in the Islamic Tradition," 50.

4. See Montgomery's introduction to Schöller, *The Oral and the Written in the Early Islam*, 1.

5. FM I:119.

6. Ibn Manẓūr, *Lisān al-ʿarab*, vol. 13, 92. A similar definition was also brought forth by al-Damīrī (d. 1405). al-Damīrī, *Ḥayāt al-ḥayawān*, vol. 1, 448.

7. Ibn Manẓūr, *Lisān al-ʿarab*, vol. 13, 92.

8. Ibn Fāris, *Muʿajam maqāyīs al-lugha*, vol. 1, 420–21.

9. See Lawrence, *The Qur'an—a Biography*, 185 and al-Ṭabarī, *The History of al-Ṭabarī*, vol. 1, 250.

10. MacDonald, "Djinn." http://dx.doi.org/10.1163/1573-3912_islam_COM_0191. Accessed January 9, 2022. Roman genii have been perceived as the guardian spirits of humans, places, and objects. Even though Meier was adamant that the words *geniī* and *jinn* are not etymologically related, he noted that the behaviour of these spirits is mostly the same. On his side, Meier was convinced that the word *jinn* is of Arabic origin. Chelhod, Nünlist, and Tritton (among others) also shared this view. See Meier, "Some Aspects of Inspiration by Demons in Islam," 424–25; Chelhod, *Les structures du sacré chez les Arabes*, 130; Nünlist, *Dämonglaube im Islam*, 24, and Tritton, "Spirits and Demons in Arabia," 715.

11. Waardenburg, "Changes of Belief in Spiritual Beings," 259. Teixidor and Albright were also among those who argued that the word *jinn* is of Aramaic origin. Albright furthermore surmised that the Arabic *jinn* comes from the Palmyrenean-Aramaic *gny*, which means "to be hidden." See Albright, "Islam and the Religions of Ancient Orient," 283 and Teixidor, *The Pantheon of Palmyra*, 77.

12. Khan, *The Heart of Sufism*, 111.

13. Ibid., 244.

14. Ali, *The Holy Qur'an with Translation and Commentary*, 319. Aloiane and Moreman analyzed how the word *jinn* was used when applied to humans, both living and dead. Aloiane, "Antropomorphic Representations of Evil in Islam," 429. Moreman, "Rehabilitating the Spirituality of Pre-Islamic Arabia," 1–21.

15. Sells, *Approaching the Qur'an*, 37.

16. Moleiro (ed.), *The Book of Felicity*, 148.

17. Quoted according to MacDonald, *Religious Attitude and Life in Islam*, 152.

18. Smith said: "Nothing is told of jinn which savages do not tell of animals. Under these circumstances it requires a very exaggerated skepticism to doubt that the jinn, with all their mysterious powers, are mainly nothing else than more or less modernized representatives of animal kinds, clothed with supernatural attributes." Smith, *Lectures on the Religion of the Semites*, 123. Wellhausen's remarks on Islamic zoology and demonology can be consulted at Zwemer, *The Influence of Animism in Islam*, 130.

19. Carboni, *The Wonders of Creation*, 38, 74. See also Nünlist, "Von Berittenen und Gerittenen," 147, and al-Azmeh, *The Emergence of Islam*, 208.

20. Ibn Barrajān, *Tafsīr Ibn Barrajān*, vol. 4, 253.

21. It should be noted, with regard to the six species of the universe, that Ibn ʿArabī did not perceive minerals as inanimate beings. As a matter of fact, Ibn ʿArabī claimed "one cannot divide [things] of the universe into living and inanimate things. We believe the universe is alive in its totality." FM III:324. See also FM I:96, 119 and Rašić, *The Written World of God*, 184.

22. FM I:132–34. Yousef maintained that jinn appeared on the Fourth Day of creation. Yousef, *Ibn ʿArabī - Time and Cosmology*, 97. Other authors gave different numbers. For instance, al-Ḥalabī (d. 1635) believed that jinn were created on Thursday, 2,000 years before Adam. al-Ḥalabī, *ʿIqd al-marjān*, 28. Al-Shiblī, however, reported that jinn were created 1,000 years before humans. Al-Shiblī, *Kitāb ʾākām al-marjān*, 23. On his side, al-ʿAyyashī (d. 932) believed that jinn were actually created 7,000 years before Adam. al-ʿAyyashī, *Tafsīr al-ʿAyyashī*, vol. 1, 80.

23. See FM I:133–34; al-Jayyānī, *Al-Baḥr al-muḥīṭ*, vol. 1, 141; Alam, *The Mughals and Sufis*, 168 and Kister, "Adam: A Study of Some Legends in Tafsīr and Ḥadīth Literature," 121.

24. FM II:106–107; Brethren of Purity, *The Case of Animals Versus Man*, 20, 29.

25. See Chittick, *In Search for the Lost Heart*, 41.

26. FM I:133.

27. al-Diyārbakrī, *Tārikh al-khamīs*, vol. 1, 33.

28. FM I:133–34. Chittick erroneously identified Iblis as the first jinni. Chittick, *The Self-Disclosure of God*, xxxi.

29. FM I:134.

30. Teuma, "The Nature of Iblis in the Qur'an," 13–14. See also al-Qazwīnī, *ʿAjāʾib al-makhlūqāt*, 172.

31. Ibn Manẓūr traced the origins of these beliefs back to the pre-Islamic times, when "ignorant people used to refer to angels as 'jinn' since they are hidden from sight." Ibn Manẓūr, *Lisān al-ʿarab*, vol. 13, 197. Ḥasan al-Baṣrī (d. 728), however, argued that the most noble of all angels are referred to as "jinn" since they are veiled from other angels on account on their superiority. Racius, "Islamic Exegeses of the Jinn," 130. In contrast, Ibn Masʿūd maintained that jinn are the tribe of angels that guard the lowest heaven. Teuma, "The Nature of Iblis in the Qur'an," 13. See also: al-Ṭabarī, *The History of al-Ṭabarī*, vol. 1, 250; al-Damīrī, *Ḥayāt al-ḥayawān*, vol. 1, 466, and al-Jīlī, *al-Insān al-kāmil*, 39.

32. Quoted according to al-Zain, *The Evolution of the Concept of Jinn*, 248. In another place, Ibn ʿArabī, however, noted that jinn are similar in nature to both angels and humans. FM I:132. Some scholars offered further explanation on the matter, claiming that jinn possess six qualities. Whereas three of these qualities were described as "angelic," jinn had three other qualities which were thought to be human in nature. Having wings, the ability to fly, and jinn's knowledge of future events were commonly referred to as the angelic qualities of the jinn folk. Eating and drinking, procreating, and having to face an inevitable death were, however, said to be the shared traits of jinn and humans. Geiger, *Judaism and Islam*, 63. See also FM I:131.

33. FM I:133. See also *Ṣaḥīḥ al-Bukhārī* #3860; Ibn Kathīr, *Tafsīr al-Qur'ān al-ʿazīm*, vol. 14, 152; al-Qazwīnī, *ʿAjāʾib al-makhlūqāt*, 172–73; al-Ghazālī, *ʾIḥyāʾ ʿulūm al-dīn*, vol. 3, 37; Ibn ʿĀbidīn, *Radd al-Muhtār*, vol. 9, 423–25, and al-Karmī, *Shifāʾ al-Ṣudūr*, 87.

34. FM I:133.

35. See FM I:131 and *Ṣaḥīḥ Muslim* #2996.

36. The word *mārij*, according to Ibn ʿArabī, comes from *marj*, which is the Arabic word for mixtures. FM I:131.

37. FM I:131. Jasad can be defined as every (corporeal) form spiritual beings adopt—irrespective of the fact if a spiritual being in question is an angel or a jinni. FM II:418. See also Chittick, "Iblīs and the Jinn in the al-Futūḥāt al-Makkiyya," 108.

38. Aristotle taught there are nine accidents: quantity, quality, relation, habitus, time, location, situation/position, action, and passion (or the state of being acted on). Neither of these categories, al-Qazwīnī noted, can be used to describe the jinn folk. al-Qazwīnī, *ʿAjāʾib al-makhlūqāt*, 32–33.

39. FM I:131.

40. FM I:85.

41. Ibn ʿArabī, *Kitāb ʿAnqāʾ mughrib*, 47.

42. See FM I:134 and Jeffery, *The Foreign Vocabulary*, 188–90.

43. FM I:131–32.

44. See FM I:133–34, 604. Whereas the word *jinn* has been used for both good and bad spirits, only evil jinn were referred to as *shayāṭīn* in Muslim cultures and societies. It was generally presumed that "devil" is any jinni that is vicious, arrogant and/or mischievous. This definition was based on the Islamic normative tradition, as can be seen from *Musnad ʾAḥmad* #14575; al-Jāḥiẓ, *Kitāb al-Ḥayawān*, vol. 6, 190 and *al-Suyūṭī, Laqṭ al-marjān*, 6. Mullā Ṣadrā Shirazī (d. 1640) had another view on the matter. He suggested that some people think that, having spent 10,000 years in the heavenly gardens, human inhabitants of the paradise will be turned to angels. Likewise, after spending 10,000 years in hell, the tormented jinn will turn to devils. Shirazī, *Divine Manifestations*, 98. It is also worth noting that the term *shayāṭīn* was used in Ibn ʿArabī's works and in the Qur'an for both jinn and humans: these are satanic humans and jinn, inspiring each other with flowery discourse to deceive (Q 6:112). Ibn ʿArabī furthermore recorded that "whomever holds onto his ingratitude is a devil." FM I:134, 271. This opinion was widely shared among Akbarians. For example, al-Kāshānī (d. 1329) noted there are "devils of mankind who are the evil, disobedient, powerful rebels and the devils of the jinn who are the illusions, images and imaginations that are veiled from the light of the spirit that disobeys the command of the intellect and rebels against obedience of the heart." Al-Kāshānī, *Tafsīr al-Kāshānī*, vol. 1, 56.

45. Neither of these names, Kubrā noted, means anything in either Arabic or Persian. However, by the means of tasting (*dhawq*), a Seeker can figure out the meaning of these names. This is how Kubrā realized that the name Qanṭarūn means "insatiable impulses," that Yūnāq means "trickster and schemer," and that the meaning of the name Istaftīn is "ʿĀʾisha of her time." Kubrā, *Fawāʾiḥ al-jamāl*, 80–81. Further information on the Prophet's companion jinn can be found at al-Azmeh, *The Emergence of Islam*, 208. The names of other famous jinn can be consulted at Fahmi, *ʾAsrār al-jinn*, 33–34.

46. FM II:466. Tendencies to refer to a qarīn as "one's own Iblis" were also documented in the works of Abū al-ʿAlā al-Maʿarrī (d. 1057) and ʿAṭṭār of Nishapur (d. 1221). Corbin, *Man of Light in Iranian Sufism*, 66.

47. FM I:133–34, 515–16. Evil jinn were often linked to the color black. Akbarians believed that white is the best of colors, the color of God, "since other colours, all of them, can turn white, whereas white does not transform into any other colour." FM II:171. Jinn's love for the color black was typically interpreted as the proof of their base nature and their remoteness from God. Alternative interpretations of jinn's love for black were offered by Ibn Taymiyya and Niẓāmī. On his side, Ibn Taymiyya argued that jinn draw strength from black since it contains the power of

heat. Al-Ashqar, *The World of Jinn*, 34. Niẓāmī, however, noted that black symbolizes all that is unseen, unknown—and evil. He recorded that "there is no colour beyond black." This is due to the fact that black was thought to be the color of Saturn, which was the last of the then-known planets. Niẓāmi furthermore noted that black is the color of India, which was often described as the land of "black infidelity" in the works of Muslim scholars. Schimmel, *Deciphering the Signs of God*, 16, 62.

48. FM I:134, FM II:466.

49. See FM I:133–34 and FM II:466–67.

50. FM I:131–34, 273–74; FM II:106–7, 466–67; FM III:99 and FM IV:232. See also Lyons, *Tales of the Marvelous*, 26 and al-Qazwīnī, *ʿAjāʾib al-makhlūqāt*, 172.

51. FM I:131–32.

52. Al-Azmeh furthermore argued that jinn—with the exception of quranāʾ—are devoid of personalities and personal character traits. This opinion was widely shared among medieval and the early modern scholars. Al-Azmeh, *The Emergence of Islam*, 206. See also Smith, *Lectures on the Religion of the Semites*, 538–41; Gaudefroy-Demombynes, *Mahomet*, 29, 32–33 and Fahd, *Anges, démons et djinns en Islam*, 190.

53. See FM I:131 and FM IV:232.

54. Quoted according to De Vaux, *L'Abrégé des merveilles*, 48.

55. For instance, desert jinn would sometimes assume the form of lit torches to warn humans of impending dangers and sorrowful events. See Yāqūt, *Muʿjam al-buldān*, vol. 1, 496 and Fahd, *Anges, demons et djinns*, 208. For Ibn ʿArabī's reports on shapeshifting and imagination of jinn see FM I:132 and al-Zain, *Islam, Arabs and the Intelligent World of Jinn*, 25.

56. Mandal al-Sulaymanī, ff.6. The facsimile of this manuscript was published in Regourd, "Images et magie," 289–94.

57. Surviving reports of Solomon and Ṣakhr were collected and analyzed in detail by Klar. Ṣakhr was described by Klar as Solomon's "demonic other" and "the prophet's unconsciousness." Klar, "And We Cast upon His Throne a Mere Body," 114. For reports on gender and appearance of doppelgangers see Lory, "Sexual Intercourse between Humans and Demons," 54; Padwick, "Notes on the Jinn and the Ghoul," 30; Tremearne, *Ban of Bori*, 138, and Zwemer, "The Familiar Spirit or Qarina," 360.

58. Daqāʾiq al-Ḥaqāʾiq (MS BnF Persian 174), ff.101.

59. For concrete examples see Izutsu, "The Theophanic Ego in Sufism," 34 and Schimmel, *The Mystical Dimension of Islam*, 112–14, 196.

60. See Sunan Abū Dāwud, #5256, as well as Berglund, "Princely Companion or Object of Offense," 545; Miller, *More Than a Sum of Its Parts*, 277; Papas, "Dog of God," 121–22; and Steingass, *A Comprehensive Persian-English Dictionary*, 690–91.

61. al-Ghazālī, *ʾIḥyāʾ ʿulūm al-dīn*, vol. 3, 37.

62. FM I:132; Bosnevi, *Sharḥ Fuṣūṣ al-ḥikam*, vol. 1, 176. See also Ibn ʿArabī, *The Meccan Revelations*, vol. 2, 80. Ibn ʿArabī's teachings were likely based on the Islamic normative tradition in this regard, for there is a hadith reading: "Whoever has seen me in a dream, then no doubt, he has seen me, for the Devil cannot imitate my appearance." *Ṣaḥīḥ al-Bukhārī* #6994; *Mishkāt al-Maṣābīḥ* #4609.

63. al-Ṭabarī, *The History of al-Ṭabarī*, 249. God designated the outward form of all other beings so as to ensure their survival. Hence the big ears of elephants, which help them protect themselves from insects, etc. Brethren of Purity, *The Case of Animals versus the Man*, 112. See also al-Qazwīnī, *ʿAjāʾib al-makhlūqāt*, 180.

64. al-Zain, Islam, *Arabs and the Intelligent World of Jinn*, 22.

65. For instance, Ibn ʿArabī associated jinn with the silent vowel /a/ in the name of the letter *bāʾ* and with the unpronounced /a/ of the *bāʾ* in prefix *bi*. FM I:85. The letters *ʿayn*, *ghayn*, *sīn*, and *shīn* were identified as "jinn letters" in Ibn ʿArabī's works, for he believed that these letters and jinn were created by the rotation of the same heavenly orbits. FM I:53. As a matter of fact, Ibn ʿArabī taught that the twenty-eight letters of the Arabic alphabet correspond to the twenty-eight stages of the act of genesis and the twenty-eight levels of existence. Jinn were thus also associated with the isolated form of the letter *bāʾ* in his works. FM II:466. See also Rašić, *The Written World of God*, 3–18.

66. FM II:467.

67. Ibn Faḍlān once mistook an aurora borealis for a battle between jinn. Some scholars, however, argued that no man has ever seen a jinni—and that those who claim otherwise are unfit to serve as legal witnesses in court. See Ibn Faḍlān, *Riḥlat Ibn Faḍlān*, 82–83 and Macdonald, *Religious Attitude and Life in Islam*, 142–43. According to Ibn ʿArabī, when God wishes for a human to be able to see jinn, He lifts the veil from their eyes. Such a person will then be able to see the jinn folk, even when they themselves do not wish to be seen. FM I:131–32, 304–305. Al-Shiblī was among the prominent opponents of the theory that jinn cannot be seen since they are colorless. Were this the case, al-Shiblī argued, God would not be able to see them either. Nünlist, *Dämonenglaube im Islam*, 107. See also Partridge, *Al-Kindi's Theory of Magical Arts*, 7.

68. FM I:132. Catching a glimpse of a jinni could sometimes lead to insanity or death of a human being—which is also the reason why god-fearing jinn are reluctant to disclose themselves to humans. Tādilī, *al-Tashawwuf ilā rijāl al-taṣawwuf*, 267.

69. Suhrawardī, *Treatises of Shihabuddin Yahya al-Shuhrawardi*, 79.

70. Donaldson, "The Belief in Jinn among the Persians," 190.

71. FM II:466–67.

72. al-Ṭabarī, *Ṭafsīr al-Tabarī*, vol. 15, 159.

73. Winkel, *Changes*, 330–36.

74. FM I:132.

75. Ibid. See also Ibn Manẓūr, *al-Lisān*, vol. 3, 55.

76. FM I:134.

77. Racius: "Islamic Exegesis of the Jinn," 129–30.

78. FM I:132. Ibn ʿArabī's tendency to switch between the term *jinn* and *jānn* when referring to the jinn folk can be consulted at FM I:131–34. See also FM II:466–67.

79. See Canaan, "The Decipherment of Arabic Talismans," 84 and Canaan, *Dämonglaube im Lande der Bibel*, 48. Since Canaan's findings were originally published in 1900 and 1929 respectively, further studies may be required to determine whether the beliefs he described are still as widespread among contemporary Palestinians. ʾAḥmar's character traits and dominion will be examined in a subchapter dealing with jinn culture and society (§2.6).

80. Fartacek, *Unheil durch Dämonen*, 58.

81. al-Jīlānī, *al-Ghunyā al-ṭālibī ṭarīq al-ḥaqq*, vol. 1, 100. Curiously enough, al-Damīrī noted al-Jānn (whom some scholars believed to be the forefather of jinn) hatched from one of Iblis's eggs. al-Damīrī, *Ḥayāt al-ḥayawān al-kubrā*, vol. 1, 466. See also Abed, "Wonders and Monsters," 245.

82. al-Ghazālī, *ʾIḥyāʾ ʿulūm al-dīn*, vol. 4, 75.

83. ʿAṭṭār, *Tadhkirāt al-ʾawliyāʾ*, 529–31. In ʿAṭṭār's version of the story, al-Khannās was described as the son of Iblis. However, other scholars used this name as one of the attributes of the Devil. For instance, al-Bayḍāwī (d. 1319) explained that Iblis is referred to as "al-Khannās" for acting like a hedgehog. According to him, shayṭān hides itself from the world like a hedgehog hides its head from predators, for the success of its endeavors depends on subtle whispering and secrecy. Harendrachandra, *Jalālu ʾd-dīn Rūmī and his Taṣawwuf*, 310–11.

84. FM II:466.

85. "Each human," Sulṭān Walad (d. 1312) noted, "is compounded of form and meaning, satanic and divine—and each and every moment the houris of paradise and the devils of hell show their faces from his inward reality." Walad, *Walad-nāmeh*, 261. See also FM III:351; Bowering, *The Mystical Vision of Existence in Classical Islam*, 187; al-Iṣfahānī, *Kitāb tafṣīl*, 73–74; Shirazī, *Divine Manifestations*, 86 and Yasien, "The Cosmology of Ikhwān al-Ṣafā," Miskawayh and al-Iṣfahānī," 672–73.

86. al-Shiblī, *Kitāb ʾākām al-marjān*, 29.

87. al-Ghazālī, *Revival of Religious Sciences*, vol. 3, 69.

88. Philips, *The Exorcist Tradition in Islam*, 75.

89. al-Shiblī, *Kitāb ʾākām al-marjān*, 43–46.

90. Nünlist, *Dämonenglaube im Islam*, 112–13.

91. See al-Jīlī, *al-ʾInsān al-kāmil fī maʿarifa al-ʾawārikh wal-ʾawāʾil*, 311–13 and FM I:32. al-Aswad noted that the notion of jinn inhabiting the lower six of the seven Earths was also widespread among the common folk in Egypt. Al-Aswad, *Religion and Folk Cosmology*, 70. Some amulets and talismans against jinn contain the images of these seven Earths. The Earths were typically depicted in seven concentric circles, each of which was likely meant to subdue a distinct class/subspecies of jinn. For instance, see Ṭabasī, *al-Shāmil fī al-bahr al-kāmil* (MS Princeton 160), ff.73.

92. al-Suyūṭī, *Laqṭ al-marjān*, 17. The behavior of ghouls and *saʿālī* presumably won Iblis's approval. Al-Suyūṭī noted that Iblis said to these devils: "Eat meat, drink intoxicating drinks and take women, for I find no collection of evils anywhere else such as I find in these three." Al-Suyūṭī, *al-Ṭibb al-nabī*, 188.

93. See al-Damīrī, *Ḥayāt al-ḥayawān*, vol. 1, 448 and Nünlist, *Dämonglaube im Islam*, 64.

94. Tritton, "Spirits and Demons of Arabia," 715.

95. al-Qazwīnī, *ʿAjāʾib al-makhlūqāt*, 178.

96. Al-Qazwīnī recorded a story from a man from Isfahīd, who told him that many *saʿālī* live nearby. Each time a *siʿlāh* is captured, it would call for help and offer ransom to its captors. When inhabitants of Isfahīd heard a forest animal calling for help in a human voice, they could be certain that the animal in question is a *siʿlāh* in disguise, and they would refrain from helping it. al-Qazwīnī, *ʿAjāʾib al-makhlūqāt*, 177–78.

97. Al-Ibshīhī (d. 1446) wrote, "there is an island in Yemen called the Island of Nasnās. On this island is a town located between two mountains." Al-Ibshīhī, *Kitāb al-Mustaṭraf*, vol. 2, 155. See also al-Qazwīnī, *ʿAjāʾib al-makhlūqāt*, 492–93. The term *nasnās* is used today for a subspecies of African Patas monkeys (Cercopithecus pyrrhonotus). Viré, "Ḳird." http://dx.doi.org/10.1163/1573-3912. Accessed February 24, 2021.

98. al-Qazwīnī, *ʿAjāʾib al-makhlūqāt*, 178. These jinn were also mentioned in the Qur'an (Q 27:39).

99. al-Jāḥiẓ, *Kitāb al-Ḥayawān*, vol. 1, 291.

100. *Musnad ʾAḥmad* #14575.

101. al-Jāḥiẓ, *Kitāb al-Ḥayawān*, vol. 1, 291.

102. MacDonald, "Ghūl." http://dx.doi.org/10.1163/2214-871X_ei1_SIM_2495. Accessed May 2, 2021.On the authority of al-Jāḥiẓ, al-Qazwīnī defined ghouls as "any type of jinn which lures the travellers and is a shape-shifter." al-Qazwīnī, *ʿAjāʾib al-makhlūqāt*, 177.

103. Fartacek, *Unheil durch Dämonen*. 63.

104. Nünlist, "Demonology in Islam," 152–70.

105. It is, however, worth noting that there are disagreements between scholars with regard to whether an *ifrit* living in the human blood is the same as *qarīn*. For instance, Blackman pointed out that Egyptians believe that each person is born with an *ifrit* in their body. Blackman was adamant that this *ifrit* is not a spiritual double of human beings (*ʾukht/qarīn*). Blackman, *The Fellahin*, 69–76, 237–38; Dols, *The Madman in Medieval Islamic Society*, 304. Seligman's research, which was conducted in Egypt in 1914, makes a distinction between an *ʾukht* and a jinni. However, in contrast to Blackman and Dols, Hornblower identified *qarīn* as a malevolent jinni and a spiritual double of humans. Unlike *qarīn*, an *ʾukht* has no impact on a person's character and behavior. Both *ʾukht* and a *qarīn* were, however, said to live in the human blood. When affronted, *ʾukht* would sometimes induce nearby jinn to harm its human host. Hornblower, "Traces of a Ka Belief in Modern Egypt and Old Arabia," 426–27. On his side, Ridgeway identified *ʾukht* with *qarīn*. al-Shamy also shared this opinion. al-Shamy, *Religion among the Folk in Egypt*, 81; Tremearne, *Ban of Bori*, 138. See also Padwick, "Notes on the Jinn and the Ghoul in the Peasant Mind of Lower Egypt," 30.

106. See *Ṣaḥīḥ al-Bukhārī* #3423 and FM I:585.

107. al-Qazwīnī, *ʿAjāʾib al-makhlūqāt*, 176.

108. Al-Rawi argued that the legends describing ghouls as necrophagies originated from Antoine Galland and his translation of *One Thousand and One Nights*. al-Rawi, "The Arabic Ghoul and its Western Transformation," 292–99. However, a few centuries earlier, the anonymous author of *Dīwnāma* also spoke of the jinn king al-Ghoul, whose daughters enjoy the taste of human flesh and blood. Shadrach, *The Book of the Deadly Names*, 2. Myths such as these are reminiscent of the legends of sirens—as can be seen in Doherty, *Siren Songs*, 138–39 and in Ferris, *Silent Urns*, xi–xiv. Creatures such as these also existed in mythologies of other cultures. See Keating, *The History of Ireland: From the Earliest Period to the English Invasion*, 171–72.

109. al-Qazwīnī, *ʿAjāʾib al-makhlūqāt*, 176–77. See also Sells, "Bānat Suʿād," 142.

110. Davidson (ed.), *A Treasury of Mystic Terms*, vol. 6, 58.

111. al-Qazwīnī, *ʿAjāʾib al-makhlūqāt*, 177.

112. Nünlist, "Von Berittenen und Gerittenen," 147, 165.

113. See Dols, *Majnūn*, 215 and Smith, *Religion of the Semites*, 90–139.

114. Ibn ʿAbd Rabbih, *al-ʿIqd al-farīd*, vol. 1, 121. Not only were jinn known for their love for horses, but they were also said to be adept in taming them. Hence, taming horses was also among the tasks Solomon's jinn were entrusted with. al-Qazwīnī, *ʿAjāʾib al-makhlūqāt*, 180.

115. See al-Suyūṭī, *Laqṭ al-marjān*, 298 and Sabzawarī, *Majmaʿ al-nūrayn*, 417.

116. See FM I:356, 564. Ibn ʿArabī said: "The Lawgiver [i.e. the Prophet] referred to camels as 'devils' and he forbade people to pray in their pens for the sole reason that they are the devils distant [from God]." FM I:356. Ibn ʿArabī's teachings were likely based on the Islamic normative tradition in this regard, for there is a hadith reading: "The Prophet said: 'Do not pray at places where camels kneel down because these are the places of devils.'" *Sunan Abī Dāwud* #493. However, it should be noted there are also hadith claiming that the Prophet sometimes prayed while facing his camel (*Sunan Abī Dāwud* #692) or while sitting on the back of his camel (*Sunan an-Nasaʾī* #1688).

117. FM I:356.

118. al-Shiblī, *Kitāb ʾākām al-marjān*, 489–91.

119. Waardenburg, *Islam: Historical, Social and Political Perspectives*, 29.

120. al-Zain, *Islam, Arabs and the Intelligible World of Jinn*, 98.

121. al-Damīrī, *Ḥayāt al-ḥayawān*, vol. 1, 41.

122. FM II:470.

123. See Meier, "Ein arabischer bet-ruf," 196 and Zwettler, "A Mantic Manifesto," 77.

124. Nünlist, "Von Berittenen und Gerittenen," 157.

125. See Dols, *Majnūn*, 3–10, 216; Izutsu, "Revelations as Linguistic Concept in Islam," 143; Sells, "Bewildered Tongue," 91, and Sells, *Approaching the Qur'an*, 49. In Egypt, if a person is eccentric or prone to anger, people would refer to them as *majnūn*. "It is [also] said that the djinn has licked his or her brain (*mukhkhu malhus*)." Golia, *Cairo, City of Sand*, 171. Understanding mental illnesses as a consequence of demonic assaults was a widespread historical phenomenon. For instance, see Katajala-Peltomaa, *Demonic Possession*, 1–27; Diamond, *Anger, Madness, and the Daimonic*, 137–80; Zvi, "Dybbuk and Devekut in the Shivhe ha-Besht," 257–305; Leigh, "The Spirit of Madness," 60–93, and Ossa-Richardson, "Possession or Insanity?," 553–75.

126. FM I:248.

127. Meier, "Ein arabischer bet-ruf," 196. See also Ibn ʿArabī, *Divine Governance of the Human Kingdoms*, 178–79.

128. FM I:131–32, 273. Avicenna's remarks on the topic can be consulted at al-Rāzī, *Sharḥ al-ʾishārā wal-tanbīhāt*, vol. 2, 655.

129. Nicholson, *Studies in Islamic Mysticism*, 171.

130. Shaffer, *Djinns, Stars and Warriors*, 71.

131. See al-ʾAlūsī, *Bulūgh al-ʿarab fī maʿarifa ʾaḥwāl al-ʿarab*, vol. 2, 216 and Ibn al-Kalbī, *Kitāb al-ʾAṣnām*, 24–27. Muslim jinn would sometimes take over this role from humans. They were thus said to have murdered a jinni named Misʿar, who used to talk to people from beneath the statues.

al-Iṣfahānī, *Dalāʾil al-nubuwwa*, 109–10. That said, there are also reports of the Muslim jinn which continued to live underneath "their" statues even after they were converted, just like before the onset of Islam! Ibn Saʿd, *Kitāb al-Ṭabaqāt al-kabīr*, vol. 1, 28.

132. al-Jawzī, *The Devil's Deceptions*, 77. In another version of the story, the devil first tries to physically restrain the man to keep him away from its tree. However, the devil's strength was no match for the righteous anger of a believer. The defeated devil then proposed him a deal. The man accepted the deal, and two days later, when he attempts to cut down the tree again, he found that all of his strength was gone. al-Qazwīnī, *ʿAjāʾib al-makhlūqāt*, 174–75. Both versions of the story reflect on the centuries-old belief that the pious and the pure are safe from the wrath of jinn. Even though the devil could not keep the woodcutter away from the tree by force, the man was ultimately defeated by his own greed.

133. See al-Jawzī, *The Devil's Deceptions*, 110 and Ibn al-Kalbī, *Kitāb al-ʾAṣnām*, 54.

134. Whereas Henninger and Nünlist surmised that jinn were worshipped among Bedouins since the ancient times, Meier maintained that jinn cults only began to appear in the late pre-Islamic times. Henninger, "La religion bédouine préislamique," 128–29; Meier, "Ein arabischer betruf," 585, Nünlist, *Dämonenglaube im Islam*, 48, and Waardenburg, *Islam*, 24.

135. Ibn Taymiyya, *Īḍāḥ al-dalāla*, 103. See also Philips (ed.), *Ibn Taymiyah's Essay on the Jinn*, 29.

136. In the present days, similar epithets and accusations of jinn worshipping are often reserved for gypsies. See Shaw, *What Is "Islamic" Art*, 289; The Brethren of Purity, *The Case of Animals versus Man*, 108, and Ibn al-Kalbī, *Kitāb al-ʾAṣnām*, 34.

137. Olomi, "Jinn in the Qur'an," 15. See also Liebling, *Legends of the Fire Spirits*, 55.

138. Wellhausen identified the main difference between a jinni and a deity as follows: "The gods are of a kind with demons, and where they are linked to a particular locale on earth, they have grown from demons, from the spirits of a place, a tree, a spring, a serpent. . . . Demons live only in a holy place; people refrain from disturbing them but do not worship them. As soon as they are approached and worshipped there, they undergo the transition to being gods." Wellhausen, *Reste arabischen Hidentums*, 212. See also Henninger, "Beliefs in Spirits among the Pre-Islamic Arabs," 4.

139. al-ʾIṣfahānī, *Kitāb al-ʾaghānī*, vol. 6, 92.

140. Bodman, *Poetics of Iblis*, 139.

141. al-Zamakhsharī, *ʾAsās al-balāgha*, 66.

142. Werth, *Spirit Possession*, 13.

143. The Brethren of Purity, *The Case of Animals versus Man*, 239.

144. Upton, *Vectors of Counter-Initiation*, 141; Bylebyl, *The Wisdom of Illuminations*, 146.

145. Punjabi Muslims thought that jinn are entitled to riches of the Earth. If the jinn folk were to be denied their due, Punjabis believed their crops would either fail—or grow so abundantly that they would be practically worthless on the market. Temple (ed.), *North Indian Notes & Queries*, 102. See also Hamadhānī, *Sifāt jazīrat al-ʿarab*, 269 and Bodman, *Poetics of Iblis*, 139.

146. al-Tūnisī, *In Darfur*, vol. 2, 29.

147. See Ibn Manẓūr, *Lisān al-ʿarab*, vol. 13, 337 and MacDonald, "Ḳarīn." http://dx.doi.org/10.1163/1573-3912_islam_SIM_3933. Accessed January 14, 2022.

148. See Ahmed, *Before Orthodoxy*, 295–99 and Graham, "The Earliest Meaning of Qur'ān," 365–68.

149. FM II:688.

150. Blackman, *The Fellahin of Upper Egypt*, 69. Padwick confirmed the existence of similar beliefs in the Lower Egypt. Padwick, "Notes on the Jinn and the Ghoul in the Peasant Mind of Lower Egypt," 30.

151. Al-Aswad, *Religion and Folk Cosmology*, 102.

152. Bronfen, *Night Passages*, 221–23. See also Argyris, "The Topic of Doppelganger," 1 and Roberts, "The Image of the Devil in C. G. Jung's Psychology," 200.

153. Ibn Manẓūr, *Lisān al-ʿarab*, vol. 1, 417. See also Tritton, "Spirits and Demons in Arabia," 722.

154. al-Safi, *Traditional Sudanese Medicine*, 448. Contrasting al-Safi's report, Trimingham observed that the term *qarīn* is not being used in Sudan for demonic doubles. According to him, only certain people were thought to have a qarīn of their own. Such people can never marry due to the jealous nature of their doubles. Trimingham, *Islam in the Sudan*, 172.

155. Al-Shamy noted that the word *qarīn* is being used in southern Egypt to denote one's human spouse as well. According to al-Shamy, "an adult male from southern Egypt stated that the tie between a man and his qarinah 'is exactly like that between a [human] husband and his wife. Four other participants in the interview session agreed.'" Al-Shamy, *Religion among the Folk in Egypt*, 80–81. Al-Aswad furthermore noted that the common folk in Egypt sometimes use the word *qarīn* for human friends and spouses. Al-Aswad, *Religion and Folk Cosmology*, 101.

156. al-Aswad, "The Ethnography of Invisible Spheres," 51; al-Zain, Islam, *Arabs and the Intelligent World of Jinn*, 57; Blackman, *Fellahin of Upper Egypt*, 73; Winkler, *Salomo und die Ḳarīna*, 71.

157. Ibn ʿArabī rejected the possibility that Bilquis was a half-human, half-jinn. He, however, emphasized the fact that this is his personal

opinion. He furthermore professed that he did not seek to refute these popular love stories on the authority of the Divine revelation. FM II:495. See also Ibn Nadīm, *Fihrist*, vol. 2, 734–45.

158. Zaydan, *al-ʾAʿmāl al-kāmila*, vol. 13, 285.

159. al-Masʿūdī, *ʾAkhbār al-Zamān*, vol. 1, 122. Other scholars, however, claimed that the Antichrist will be a pure-blood jinni. Ibn Kathīr, *The Signs before the Day of Judgment*, 21–22, 52.

160. See al-Ashqar, *The World of Jinn*, 22. King Solomon was said to have fathered at least one *shiqq* and/or *nasnās* himself. Klar, "And We Cast upon His Throne a Mere Body," 107.

161. al-Damīrī, *Ḥayāt al-ḥayawān*, vol. 1, 185.

162. Knyush, *Ibn Arabi in the Later Islamic Tradition*, 68.

163. Krawietz, "Ten Theses on Working with Jinn (Demons) in Islamic Studies," 334.

164. See Bosnevi, *Sharḥ Fuṣūṣ al-ḥikam*, vol. 1, 77 and Knyush, *Ibn Arabi in the Later Islamic Tradition*, 68.

165. FM II:495.

166. For instance, there is a story of the female jinni Nahhada, whose behavior was similar to Ibn ʿArabī's consort. Although she eventually married her human lover, Nahhada refused to live with him, and she only ever visited their family home when she felt longing for her husband. She was, however, fiercely possessive of him and did not hesitate to harm the women she perceived as competition. *Tales of the Marvellous, News of the Strange*, 254.

167. al-Ghazālī, *ʾIḥyāʾ ʿulūm al-dīn*, vol. 4, 75. See also Winkler, *Salomo und die Ḳarīna*, 71.

168. Lory noted: "It is said that the world of jinn is completely parallel to that of humans—but they have no mirrors, and that is why they are frightened to discover their own image in a mirror when they enter the human world." Lory, "Sexual Intercourse between Humans and Demons in the Islamic Tradition," 61.

169. Blackman, *The Fellahin of Upper Egypt*, 71.

170. Zwemer, "The Familiar Spirit of Qarina," 367–68.

171. Canaan, "Deciphering Arabic Talismans," 86.

172. Ibid.

173. al-Tilimsānī, *Kitāb shumūs al-ʾanwār*, 114–15.

174. See Ibn Manẓūr, *Lisān al-ʿarab*, vol. 4, 566 and Tengour, "Représentations et croyances dans l'Arabie du VIIe siècle." https://journals.openedition.org/insaniyat/12994. Accessed January 15, 2022.

175. Some jinn tend to be benevolent towards humans with whom they share a tribe. Such was the case of Zuhair b. Numair, the companion jinni of the poet Ibn Shuhaid (d. 1035). Both the poet and the jinni came from the tribe Banū Ashjaʿ. Ibn Shuhaid, *Risālat at-tawābī*, 52.

176. Ibn Maybudī claimed that the jinn of Niṣībīn were Jewish. He furthermore argued that these jinn converted to Islam once they heard Muhammad's sermon in Mosul. Their names were Ḥaṣā, Maṣā, Shāṣir, Nāṣir, Afḥam, Yarid, Īnān, Zawbaʿa, and ʿUmar b. Jābir. *Nünlist, Dämonenglaube im Islam,* 78. Other scholars, however, maintained that the jinn of Niṣībīn were Bedouins from Banu ʿAmīr tribe. al-Kāshāni, *Tafsīr al-ṣāfī,* vol. 7, 17. See also Browne, *A Literary History of Persia,* vol. 1, 263 and Brethren of Purity, *The Case of Animals versus Man,* 108.

177. FM I:133–34.

178. *Mandal al-Sulaymanī,* ff.6.

179. The term *ʿilm al-nujūm,* the science of stars, was used for both astronomy and astrology in Muslim cultures and societies. The two disciplines were often indistinguishable in medieval Islam.

180. *Majmūʿ min kull fann yabḥarh annahu jawāhir al-kalām,* ff.105–6; Winkler, *Salomo und die Ḳarīna,* 40. The belief in correspondences between jinn clans and the zodiac signs survive in the popular culture today. Comparable beliefs could also be found in different contexts and traditions—as can be seen from Thomas, *Religion and the Decline of Magic,* 425–26, 755–56; Hegedus, *Early Christianity and Ancient Astrology,* 125–31, and Wedel, *Astrology in the Middle Ages,* 60–75. See also Tremearne, *Ban of the Bori,* 97.

181. Zadih, *Wonders and Rarities,* 190. It should, however, be noted that the Greek word *daimōn* could also serve to denote pagan gods in general. Graeco-Egyptian *daimones* and the reception of hermeticism in Islamic culture were closely studied by Coulon, Gieseler-Greenbaum, Upton, and Von Franz—among others. See Coulon, *La magie islamique,* 918–32; Gieseler-Greenbaum, "Porphyry of Tyre on the Daimon, Birth and the Stars," 102–139; Gieseler-Greenbaum, *The Daimon in Hellenistic Astrology,* 1–11; Upton, *Vectors of Counter-Initiation,* 141; Ronis, *The Demons in the Details,* 58–70; von Franz, *Projection and Recollection,* 108; and von Franz, "Daimons and the Inner Companion," 177–87.

182. Noble, *Philosophizing the Occult,* 1–46.

183. Elmore, "Qur'ānic Wisdom, Prophetology and Ibn ʿArabī's Fuṣūṣ al-ḥikam," 93–94.

184. FM I:187. Spirits of the planets (*ʾarwāḥ al-kawākib*) which were described by Ibn ʿArabī in Chapter 25 of *al-Futūḥāt* are likely identical with the aforementioned jinn of light.

185. Ibn Rushd, *Incoherence of the Incoherence,* 323.

186. See al-Tahanāwī, *Mawsūʿat istilāḥāt al-ʿulūm al-islāmiya,* vol. 2, 261. Saif later identified spirits of planets as multiplications and manifestations of the World Soul. Saif, "Between Medicine and Magic," 318. See also Canaan, *Aberglaube und Volksmedizin,* 22–23.

187. Brethren of Purity, *On God and the World*, 64–65.

188. *Picatrix*, 85; Brethren of Purity, *The Case of Animals versus Man*, 238.

189. See Canaan, "Deciphering Arabic Talismans," 84–85 and Liebling, *Legends of the Fire Spirits*, 87. Scholem pointed out the parallels between the symbolism of colors in Islamic and Jewish magic, where we also find demon-kings being referred to as the Red King, the Golden King, etc. Scholem, "Some Sources of Jewish-Arabic Demonology," 2–3.

190. Gruber, "In Defense and Devotion," 95–123. See also: Allen, "Two Ways of Dealing with the Jinn in the Ottoman World." https://thicketandthorp.com/2018/07/04/two-ways-of-dealing-with-the-jinn-in-the-ottoman-world/. Accessed May 27, 2021.

191. Canaaan, "Deciphering Arabic Talismans," 83–84.

192. Brethren of Purity, *The Case of Animals versus Man*, 127. Another depiction of jinn as sedentary nobility can be found in al-Masʿūdī's *Kitāb al-Tanbīh wal-Ishrāf*, where Alexander the Great meets the jinn chief Zakhraf. See Doufikar-Aerts, "Dionysus, Enoch and Zakhraf," 118.

193. al-Damīrī, *Ḥayāt al-ḥayawān*, vol. 1, 475.

194. al-Wansharīsī, *al-Miʿyār al-muʿrib*, vol. 11, 171.

195. FM I:585.

196. *The Book of Curiosities*, 512–13.

197. al-Dhubiyānī, *Diwān al-Nābighah al-Dhubiyānī*, 20–21.

198. In contrast, Solomon would need to apply his seal on a brass surface in order to control demons. Iafrate, *The Long Life of Magical Objects*, 53.

199. al-Qazwīnī, *ʿAjāʾib al-makhlūqāt*, 181.

200. According to al-Damīrī, once it reaches a certain age, *ʾashkāl* grows a pair of wings and flies. Ants are the natural enemies of *ʾashkāl* due to their size. The beautiful nests of these insects were said to have inspired ancient Egyptians to build sarcophagi. Some sources, however, claimed that a termite, not *ʾashkāl*, betrayed Solomon to jinn. Brethren of Purity, *The Case of Animals versus Man*, 295.

201. al-Maʿarrī, *Risālat al-ghufrān*, 94.

202. Even Iblis the Devil would sometimes show mercy to poets. In a folktale documenting his encounter with Sul, the Devil demands to be worshipped in return for helping Sul find his bride. Rather than obeying the Devil, the young man repeats his entreaties in verses. Impressed by the quality of his verses, Iblis rewarded him handsomely before reuniting him with his bride. *Tales of the Marvelous, News of the Strange*, 252–53.

203. Ibn Shuhaid, *Risālat at-tawābī*, 54.

204. Ibid., 52–54. See also Meier, "Some Aspects of Demonic Inspiration in Islam," 429.

205. al-Azmeh, *The Emergence of Islam*, 207–8.

206. al-Iṣfahānī, *ʾAkhbar al-Nisaʾ*, 135.

207. FM II:274. It is, however, worth noting that different jinn had different reason for helping humans with their verses. For instance, Zuhair b. Numair was said to have been a great admirer of poetry. This is why this jinni took pity on Ibn Shuhaid when the poet found himself unable to write as he was mourning the loss of a person dear to him. However, mischievous jinn would sometimes make an untalented human famous on a whim, for no reason in particular. Ibn Shuhaid, *Risālat at-tawābī*, 52. See also Kennedy, "Some Demon Muse: Structure and Allusion," 120–21.

208. al-Qazwīnī, *ʿAjāʾib al-makhlūqāt*, 172–73.

209. Yāqūt, *Muʿjam al-buldān*, vol. 4, 118.

210. al-Qazwīnī, *ʿAjāʾib al-makhlūqāt*, 182–83; al-Hujwīrī, *Kash al-Maḥjūb*, 402–3.

211. al-Zain, *The Evolution of the Concept of Jinn*, 59.

212. al-Sharānī, *Lawāqiḥ al-ʾanwār fī ṭabaqāt al-ʾakhyār*, vol. 1, 74.

213. Shaw, *What Is Islamic Art?*, 67, 71. Some scholars, however, believed that jinn are prone to gathering at the sound of a blowing pipe. This is why pipes were sometimes used in jinn summoning rituals. See Zwemer, *The Influence on Animism on Islam*, 130 and Rouget, *Music and Trance*, 279.

214. See Savage-Smith's introduction to Savage Smith (ed.), *Magic and Divination in Early Islam*, xiii. See also Walker, *Spiritual and Demonic Magic*, 75–76.

215. Fanger, *Rewriting Magic*, 112, 117.

216. See Fartacek, *Unheil durch Dämonen*, 61 and Ibn Khaldūn, *al-Muqaddima*, 625.

217. Ibn Waṣīf, *ʾAkhbār al-zamān*, 92–93.

218. See Ibn Taymiyya, *Īḍāḥ ad-dalāla*, 103 and Zadeh, "Commanding Demons," 142–44.

219. For instance, see FM II:583 and FM III:288.

220. FM I:273–74.

221. See Q 2:102, 17:18 and *Ṣaḥīḥ Muslim* # 5538. See also Coulon, *La magie islamique*, 81–82; Kabbani, *Angels Unveiled*, 171; al-Kāshāni, *Tafsīr al-Kāshānī*, vol. 1, 303 and Zbinden, *Die Djinn des Islam*, 12. Comparable notions of evil spirits, the teachers of magic, were widespread in Catholic Europe. Thomas, *Religion and the Decline of Magic*, 265, 564.

222. al-Qayṣarī, *Muqaddima*, 156–58.

223. al-Maʿarrī, *Risālat al-ghufrān*, 288. MacDonald subsequently found the inscriptions identifying this language as Himyarite. Porter, "The Use of the Arabic Script in Magic," 136. When it comes to the Arabic grammar studies, jinn were said to admire Sibawayh's teachings in particular. al-Suyūṭī, *Laqṭ al-marjān*, 104.

224. al-Qayṣarī, *Muqaddima*, 334. See also Brethren of Purity, *The Case of Animals versus Man*, 136 and al-Ghazālī, *The Incoherence of the Philosophers*, 3.

225. FM III:67.

226. FM I:50.

227. Some scholars believed that the Devil was the first freethinker in history and the first one to rely on reasoning by analogy. The proverb "the Devil was the first to reason by analogy" (*ʾawwal man qāsa al-shayṭān*) was traditionally attributed to Jaʿfar al-Ṣādiq (d. 765). Virani, *The Ismailis in the Middle Ages*, 158. See also sl-Ṭūsī, *al-ʾIstibṣār*, vol. 2, 93.

228. FM I:134; FM II:467.

229. Quoted according to Stroumsa, *Freethinkers in Medieval Islam*, 130–31.

230. Shīrāzī, *Divine Manifestations*, 81.

231. FM II:532.

232. FM II:281, 628. When doubts and questions come to mind with regard to a word of God, Ibn ʿArabī argued that the only proper approach is to recite the ayah: My Lord, increase me in knowledge! (Q 20:114). Other than that, a skeptic should refrain from questions, analyses and discussions at all cost, for this would only serve to demonstrate their lack of faith. Ibn ʿArabī, *Divine Governance of the Human Kingdom*, 19. See also Izutsu, *The Concept of Belief in Islamic Theology*, 85.

233. FM I:192–93; FM III:99.

234. FM II:78.

235. FM I:281–82, 627; FM III:142, 251. Kant believed that only a free, rational agent can be a subject and an object of the moral law, and jinn fulfil these criteria. Kant, *Groundwork of the Metaphysics of Morals*, 63–64.

236. FM II:105–6.

237. al-Suyūṭī, *Laqṭ al-marjān*, 103, 221.

238. al-Qushayrī, *Epistle of Sufism*, vol. 2, 141.

239. FM I:333.

240. See FM I:119, 259 and Rašić, *The Written World of God*, 49.

Chapter 3

1. Byatt, *The Djinn in the Nightingale's Eye*, 134–35.

2. Ibn ʿArabī, *Kitāb al-Isrāʾ*, 57.

3. The later-date variations and interpretations of Ibn ʿArabī's diagram of the Great City were closely examined by Elmore. These can be consulted at Elmore, *Fabulous Gryphon*, 452–54. Elmore furthermore suggested that the Great City as a whole can be seen as the human heart,

which corresponds to the Kaaba on macrocosmic level. Ibid., 361. Compare Elmore's interpretations with al-Ghazālī, *Kitāb sharḥ ʿajāʾib al-qalb*, 18–19.

4. Affifi, *The Twenty-Nine Pages*, 53; Chittick, *Sufi Path of Knowledge*, 17. See also Murata, *Chinese Gleams of Sufi Lights*, 52; Murata, "Masculine-Feminine," 169; and Nasr, *The Garden of Truth*, 6–12.

5. Ibn ʿArabī, *al-Futūḥāt al-Makkiyya*, I:85. Hereafter referred to as FM.

6. FM I:216, 394.

7. FM IV:7.

8. FM I:202; FM III:99.

9. See FM I:560–61, FM III:237, and Ibn ʿArabī, *Divine Governance of the Human Kingdom*, 97–101.

10. Ibn ʿArabī, "R. fī al-maʿrifa al-nafs wal-rūḥ," 156–57. See also Ibn ʿArabī, "al-Tadbirāt al-ilahiyya," 131 and FM I:732.

11. For example, see Chittick, *Sufi Path of Knowledge*, 17, al-Qayṣarī, *Muqaddima*, 181–85, and Ibn ʿArabī, *Divine Governance of the Human Kingdoms*, 37–38.

12. FM I:138; FM III: 399. Ibn ʿArabī, "al-Tadbirāt al-ilahiyya," 129–30, 168.

13. FM II:331. The original ayah can be consulted at Q 4:171.

14. FM IV:68.

15. Chittick, *Ibn Arabi, Heir to the Prophets*, 108.

16. Ibn ʿArabī, "R. fī al-maʿrifa al-nafs wal-rūḥ," 152. The most common interpretation of this statement is that human beings were created in God's form. Hence, the one who knows himself knows his Lord. Chittick, however, argued that the statement in question served to underline that human knowledge, all of it, is the articulation of human awareness and consciousness, "an internal image of an external image." Chittick, *Ibn Arabi, Heir to the Prophets*, 108. Another interpretation was proposed by Avicenna, who noted "that philosophers and pious saints have held fast to the Tradition: Whoever knows himself, knows his Lord. They also say: Whoever fails to know himself is more likely to fail to know his Creator. How can anyone be trusted as a reliable authority when they fail to know themselves? Even further than this, God Almighty points out in the Quran: And be not like those who forgot God and He caused them to forget themselves (Q 59:19). Is not God's making the forgetting of self to depend upon forgetting God done so as to awaken one's attention to the remembrance of Him with the remembrance of one's self? Is not the knowledge of God bound to the knowledge of one's self, one's soul"? Quoted according to Bakhtiar, *Avicenna On the Science of the Soul*, 6.

17. FM II:568.

18. Ibn ʿArabī, "R. fī al-maʿrifa al-nafs wal-rūḥ," 152. See also FM I:113, Absar, "Qur'anic Concepts of Human Psyche," 30–31, and Izutsu, "The Theophanic Ego in Sufism," 27.

19. Quoted according to Omsby, *Between Reason and Revelation*, 95.

20. Hence, Hakim's "reader or listener is warned that when we refer to 'the spirit' when quoting Ibn ʿArabī, his text may use the word 'soul.'" Hakim, "The Paths to God," https://ibnarabisociety.org/the-paths-to-god-souad-hakim/. Accessed February 18, 2022.

21. Shazad, "Ibn 'Arabī's Metaphysics of the Human Body," 509. It is, however, worth nothing that Ibn ʿArabī sometimes contrasted the darkness of the human body with *nafs* and the Creator. FM IV:422.

22. Al-Qayṣarī, *Muqaddima*, 181–85.

23. FM I:564, 575. Murata claimed that similar notions can be found in both Sufism and Confucianism. Murata, "Reading Islamic Texts from the Standpoint of Ying and Yang," 109.

24. FM II:568.

25. Ibn ʿArabī, "R. fī al-maʿrifa al-nafs wal-rūḥ," 152.

26. al-Bayhaqī, *Kitāb al-zuhd al-kabīr*, 190; Bakhtiar, *Qur'anic Psychology of the Self*, 85.

27. *Mathnawī* III:2554, 3197, 4053. See also Murata, "Angels," 336.

28. al-Rāzī, *Rasāʾil al-falsafiyya*, 177–78. Suhrawardī's teachings can be consulted at: Suhrawardī, *Philosophy of Illumination*, 148–50.

29. al-Birūnī, *al-ʾĀthār al-bāqiyya ʿan al-qurūn al-khāliyya*, 284–85.

30. Among the prominent supporters of this theory was ʿAbd al-Jalīl Laknawī (d. 1634). He famously described *nafs* as the follower of "the great lover Iblis, who is the locus of manifestation for the Divine Name the Misguider (*al-mudhill*)." *Rūḥ* was, however, described as the follower of the prophet Muhammad and the Divine Name *al-Hādī*, the One Who Guides. Chittick, *In Search of the Lost Heart*, 173.

31. al-Qushayrī, *Epistle on Sufism*, 109.

32. For example, all human souls that were separated from their bodies were referred to as "jinn" in al-Bayḍāwī's works. Bayḍāwī, *ʾAnwār al-tanzīl wa-asrār al-taʾwīl*, vol. 2, 361.

33. *The Book of Curiosities*, 512.

34. *Picatrix*, 204.

35. For instance, see FM I:333. Some Sufis were also referring to the human soul as "Iblis"—Abū al-ʿAlā al-Maʿarrī and ʿAṭṭār used this name as a synonym for one's qarīn. Chittick, *The Heart of Islamic Philosophy*, 219; Corbin, *Man of Light in Iranian Sufism*, 66. See also Izutsu, "Revelations as Linguistic Concept in Islam," 135 and Izutsu, *God and Man in the Qur'an*, 177.

36. See FM II:177, 196, 688 and Ibn ʿArabī, *The Meccan Revelations*, vol. 2, 80. That said, different Sufis had different lists of the traits and desires of the lower soul. For example, al-Tirmidhī believed there are 100 traits and desires the Devil seeks to inspire in humans—one trait for each of the Names of God. These are: disbelief (*kufr*), ignorance (*jahl*), pride

(*kibr*), grudge (*ḥiqd*), cunning (*makr*); deceit (*khidāʿ*), cheating (*ghishsh*), spite (*ghill*), perfidy (*khiyāna*), enmity (*ʿadāwa*), falsehood (*kidhb*), dissimulation (*zūr*), slander (*buhtān*), niggardliness (*bukhl*), wickedness (*sharr*), gossiping (*namīma*), backbiting (*ghība*), anger (*ghaḍab*), cowardice (*jubn*), cajolery (*mudāhana*), affectation (*riyāʾ*), fame (*sumʿa*), doubt (*shakk*), polytheism (*shirk*), bias (*mayl*), innovation (*bidʿa*), error (*ḍalāla*), transgression (*ghayy*), enticement (*khilāba*), seduction (*ghurūr*), oppression (*jawr*), injustice (*ẓulm*), iniquity (*baghy*), apathy (*qillat al-mubālāh*), levity (*khiffa*), instability (*ṭaysh*), sport (*laʿb*), frivolity (*ʿabath*), pastime (*lahw*), inattentiveness (*sahw*), heedlessness (*ghafla*), taking delight in this world (*surūr bil-dunyā*), taking joy in this world (*faraḥ bil-dunyā*), precipitation (*ʿajala*), boorishness (*faẓāẓa*), uncouthness (*ghilẓa*), roughness (*khushūna*), harshness (*ʿunf*), disdain (*anafa*), arrogance (*istikbār*), glorying in this world (*fakhr bil-dunyā*); haughtiness (*khuyalāʾ*); contumely (*tajabbur*), confusion (*ḥayra*), idleness (*kasal*), sloth (*thiqal*), incapacity (*ʿajz*), procrastination (*taʾkhīr*), ennui (*malāla*), error (*khaṭaʾ*), forgetfulness (*nisyān*), lust (*shahwa*), delusion (*wahm*), suspicion (*tuhma*), dubiety (*shubha*), hope (*amal*), falsity (*bāṭil*) superciliousness (*tīh*), impudence (*safah*) laughter (*ḍaḥk*), folly (*ḥumq*), apprehension (*jazaʿ*), ingratitude (*kufrān*), search for aggrandizement (*ṭalab al-ʿuluww*), love of this world (*ḥubb al-dunyā*), extravagance (*isrāf*), popularity (*maḥmadat al-nās*), unlawfulness (*ḥarām*), adornment (*zīna*), greed (*ḥirṣ*), indecency (*faḥsh*) cruelty (*qasāwa*), voracity (*sharah*), insolence (*ashar*), wantonness (*baṭar*), despondency (*qunūṭ*), odiousness (*samāja*), phantasy (*takhayyul*), pomp (*badakh*), duplicity (*khatl*), praise (*madḥ*), desire (*tamannī*), self-importance (*nakhwa*), prying (*tajassus*), fraud (*ghabn*), misgiving (*rība*), querulousness (*shikāya*), swearing on oath (*ḥilf*), vainglory (*ṣalif*). Al-Geyoshi, "Al-Tirmidhi's Conception of the Struggle between Qalb and Nafs," 7–8.

37. Ibn ʿArabī noted that limbs of the human body sometimes complain to God about the soul forcing them to do evil in order to satisfy the Devil. FM I:287, 573. The human bodily motions were also associated with the animal spirit in Ibn ʿArabī's works. Ibn ʿArabī, "R. fī al-maʿrifa al-nafs wal-rūḥ," 153–54.

38. Schimmel, *Mystical Dimensions of Islam*, 112. See also Bakhtiyar, *Qur'anic Psychology of the Self*, 43–44 and FM I:112.

39. See Adamson, al-Rāzī, 57, 70 and Ibn ʿArabī, "R. fī al-maʿrifa al-nafs wal-rūḥ," 153–54.

40. Ibn ʿArabī said: "Then there are pleasures and desires that are obtained by the animal soul through the sensory faculties. These include eating, drinking, sexual intercourse, clothes, fragrances, fine musical tones that reach the ears—as well as physical forms which invoke the desire of the eye such as swelling breasts, lovely faces, intricate colors, trees and rivers." FM I:317. The rational soul was thought to be responsible for

cognitive abilities, memory, and perception. Ibn ʿArabī, "R. fī al-maʿrifa al-nafs wal-rūḥ," 153–54. On his side, Chittick identified the rational soul with the Divine Spirit. Chittick, "Death and the World of Imagination," 63.

41. FM III:237.

42. al-Qayṣarī, *Muqaddima*, 184–85.

43. Leaman identified *al-nafs al-ʾiblīsiyya* as the lowest stage of the soul's descent. Leaman, *The Qur'an: A Philosophical Guide*, 84.

44. Elmore, "Ibn al-ʿArabī Testament on the Mantle of Initiation" 15.

45. FM III:237; Ibn ʿArabī, "Kunh mā lā budda lil-murīd minhu," 527.

46. FM II:563.

47. Quoted according to Valiuddin, *Contemplative Disciplines in Sufism*, 9. Symbolic interpretations of the fruits and branches of Zaqqum can be consulted at: *Shīrāzī, Divine Manifestations*, 151.

48. Chapter 113 of *al-Futūḥāt* explicitly linked all that is hateful to God within the soul to devils. FM II:195. That being said, it should be noted that Chapter 353 of *al-Futūḥāt* allows for the possibility that at least some blameworthy traits and impulses were caused by external circumstances unrelated to jinn. For instance, Ibn ʿArabī noted that the inability to fulfill one's desires can lead to anger, which was traditionally linked to jinn in Islamic normative tradition. FM III: 237.

49. Ibn ʿArabī, *Kitāb ʿAnqāʾ mughrib*, 47.

50. Ibn ʿArabī, "R. fī al-maʿrifa al-nafs wal-rūḥ," 159.

51. FM II:583.

52. In the attempt to differentiate between the whispering of nafs and devils, Bakhtiar noted that the lower soul only cares about getting what it wants. Unlike jinn, the lower soul neither knows nor cares whether something is good or bad. Hence, it does not deliberately induce humans to sin. Jinn, however, deliberately try to incite humans to evil. Bakhtiar, *Qur'anic Psychology of the Self*, xiv.

53. Ibn ʿArabī, *Mashāhid al-ʾasrār al-qudsiyya*, 45–46. Beneito's interpretation of this vision can be consulted at Ibn ʿArabī, *Contemplations of the Holy Mysteries*, 36.

54. Ibn ʿArabī, *Rūḥ al-quds*, 23.

55. Ibn ʿArabī, *Divine Governance of the Human Kingdoms*, 194.

56. İpşiroğlu's writings can also be consulted at Parman, "The Demon as Human Double," 134.

57. See al-Zain, *The Evolution of the Concept of the Jinn*, 290–92, 382–83; Corbin, *The Man of Light in Iranian Sufism*, 94–116; Hadromi-Allouche, *Between the Pure Milk and the Froth*, 42–60; Klar, "And We Cast upon His Throne a Mere Body," 113–16; Nasser, "The Jinn: Companion in the Realm of Dreams and Imaginatiom," 149–50, Nünlist, "Demonology in Islam," 152–70, and Parman, "The Demon as Human Double," 132–33. Jungian

notions of the shadow can be consulted at Von Franz, *Spiegelungen der Seele*, 128.

58. Hadromi-Allouche, *Between the Pure Milk and the Froth*, 41–60.

59. The state of the soul that is receptive to influences from the Unseen was sometimes referred to as "*al-nafs al-mulhama*." Ali defined *al-nafs al-mulhama* as the station of the soul which is above *al-nafs al-lawwāmah* and below *al-nafs al-muṭma'inna* in excellence. Ali, *Philosophical Sufism*, 161. See also Nasr, "Happiness and the Attainment of Happiness," 78.

60. FM I:287; al-Qayṣarī's, *Muqaddima*, 152. There are also instances where Ibn ʿArabī claimed nafs is the recipient of ʾilhām. FM I:286.

61. Ibn ʿArabī's teachings were likely based on the 110th ayah of the surah *al-ʾAnʿām*, which reads: "We are turning (*nuqallibu*) their hearts and eyes away from the Truth even as they did not believe in the first instance—and We leave them in their insurgence to stumble blindly" (Q 6: 110). In Chapter 3 of *al-Futūḥāt*, Ibn ʿArabī explained that each time when a Seeker feels there is a strife between different inrushes in their heart means that God just turned over their heart between His fingers. The two fingers of God represent the mutually opposing inclinations to do good or evil and for incoming notions that can be either beautiful or ugly. FM I:95–96. It is, however, worth noting that Ibn ʿArabī taught that only God has the power to turn the human heart towards one thing or another—irrespective of the source of *khawāṭir* it received. FM II:171.

62. FM I:287–29, 281–84; FM II:195; FM III:198–99.

63. Ibn ʿArabī, "K. Kunh mā lā budda lil-murīd minhu," 526.

64. FM II:195.

65. FM II:344; FM III:239.

66. FM II:688.

67. FM I:286–87.

68. FM I:281–84. See also Ibn ʿArabī, *The Meccan Revelations*, vol. 2, 78–81.

69. *Ṣaḥīḥ al-Bukhārī* #4953; Zwemer, *The Influence of Animism in Islam*, 127.

70. Meier, "Some Aspects of Inspiration by Demons in Islam," 427–28.

71. FM I:405. See also: Ibn ʿArabī, *Contemplations of the Holy Mysteries*, 113 and Morris, *Reflective Heart*, 66.

72. FM I:283.

73. See Al-Geyoshi, "al-Tirmidhi's Conception of the Areas of Interiority," 169 and al-Qayṣarī, *Muqaddima*, 306.

74. Yazaki, *Islamic Mysticism and Abu Talib Al-Makki*, 98.

75. Al-Tustarī, *Tafsīr al-Tustarī*, 71.

76. *Ṣaḥīḥ al-Bukharī* #52. See also Ibn ʿArabī, *Divine Governance of the Human Kingdoms*, 20, 42.

77. FM I:283; Ibn ʿArabī, *The Meccan Revelations*, vol. 2, 84–85.

78. FM II:171. Idolatry was the worst of the sins which were associated with the layers of hell in Ibn ʿArabī's works. These sins are: disbelief in pilgrimage, disbelief in Ramadan, disbelief in giving alms, disbelief in prayer, and idolatry. Rašić, *The Written World of God*, 162.

79. Ibn ʿArabī claimed to have written a detailed analysis explaining the properties of the four jinn letters and what makes them special when compared to other letters of the Arabic alphabet in the now-lost manuscript of *K. al-Mabādī wal-ghāyāt*. FM I:53.

80. Akkach, *Cosmology and Architecture*, 92–95.

81. FM I:302.

82. Ibn ʿArabī, *Divine Governance of the Human Kingdoms*, 220.

83. FM I:283, 303. See also Ibn ʿArabī, *Divine Governance of the Human Kingdoms*, 151.

84. The left and the right side of the human body were compared in *al-Futūḥāt* to the scale, with the right side standing for virtue and justice. Left is the side of human weaknesses and sin—"and a man belongs to whichever side he is inclined to." FM III:6.

85. FM I:333. Ibn ʿArabī likely got these questions from *Ṣaḥīḥ al-Bukhārī* #3276.

86. FM I:281–82, 333.

87. Quoted according to Ibn ʿArabī, *The Meccan Revelations*, vol. 2, 80–81. See also FM I:281–82; FM II:183, 319 and FM IV:105.

88. FM I:282. Ibn ʿArabī sometimes compared Shia to pigs in his works. FM II:8.

89. This argument was commonly cited in Sufi literature as a warning against the Devi's deceptions. Awn, *Satan's Tragedy and Redemption*, 70.

90. Ibn ʿArabī, *Divine Governance of the Human Kingdom*, 211. See also Ibn ʿArabī, "K. Kunh mā lā budda lil-murīd minhu," 529.

91. Ibn ʿArabī, *The Meccan Revelations*, vol. 2, 80.

92. Ibn ʿArabī, "K. Kunh mā lā budda lil-murīd minhu," 529–30; FM I:112.

93. FM II:227.

94. FM I:33; FM III:344.

Chapter 4

1. Ibn ʿArabī, *The Seven Days of the Heart*, 50.

2. Ibn ʿArabī, *Contemplations of the Holy Mysteries*, 80.

3. Ibn ʿArabī said: "Wearing patched clothes is being referred to as the Green Death since the state of a human is akin to earth. In other

words, the variety of plants and flowers on earth is akin to the variety of patches. The Black Death is likened to enduring assaults [from others], which makes the soul sad. Sadness is the darkness of the soul and it is akin to the color black. The red death stands for opposing nafs. This is like the red color of blood, because opposing its caprices slays the soul." Ibn ʿArabī, *al-Futūḥāt al-Makkiyya*, I:258 (hereafter referred to as FM). Whereas Chapter 47 of *al-Futūḥāt* explicitly links the Red Death to opposing the (lower) soul, in another place, Ibn ʿArabī noted that all four deaths can be collectively defined as the stages of "mortification" of the lower soul and/or a qarīn. FM II:187–88; FM III:288. Alternatively, in this context, "death" can be taken as a reference to spiritual wayfaring and entering the spirit world before the death of the physical body FM IV:424.

4. Quoted according to Corbin, *Man of Light in Iranian Sufism*, 66. See also al-Sharnūbī, *Sharḥ Tāʾiyyat al-sulūk ilā malik al-mulūk*, 57. The term "Red Death" was also used in Ibn ʿArabī's works for the mere act of opposing the lower soul. FM II:194–95.

5. FM I:134.

6. The prophetic narratives concerning the cleansing of the Prophet's heart have been collectively referred to as *sharḥ al-ṣadr* in the Islamic normative tradition. The comparative analyses of these hadith were previously conducted by Hadromi-Allouche and Rubin. Hadromi-Allouche, *Between Pure Milk and the Froth*, 147–50; Rubin, *The Eye of the Beholder*, 62–64. See also Young, "Concerning the Station of Purity," 33–34.

7. al-Birūnī, *al-ʾĀthār al-bāqiyya ʿan al-qurūn al-khāliyya*, 261–62.

8. Blackman, *The Fellahin of the Upper Egypt*, 74. Another Christian prayer/amulet against quranāʾ was discovered by Canaan in a book entitled *K. ṣalātu al-qiddīs Kabriānus*. It consisted of the following inscription: "Do not allow (O God), by the power of Your Name, the unclean and the accursed Satan (*qarīneh*) to prevail over or injure (the person carrying) this book." Canaan, "The Decipherment of Arabic Talismans," 80.

9. See al-Bayhaqī, *Kitāb al-zuhd al-kabīr*, 190 and Khalil, "Ibn al-ʿArabī on the Trials and Virtues of Hunger and Fasting," 579. Legends also speak of another jinn-slaying sword, al-Maʿathūr. The sword named al-Maʿathūr was said to have been forged by jinn, and it was inherited by ʿAlī after the death of the Prophet. Wheeler, *Mecca and Eden*, 34.

10. Shah, *The Commanding Self*, 8.

11. "My Lord,'" Ibn ʿArabī prayed, "bring me close to You with the closeness of those who truly know [You]. Purify me from the attachments of the natural constitution. Eliminate the blood-clot of blameworthiness from my heart, that I may be one of the completely purified ones." Ibn ʿArabī, *Seven Days of the Heart*, 26.

12. FM II:196. Ibn ʿArabī specified that the vegetable soul and the desiring soul are the only aspects of the human soul that perish when a person enters the heavenly gardens—possibly due to the fact that these aspects of the soul are in charge of the well-being of the physical body. However, entering paradise and death have no impact on one's ability to feel anger and/or on the so-called wrathful soul (*al-nafs al-ghaḍabiyya*). FM III:237.

13. FM I:113–14. In his commentary of Ibn ʿArabī's *al-Tadbīrāt al-Ilāhiya*, Halveti noted that God made the lower soul desirous of evil so that a person realizes they would only ever triumph against evil with the strength and support of their Lord. Ibn ʿArabī, *Divine Governance of the Human Kingdom*, 45.

14. FM I:37. See also FM I:393; FM III:464.

15. FM II:662. Cf. Chodkiewicz, *Ocean without Shore*, 42. See also FM I:227.

16. FM I:227.

17. FM I:125–26, 362. Some Akbarians defined Sufism in general as the submission to and affirmation of the will of God. Ibn ʿArabī, *Divine Governance of the Human Kingdom*, 16.

18. Ibn ʿArabī claimed that no other scholar managed to get to the heart of this matter before him. FM I:362. That said, the problem of evil represented by Iblis the Devil and other evil jinn was addressed by numerous other scholars who were writing before Ibn ʿArabī's time. These include the Brethren of Purity, Jaʿfar b. Manṣūr al-Yaman (d. 957), Abū Yaʿqūb al-Sijistānī (d. 971), Avicenna (d. 1037), Ḥamīd al-Dīn al-Kirmānī (d. 1020), and Nāṣir-i Khusraw (d. 1088), to name a few. Whereas the present study is limited to Ibn ʿArabī's writings on the topic, the historical overview on how the problem of evil was tackled in Islamic religious philosophy can be consulted at Sherman, *Islam and the Problem of Black Suffering* (2009) and Rustom-Faruque, *From the Divine to the Human* (2023). See also De Smet, "The Demon in Potentiality and the Devil in Actuality," 601–25 and Baffioni, "The Figure of Iblīs in the Ikhwān al-Ṣafāʾ-related Esoteric Literature," 113–41.

19. Nasr, *Islamic Spirituality*, 356.

20. FM III:351. Ibn ʿArabī's stand on the matter was likely inspired by the surah *al-Anʿam*, which reads: *Satanic humans and jinn, inspire each other with flowery discourses to deceive. If your Lord had so wanted, they wouldn't have done it* (Q 6:112). He cited the aforementioned ayah in Chapter 55 of *al-Futūḥāt*. FM I:281. That said, İsmail Hakkı Bursevī (d. 1752) was among the Akbarians who argued that only Muhammad, as the seal of the prophets (*khātam an-nabīyīn*), was protected from satanic inrushes. No

other messenger, Bursevī maintained, was granted this protection. Bursevī, *Tafsīr rūḥ al-bayān,* vol. 7, 189–90. In contrast, Ibn ʿArabī explicitly named Jesus as one of the prophets who were protected from satanic whispers. FM I:283. Hence, it can be safely assumed that Ibn ʿArabī did not hold Jesus's qarīn responsible for corrupting the text (*taḥrīf al-naṣṣ*) of the Bible. As for Torah, Ibn ʿArabī explained that this text was corrupted by humans after it was revealed to them, as people began "writing and verbalizing" their books. For the surah *al-Baqarah* reads: *humans knowingly corrupted the Torah after they have understood it* (Q 2:75). That said, it remains unclear why God did not protect the holy books of Jews and Christians from substitution (*tabdīl*) and corruption (*taḥrīf*) altogether. FM III:351.

21. Ibn ʿArabī hinted that this was the tactic the Devil used against Jesus. FM I:283.

22. Like Iblis, angels initially opposed the idea Adam should be made the Divine viceregent. They said: "The man serving as a viceregent will pollute the Earth and shed blood." FM II:68.

23. FM I:4, 125–26; FM III:56, 373, 528. See also Ridgeon, "A Sufi Perspective of Evil," 113. Murata divided evil beings, thoughts, and deeds in Ibn ʿArabī's work into four basic categories. These are (1) thoughts, actions, and occurrences that have failed to meet the conventions established by God in the form of revealed laws, (2) a general lack of agreeableness with the constitution, (3) the failure to attain perfection, and (4) the failure to fulfill individual goals and desires. According to Murata, "all four [of these categories] go back to nonexistence." Murata "Good and Evil in Islamic Neoconfucianism," 128.

24. FM III:315, 389. Al-Māturīdī noted Magians once believed that God admired the beauty of creation so much that "He came to fear that which was in opposition to it and He pondered over this thought, from which Iblis emerged. . . . Thus, all evil is from Iblis, and from God (Allāh) is all goodness." al-Māturīdī, *Kitāb al-Tawḥīd,* 172. For a detailed overview of al-Māturīdī's teachings, see Erlwein, *Arguments for God's Existence in Classical Islamic Thought,* 106.

25. FM II:575. See also FM I:286 and FM III:389.

26. FM I:286.

27. See Butler, "Reading Satan, Remembering the Other," 162; Bodman, "Stalking Iblis," 248 and Grunebaum, "Observations on the Muslim Concept of Evil," 117–34.

28. FM II:575.

29. FM III:389.

30. In this context, the two fingers represent the demonic and angelic force/companions (*qarīnān*) fighting in the human heart. This can also be read as a reference to God, as He is making the heart leaning towards

one of these forces or another. The Prophet said: "The hearts of all men are between two of the Compassionate's fingers as if they were one heart which He turns about as He wills." *Mishkāt al-maṣābīḥ* #89. Ibn ʿArabī explained both these fingers/forces are the reflections of God's kindness. For the satanic forces can also lead to the salivation of mankind. FM I:362.

31. Ibid.

32. FM II:492.

33. Quoted according to Burckhardt, *Introduction to Sufi Doctrine*, 11.

34. Ibn ʿArabī, *Divine Governance of the Human Kingdom*, 220–21. See also Ibn ʿArabī, "K. Kunh mā lā budda lil-murīd minhu," 551 and FM I:259.

35. FM I:362; Ibn ʿArabī, *Divine Governance of the Human Kingdom*, 220–21.

36. In other words, God needs an object of vengeance to disclose Himself as the Avenger (*al-Muntaqim*)—whereas the Name the Compassionate is disclosed when the Divine vengeance is removed from its target object. FM II:93. Comparable teachings can also be found in al-Makkī's works. For example, al-Makkī confirmed it is necessary for sinners to exist so that God can demonstrate His compassion. Like Ibn ʿArabī, al-Makkī argued that the existence of evil jinn and Iblis is indispensable in this world. Yazaki, *Islamic Mysticism and Abu Talib Al-Makki*, 21. In *Mathnawī*, Rūmī also claimed evil must exist so that people would be able to know what is good. Rūmī wrote: "The bone-setter, where should he try his skill; but on the patient lying with broken leg? . . . Gazing on youthful Joseph amorously//And lo, another scene by the same hand,// Hell-fire and Iblis with his hideous crew: Both master-works, created for good ends//To show His perfect wisdom and confound the skeptics who deny His mastery.// Could He not evil make, He would lack skill//Therefore He fashions infidel alike and Muslim true,// That both may witness bear to Him, and worship One Almighty Lord." Quoted according to Nicholson's translation in Nicholson, *The Mystics of Islam*, 69–70.

37. FM II:16.

38. FM I:49.

39. FM I:36–37; FM II:69, 104–5; FM III:129, 409. See also Ali, *Philosophical Sufism*, 105.

40. al-Ghazālī, *Revival of Religious Sciences*, vol. 2, 55.

41. Schimmel, *Mystical Dimensions of Islam*, 198. The original verses can be consulted at *Mathnawī* VI:2660.

42. ʿAlqama b. Ṣafwān was the most famous of these heroes. According to legend, he fought the whole night against a *shiqq*. At dawn, al-Qazwīnī noted, both he and the jinni he fought with succumbed to their injuries. Al-Qazwīnī furthermore noted that some people believe a ghoul can be easily converted to Islam and/or subdued with the word of God.

Others, however, claimed that the ghoul's nature can neither be tamed nor refined, even if a ghoul was to be separated from its natural habitat and other members of its species. al-Qazwīnī, *ʿAjā'ib al-makhlūqāt*, 177–78. The first strike of a sword was thought to be decisive when fighting a ghoul. If the first strike was not fatal, the wounded ghoul would prove to be indestructible. See al-Rawi, "The Arabic Ghoul and Its Western Transformation," 296–97; al-Azmeh, *The Emergence of Islam in Late Antiquity*, 209 and Allen, *The Arabic Literary Heritage*, 109.

43. FM I:188.

44. Ibid.

45. FM I:187–88.

46. To punish a jinni, God would rather expose it to cold temperature. FM I:134, 297. Due to their fiery nature, jinn are naturally drawn towards hot and dry landscapes. Sayyidī ʿAbd al-ʿAzīz al-Dabbāgh thus noted that jinn could also be harmed by exposure to wind and water. "If it were decreed that one of them enter water, he'd be extinguished and dissolve, the way one of us would burn up and dissolve if he entered a fire." Al-Lamaṭī, *al-Dhahab al-Ibrīz*, 112.

47. FM I:131–32.

48. Nasser, "The Jinn," 152.

49. FM I:202, 274.

50. Iafrate, *The Long Life of Magical Objects*, 50. See also: Klar, "And We Cast upon His Throne a Mere Body," 112.

51. FM I:134; FM II:467.

52. Tehrani, *Lubb al-lubb*, 43.

53. al-Qazwīnī, *ʿAjā'ib al-makhlūqāt*, 180.

54. Ibn ʿArabī, *K. al-Khalwa* (MS Carulla #2080),ff.22. We are immensely grateful to Stephen Hirtenstein for his invaluable insights with regard to the content of Ibn ʿArabī's *K. al-Khalwa.*

55. Ibn Taymiyya, *Īḍāḥ al-dalāla*, 103.

56. Ibn ʿArabī, *K. Maḥajja al-bayḍā'*, ff.1a. The earliest copies of Ibn ʿArabī's *K. al-Khalwa* were dated between 638 and 656 A.H.

57. Bonmariage (ed.), *Dā'irat al-aḥruf al-abjadiyya*, 60–65. A much-copied talisman of this type can also be found in al-Būnī, *Shams al-maʿārif*, ff.11.

58. FM I:67–69, 75. Ibn ʿArabī divided the letters of the Arabic alphabet into Divine, angelic, human, and jinn letters. Although the letter *dāl* is also angelic in nature, Ibn ʿArabī believed its dominion is over animals. See Rašić, *The Written World of God*, 34.

59. Canaan's collection contains some fifteen amulets and talismans against qarīn(a). These were cataloged and described in Probert, *Exploring the Life of Amulets in Palestine*, 227–39. See also Canaan, "The Decipherment of Arabic Talismans," 86. Drawing talismans on the palms of young boys

was not unusual in the Middle East. For instance, Lane documented the spiritual practices of the shaykh ʿAbd al-Qādir al-Maghribī, who was famous in Cairo for the visions he induced in people. Al-Maghribī openly professed that he worked with the assistance of jinn, though he claimed that all of his jinn-helpers were both benevolent and pious. Still, the presence of a young boy was required in his rituals—though the shaykh explained that a virgin girl, black female slave, and/or a pregnant woman could also be used. Al-Maghribī drew magic squares and sigils on the palms of his helpers to induce people to see the desired visions. Lane, *An Account of the Manners and Customs of the Modern Egyptians* vol. 1, 349–57.

60. al-Dīrbī, *K. Mujaribāt*, 73–77.

61. Schaefer produced a complete transcription of one such supplication, which is currently kept in Taylor-Schechter Geniza Collection of the Cambridge University Library under the reference number T-S AR 38.135. This supplication was intended to serve as a part of an amulet consisting of two shorter pieces of paper. Among other things, the amulet sought to invoke Gabriel's protection against evil jinn, like the Coptic magic square Blackman purchased. The full text of the supplication it contained can be consulted at Schaefer, *Enigmatic Charms*, 85–88. Another curious charm against ʾUmm al-Ṣibyān and other evil spirits was purchased by Fodor in the mid-twentieth century. It consisted of a scroll and a case. The scroll containing the accompanying supplication was pierced by several needles, which were meant to ensure protection against jinn. The scroll was then placed in the case containing more needles and a piece of triangular cloth, "probably from a woman's dress." Fodor, *Amulets from the Islamic World*, 85.

62. The term *walhān* has been commonly used with regard to the Devil causing distractions and disturbing the senses. Yazaki, *Islamic Mysticism and Abu Talib Al-Makki*, 97.

63. This was likely meant as a reference to the opening ayahs of the surah *aṭ-Ṭāriq*: *By the heaven and the nightly star (ṭāriq)! What will make you realize what the nightly star is? It is the star of piercing brightness—for there is no soul without the angel recording its deeds* (Q 86:1–4).

64. Ibn ʿArabī, *Rasāʾil Ibn ʿArabī*, 254. Donaldson noted how the spiritual healers and the professional prayer-writers she consulted with would always compose three prayers for the sick once they determined that a qarīn was the cause of sickness. One of these prayers was supposed to be sewn up in a case, cowered with green cloth, and tied to the right arm of a patient. The second prayer was supposed to be buried in a graveyard, and the third prayer was meant to be burned on a Saturday night. The spiritual healers ensured Donaldson a person tormented by their qarīn was bound to get healthy as soon as these rituals were completed. Donaldson, "The Belief in Jinn among the Persians," 187.

65. FM II:300.

66. FM I:330.

67. Ibn Manẓūr, *Lisān al-ʿarab,* vol. 4, 185–86. See also al-Nābulsī, *Hadiyyat al-Murād fī Sharḥ Hadiyyat Ibn al-ʿImad,* 68–70.

68. Ibn ʿArabī's remarks on camel meat and camels can be consulted at: FM I:74, 356, 564. See also al-Suyūṭī, *al-Ṭibb al-nabī,* 72, 190 and Probert, *Exploring the Life of Amulets in Palestine,* 237. Mentally ill patients were sometimes beaten with branches of a pomegranate tree to drive out their jinn. See Canaan, *Mohammadan Saints and Sanctuaries in Palestine,* 716; Stephan, "Lunacy in Palestine Folklore," 8; and Tritton, "Spirits and Demons of Arabia," 716.

69. Ibn Manẓūr, *Lisān al-ʿarab,* vol. 4, 185–86. Ibn Manẓūr's opinion appears to have been relatively widespread among scholars, as can be seen from Zadeh, "Commanding Demons and Jinn," 131–55.

70. FM I:604. Ibn ʿArabī's K. Kunh *mā lā budda lil-murīd minhu* offers another view on the matter. Here Ibn ʿArabī wrote that fasting increases the spiritual energy for obeying God, while at the same time reducing laziness of a person. Ibn ʿArabī, "K. Kunh mā lā budda lil-murīd minhu," 525. Najm al-Dīn Kubrā, however, claimed that fasting is efficient since it narrows blood vessels, thus preventing a qarīn from circulating through the body. Kubrā, *Fawāʾiḥ al-jamāl wa-fawātiḥ al-jalāl,* 80–81.

71. Zwemer, "The Familiar Spirit or Qarina," 367–68.

72. *Ṣaḥīḥ Muslim* #5616. Muslim saints and jinn were both thought to be capable of invading human dreams to make requests or to deliver a message. Noble, *Philosophizing the Occult,* 16; Yılmaz, *Caliphate Redefined,* 239–40. According to Meier, "dreams, poetry, and religious inspiration were already linked in the popular consciousness of ancient Arabia, and this trinity was apt to be judged rather negatively." Meier, "Some Aspects of Inspiration by Demons in Islam," 423, 427–28.

73. Sabzvārī, *Tuḥfah Yi-ʿAbbāsī,* 153.

74. FM I:274.

75. Ibn ʿArabī, *Risāla rūḥ al-quds,* 11–12.

76. FM I:333–34.

77. Powers, *Introduction to Tibetan Buddhism,* 426.

78. As Allione explained: "The process of feeding our demons is a method for bringing our shadow into consciousness and accessing the treasure it holds, rather than repressing it." Allione, *Feeding Your Demons,* 54–55.

79. Murata, *Tao of Islam,* 270. "Indeed," Klar noted in support of this opinion, "the mystical philosophy of renouncing worldly goods, being wary of indulgence, avoiding the temptation of women, is expressed time

and time again throughout the various versions of the tale." Klar, "And We Cast upon His Throne a Mere Body," 115.

80. FM II:196.

81. Ibn ʿArabī, "Kunh mā lā budda lil-murīd minhu," 527.

82. Ibn ʿArabī, "Kunh mā lā budda lil-murīd minhu," 529–30. Some scholars, however, believed that the Devil's strength and cunning will only increase as a Seeker advances in rank and virtue. Rustom, *Qur'anic Exegesis in the Later Islamic Philosophy*, 252.

83. Ibn ʿArabī, "K. Kunh mā lā budda lil-murīd minhu," 527.

84. Ibn ʿArabī, *Divine Governance of the Human Kingdom*, 221–22.

85. Elmore, "Ibn al-ʿArabī Testament on the Mantle of Initiation," 14.

86. Morris, "Listening for God: Prayer and the Heart in the al-Futūḥāt," https://ibnarabisociety.org/listening-for-god-part-3-james-morris/. Accessed May 14, 2022.

87. Corbin, *Man of Light in Iranian Sufism*, 93–94.

88. Ibn ʿArabī, *Mawāqiʿ al-nujūm*, 112.

89. See Ahmed-Amer (eds.), *Counselling Muslims*, 19–21; al-Azmeh, *The Emergence of Islam in Late Antiquity*, 208–10; Canaan, *Mohammadan Saints and Sanctuaries in Palestine*, 123–25; Curtiss, *Primitive Semitic Religion Today*, 189; Dols, *The Madman in Medieval Islamic Society*, 237; Lebling, *Legends of the Fire Spirits*, 72–76, 81–82; Stephan, "Lunacy in Palestine Folklore," 7–8; and al-Zain, Islam, *Arabs and the Intelligible World of Jinn*, 70–88.

90. Kubrā, *Fawāʾiḥ al-jamāl wa-fawātiḥ al-jalāl*, 80.

91. al-Qushayrī, *Epistle of Sufism*, 182.

92. FM II:195.

93. FM II:466–67. The original Qur'anic references can be consulted at: Q 17:64 and Q 38:82–83.

94. FM I:334. In the eleventh century, Nāṣir Khusraw (d. 1088), however, lamented that, at this point, humans turned so evil that it would be appropriate to say the real devils are made of clay and not of fire. Schimmel, *Deciphering the Signs of God*, 232.

95. Zwemer, "The Familiar Spirit of Qarina," 367–68. Unscrupulous parents would sometimes disguise male children as females in the hope of deceiving the more wicked, female qarīn which would normally accompany male children. Canaan, *Dämonglaube im Lande der Bibel*, 47.

96. FM I:515–16; FM II:15, 300. See also Zwemer, "The Familiar Spirit of Qarina," 364.

97. Quoted according to FM I:666. See also FM I:333. Some Akbarians, however, argued that it would be better to strive hard on the spiritual path without any real conviction than abandon the spiritual exercises altogether. Such a person, although not a believer in the true sense of the

word, would still catch a glimpse of the Divine light entering their heart and guiding them to the path of salvation. For instance, Halveti argued that the Devil would not dare to harm a person for as long as they stayed close and true to their heart and God. Ibn ʿArabī, *Divine Governance of the Human Kingdom*, 152.

98. Ibn ʿArabī was adamant that one must bow down to God—both inwardly and outwardly, with their heart and body alike—in order to experience a *tajallī*. In other words, Ibn ʿArabī believed that the human heart prostrates in prayer alongside the body, provided that a prayer is sincere. It is at this moment, when a person bows down to God both inwardly and outwardly, that a Divine self-disclosure occurs. FM I:515–16. See also Abrahamov, *Ibn ʿArabī and the Sufis*, 54.

99. FM I 515–16. The original reference can be consulted at *Ṣaḥīḥ Muslim*, #2814a.

100. The whole setting, music, and choreography of the Lo Gue dance were meant to symbolize the fiery nature of jinn. The masked figure representing a personal jinni would be carefully selected for their long limbs, lean figure, and domineering appearance. Their appearance coincidentally corresponds to the description of quranāʾ from *Mandal al-Sulaymanī* down to their "hair like sticks." *Mandal al-Sulaymanī*, ff.6; Bravmann, "Gyinna-Gyinna: Making the Jinn Manifest,"154–56. Further information on the Lo Gue dance can be found in another paper, which was published by Bravmann under the same title. Bravmann, "Gyinna-Gyinna: Making the Djinn Manifest," 48.

101. Ibn ʿArabī, *Risāla rūḥ al-quds*, 11–12; FM I:2–3, 133.

102. al-Damīrī, *Ḥayāt al-ḥayawān* vol. 1, 450–51. See also al-Jawziyya, *al-Tafsir al-qayyim*, 461 and Al-Tustarī, *Tafsīr al-Tustarī*, 251.

103. For an overview of disparate theories and opinions on jinn entering paradise see al-Shibilī, *Kitāb ʾākām al-marjān fī ʾaḥkām al-jānn*, 133–39.

104. Ibn Barrajān, *Tafsīr Ibn Barrajān*, vol. 5, 189. Ibn Barrajān even went as far as describing jinn doppelgangers (quranāʾ) of the righteous people (*ʾahl al-ṣalāḥ*) as angels. Ibid.

105. Ibn Manẓūr described ʿAbqar "as a place in the desert, full of jinn." Ibn Manẓūr, *Lisān al-ʿarab*, vol. 4, 535. Yāqūt believed it to be located in Yemen or near Yamāmah. Yāqūt, *Muʿjam al-buldān* vol. 4, 79. See also Jawād, *al-Mufaṣṣal fī tārīkh al-ʿarab qabla al-ʾislām* vol. 6, 718–73 and Brethren of Purity, *The Case of Animals versus Man*, 20–29.

106. ʿAṭṭār, *Manṭiq aṭ-ṭayr*, 132–33. The contemporary Bedouin notions of the jinn folk can be consulted at Bodman, *Poetics of Iblis*, 139.

107. ʿAṭṭār, *Manṭiq aṭ-ṭayr*, 133. Ibn ʿArabī also claimed that the Devil was powerless to either strike or tempt Jesus because of his purity FM I:283. These and similar teachings were likely based on the Islamic

normative tradition, for there are hadith indicating that Jesus was as pure and as obedient to God from birth. When a normal human being is born, their devil touches both sides of their body with its two fingers. A devil, however, failed to do so with Jesus, so it touched the placenta covering the baby instead. *Ṣaḥīḥ al-Bukhārī* #3286.

108. Ibn ʿArabī, *Divine Governance of the Human Kingdom*, 66.

109. FM II:466–67.

110. FM I:134; FM II:114, 466–67.

111. FM I:278. Similar tendencies in Sufi literature can be consulted at: al-Mayhānī, *ʾAsrār al-tawḥīd*, 310; al-Niffari, *Trois auvres inédites de mystiques musulmans*, 207–8, and al-Kharrāz, *Rasāil al-Kharrāz*, 45.

112. Ibn ʿArabī, "Risālat fī al-maʿrifa al-nafs wal-rūḥ," 155–56.

113. ʿAyn al-Quḍāt, *Tamhīdāt*, 186.

Bibliography

Abed, Sally. "Wonders and Monsters in the Travels of John Mandeville and in Abu Hamid al-Gharnāti's Tuhfat al-Albāb." In *Imagination and Fantasy in the Middle Ages and Early Modern Time*, edited by Albrecht Classen, 487–551. Berlin: De Gruyter, 2020.

ʾAbū Jāmūs, Muḥammad b. ʿUmar al-Buḥayrī al-Maḥallī. *al-Qurʿah al-kubrā* (MS USJ 00277). Beirut: Bibliothèque Orientale at the Université Saint-Joseph, c. 1666.

Abrahamov, Binyamin. *Ibn ʿArabī and the Sufis*. London: Anqa, 2014.

Absar, Ahmad. "Qur'ānic Concepts of Human Psyche." In *Qur'anic Concepts of Human Psyche*, edited by Zafar Afaq Ansari, 15–38. Herndon: International Institute of Islamic Thought, 1992.

Adamson, Peter. *Al-Rāzī*. Oxford: Oxford University Press, 2021.

ʿĀdil Shah, ʿAlī. *Nujūm al-ʿulūm* (MS Chester Beatty 02). Dublin: Chester Beatty Library, 1570.

Affifi, Abdul Ela. *The Twenty-Nine Pages: An Introduction to Ibn 'Arabi's Metaphysics of Unity*. London: Beshara Publications, 1998.

Ahmed, Sameera, and Mona Amer, eds. *Counselling Muslims Handbook of Mental Health Issues and Interventions*. London: Routlege, 2011.

Ahmed, Shahab. *Before Orthodoxy: The Satanic Verses in Early Islam*. Cambridge: Harvard University Press, 2017.

al-ʿAjmī, Daghash. *Ibn ʿArabī, ʿaqīdatuhu wa mawqifu ʿulamāʾ minhu*. Kuwait City: Maktaba ʾAhl al-ʾathar, 2011.

Akkach, Samer. *Cosmology and Architecture in Premodern Islam: An Archetectual Reading of Mystical Ideas*. Albany: State University of New York Press, 2006.

Alam, Muzaffar. *The Mughals and the Sufis: Islam and Political Imagination in India, 1500–1750*. Albany: State University of New York Press, 2021.

Albright, William. "Islam and the Religions of Ancient Orient." *Journal of the American Oriental Society* 60 (1940): 283–301.

Ali, Mukhtar. *Philosophical Sufism. An Introduction to the School of Ibn al-'Arabi*. London: Routlege, 2022.

Ali, Yusuf. *The Holy Qur'an with Translation and Commentary*. Oak Brook: American Trust Publications, 1977.

Allen, Jonathan. "Two Ways of Dealing with the Jinn in the Ottoman World." https://thicketandthorp.com/2018/07/04/two-ways-of-dealing-with-the-jinn-in-the-ottoman-world/. Accessed May 27, 2021.

Allen, Roger. *The Arabic Literary Heritage: The Development of Its Genres and Criticism.* Cambridge: Cambridge University Press, 1998.

Allione, Tsultrim. *Feeding Your Demons*. New York: Little, Brown and Company, 2008.

Almond, Ian. *Sufism and Deconstruction: A Comparative Study of Derrida and Ibn 'Arabi.* London: Routlege, 2009.

Aloiane, Zourabi. "Anthropomorphic Representations of Evil in Islam." *Orientalia Academiae Scientiarum Hungaricae* 49 (1957): 423–34.

al-ʾAlūsī, Muḥammad Shukhrī. *Bulūgh al-ʿarab fī maʿarifa ʾaḥwāl al-ʿarab*. Cairo: al-Maktaba al-ahlīya, 1924.

Anushiravani, Alireza. "The Image of Satan in Rumi's "Mathnawi," Dante's 'Divine Comedy' and Milton's 'Paradise Lost.'" PhD diss., University of Illinois, 1992.

Argiris, Panagiotis. "The Topic of the 'Doppelgänger' (the Double) in the Literature of the Fantastic." https://rb.gy/euhk7e. Accessed January 14, 2022.

Aristotle. *Metaphysics*. London: Penguin Books, 1998.

al-Ashqar, Umar Sulaiman. *The World of Jinn and Devils*. Riyadh: Al-Basheer Publications & Translations, 1998.

al-Aswad, Sayed. "The Ethnography of Invisible Spheres." *Anthropology* 46 (2001): 51.

al-Aswad, Sayed. *Religion and Folk Cosmology: Scenarios of the Visible and Invisible in Rural Egypt.* Westport: Greenwood, 2002.

ʿAṭṭār, Farīd ud-Dīn. *Manṭiq aṭ-ṭayr: The Conference of the Birds*. Translated by C. S. Nott. New York: Yanus Press, 1954.

ʿAṭṭār, Farīd ud-Dīn. *Tadhkirāt al-ʾawliyāʾ*. Edited by Muhammad Istilami. Tehran: 1927.

Awn, Peter. *Satan's Tragedy and Redemption: Iblīs in Sufi Psychology*. Leiden: E. J. Brill, 1983.

al-ʿAyyashī, Muhammad b. Masʿūd. *Tafsīr al-ʿAyyashī: A Fourth/Tenth Century Shīʿī Commentary of the Qur'an*, vol. 1. Translated by Meir Bar-Asher. Birmingham: Ami Press, 2020.

ʿAyn al-Quḍāt. *Tamhīdāt*. Edited by ʿAfīf ʿUsayrān. Tehran: Intishārāt-i Manūchihrī, 1994.

al-Azmeh, Aziz. *The Emergence of Islam in Late Antiquity: Allah and His People*. Cambridge: Cambridge University Press, 2014.

Badeen, Edward, and Birgit Krawietz. "Eheschließung mit Dschinnen nach Badr al-Dīn al-Shiblī." *Wiener Zeitschrift für die Kunde des Morgenlandes* 92 (2002): 33–51.

Baffioni, Carmela. "The Figure of Iblīs in the Ikhwān al-Ṣafāʾ-related Esoteric Literature." In *Raison et quête de la sagesse: Hommage à Christian Jambet*, edited by Mohammad Ali Amir-Moezzi, 113–41. Turnhout: Brepols, 2020.

Bakar, Osman. "The Unity of Science and Spiritual Knowledge: The Islamic Perspective." *Seventeenth International Conference on the Unity of Sciences Internal Conference Proceedings* 1 (1988): 1–20.

Bakhtiar, Laleh. *Avicenna on the Science of the Soul*. Chicago: KAZI Publications Inc, 2013.

Bakhtiar, Laleh. *Quranic Psychology: The Islamic View Moral Psychology: Textbook on Islamic Moral Psychology*. Chicago: KAZI Publications Inc., 2019.

Basharin, Pavel. "Образ джиннов в мусульманской магии." *Umbra* 8 (2019): 106–51.

Bauden, Frédéric (ed.). *Al-Maqrīzī's al-Khabar ʿan al-bashar*, vol. 8. Leiden: Brill, 2022.

Bayḍāwī, Nāṣir al-Dīn. *ʾAnwār al-tanzīl wa-ʾasrār al-taʾwīl*. 2 vols. Edited by Winand Fell and Heinrich Leberecht Fleischer. Leipzig: Sumtibus F. C. G. Voegeli, 1848.

al-Bayhaqī, ʾAḥmad b. al-Ḥusayn. *Kitāb al-zuhd al-kabīr*. Edited by Taqī al-Dīn al-Nadwī Maẓāhirī. Kuwait: Dār al-Qalam, 1983.

Beneito, Pablo. "On the Divine Love for Beauty." *Journal of the Muhyiddin Ibn 'Arabi Society* 28 (1995): 1–22.

Berglund, Jenny. "Princely Companion or Object of Offense: The Dog's Ambiguous Status in Islam." *Society and Animals* 22 (2014): 545–59.

al-Birūnī, Muḥammad b. ʾAḥmad. *al-ʾĀthār al-bāqiyya ʿan al-qurūn al-khāliyya*. Cairo: al-Maktaba al-thaqāfa al-dīniyya, 2008.

Blackman, Winifred. "The Karīn and Karīneh." *Journal of the Royal Anthropological Institute of Great Britain and Ireland* 56 (1926): 163–69.

Blackman, Winifred. *The Fellahin of Upper Egypt*. London: Frank Cass & Company, 1968.

Bodman, Whitney. "Poetics of Iblis: Qur'ānic Narrative as Theology." PhD diss., Harvard University, 2004.

Bodman, Whitney. "Stalking Iblis: In Search of an Islamic Theodicy." In *Myths, Historical Archetypes and Symbolic Figures in Arabic Literature: Towards a New Hermeneutic Approach*, edited by A. Neuwirth, 247–71.

Baden-Baden: Ergon Verlag - ein Verlag in der Nomos Verlagsgesellschaft mbH & Co. KG, 1999.

Bonmariage, Cécile, ed. *Dā'irat al-aḥruf al-abjadiyya: Le cercle des lettres de l'alphabet*. Leiden: Brill, 2017.

The Book of Curiosities. An Eleventh-Century Egyptian Guide to the Universe. Edited and translated by Emilie Savage-Smith. Leiden: Brill, 2014.

Bosnevi, Abdullah. *Sharḥ Fuṣūṣ al-ḥikam*. Translated by Rašid Hafizović. Sarajevo: Institute Ibn Sina, 2009.

Bowering, Gerhard. *The Mystical Vision of Existence in Classical Islam: The Qur'anic Hermeneutics of the Sufi Sahl At-Tustari (d. 283/896)*. Berlin: De Gruyter, 1979.

Bravmann, Rene. "Gyinna-Gyinna: Making the Djinn Manifest." *African Arts* 10 (1977): 46–52.

Bravmann, Rene. "Gyinna-Gyinna. Making the Jinn Manifest." *The Performance Arts in Africa: A Reader*, edited by Frances Hearding, 149–56. London: Routlege, 2002.

Brethren of Purity. *On God and the World: An Arabic Critical Edition and English Translation of Epistles 49–51*. Edited and translated by Wilfred Madelung, Cyril Uy, and Carmela Baffioni. Oxford: Oxford University Press, 2019.

Brethren of Purity. *The Case of Animals Versus Man in Front of the King of the Jinn: An Arabic Critical Edition and English Translation of Epistle 22*. Edited and translated by Lenn E. Goodman and Richard McGregor. Oxford: Oxford University Press, 2012.

Bronfen, Elisabeth. *Night Pasages: Philosophy, Literature and Film*. New York: Columbia University Press, 2008.

Browne, Edward. *A Literary History of Persia*. Cambridge: Cambridge University Press, 1964.

al-Būnī, 'Aḥmad. *Shams al-ma'ārif wa laṭā'if al-'awārif* (MS Arabe 6681). Paris: Bibliothèque Nationale de France, c. 19th century.

Burckhardt, Titus. *Introduction to Sufi Doctrine*. Somerville: World Wisdom Books, 2008.

Bursevī, İsmail Hakkı. *Tafsīr rūḥ al-bayān*. 10 vols. Damascus: al-Maṭba'ah al-'Uthmānīyah, 1928.

Butler, Jean. "Reading Satan, Remembering the Other." *Numen: Cultural Memory and Islam* 58 (2011): 157–87.

Byatt, Antonia Susan. *The Djinn in the Nightingale's Eye*. London: Chatto and Windus, 1994.

Bylebyl, Michael. "The Wisdom of Illuminations: A Study of the Prose Stories of Suhrawardī." PhD diss., University of Chicago, 1976.

Bynum, Caroline. "Wonder." *American Historical Review* 102 (1997): 1–26.

Canaan, Taufik. *Aberglaube und Volksmedizin im Lande der Bibel*. Hamburg: L. Friederichsen & co., 1914.

Canaan, Taufik. *Dämonenglaube im Lande der Bibel*. Leipzig: J. C. Hinrichs'sche Buchhandlung, 1929.

Canaan, Taufik. *Mohammadan Saints and Sanctuaries in Palestine*. London: Luzac & Co., 1927.

Canaan, Taufiq. "The Decipherment of Arabic Talismans." In *Magic and Divination in Early Islam*, edited by Emilie Savage-Smith, 69–151. Burlington: Ashgate, 2004.

Canova, Giovanni. "Uno sheykh-serpente dell'Alto Egitto: al-Harīdī." *Quaderni di Studi Arabi* 10 (1992): 201–14.

Carboni, Stefano. *The Wonders of Creation and the Singularities of Painting: A Study of the Ilkhanid London Qazwini*. Edinburgh: Edinburgh University Press, 2020.

Chelhod, Joseph. *Les structures du sacré chez les Arabes*. Paris: Adrien Maisonneuve et Larose, 1964.

Chittick, William. "Death and the World of Imagination: Ibn al-ʿArabī's Eschatology," *The Muslim World* 78 (1988): 51–82.

Chittick, William. "Iblīs and the Jinn in the al-Futūḥāt al-Makkiyya." In *Classical Arabic Humanities in Their Own Terms: Festschrift for Wolfhart Heinrichs on His 65th Birthday*, edited by Beatrice Gruendler and Michael Cooperson, 99–126. Leiden: Brill, 2008.

Chittick, William. "Ibn ʿArabī." In *The Stanford Encyclopaedia of Philosophy*, edited by Edward N. Zalta. Stanford University, 2020. https://plato.stanford.edu/entries/ibn-arabi/.

Chittick, William. "Ibn ʿArabī's own Summary of the Fuṣūṣ." *Journal of the Muhyiddin Ibn Arabi Society* 1 (1982): 88–128.

Chittick, William. "The Wisdom of Animals." *Journal of the Muhyiddin Ibn ʿArabi Society* 44 (2009): 27–37.

Chittick, William. *In Search for the Lost Heart: Explorations in Islamic Thought*. Albany: State University of New York Press, 2012.

Chittick, William. *Science of the Cosmos, Science of the Soul: The Pertinence of Islamic Cosmology in the Modern World*. London: Oneworld Publications, 2007.

Chittick, William. *Sufi Path of Knowledge: Ibn al-Arabi's Metaphysics of Imagination*. Albany: State University of New York Press, 1989.

Chittick, William. *The Heart of the Islamic Philosophy: The Quest for Self-Knowledge in the Teachings of Afḍal al-Dīn Kāshānī*. Oxford: Oxford University Press, 2001.

Chodkiewicz, Michel. *Ocean without Shore: Ibn Arabi, the Book and the Law*. Albany: State University of New York Press, 1993.

Clark, Jane, and Stephen Hirtenstein. "Establishing Ibn ʿArabī's Heritage: First Findings from the MIAS Archiving Project." *Journal of the Muhyiddin Ibn ʿArabi Society* 52 (2012): 1–32.

Corbin, Henry. *The Man of Light in Iranian Sufism*. New York: Omega Publications, 1994.

Cornell, Rika. "Soul of a Woman Was Created Below." *Probing the Depths of Evil and Good: Multireligious Case Studies,* edited by Jerald. D. Gorth, Henry Jansen, and Hendrik M. Vroom, 257–80. Amsterdam: Rodopi, 2007.

Coulon, Jean-Charles. "La magie islamique et le «corpus bunianum» au Moyen Âge." PhD diss., Paris-Sorbonne University, 2013.

Coulon, Jean-Charles. "ʿAnāq bt. Adam, the Islamic Story of the Very First Witch: Gender and the Origins of Evil Magic." *Journal of Women of the Middle East and the Islamic World* 17 (2019): 135–67.

Craig, Leigh Ann. "The Spirit of Madness: Uncertainty, Diagnosis, and the Restoration of Sanity in the Miracles of Henry VI," *Journal of Medieval Religious Cultures* 39 (2013): 60–93.

Curtiss, Samuel Ives. *Primitive Semitic Religion Today: A Record of Researches, Discoveries and Studies in Syria, Palestine and the Sinaitic Peninsula.* Chicago: Fleming H. Revel Company, 1902.

Dajani, Samer. *Sufis and Sharia: The Forgotten School of Mercy*. Edinburgh: Edinburgh University Press, 2023.

Dallos, Edina. "Albasty: A Female Demon of Turkic Peoples." *Acta Ethnographica Hungarica* 2 (2019): 413–23.

al-Damīrī, Kamāl al-Dīn. *Ḥayāt al-ḥayawān al-kubrā.* 2 vols. Edited by A. S. G. Jayakar. Bombay: Taraporevala, n.d.

Daqāʾiq al-Ḥaqāʾiq (MS BnF Persian 174). Paris: Bibliothèque Nationale de France, c. 1272.

Daston, Lorraine, and Katherine Park. *Wonders and the Order of Nature 1150–1750*. Princeton, NJ: Princeton University Press, 2001.

Davidson, John, ed. *A Treasury of Mystic Terms, Volume 6: The Soul in Exile.* New Delhi: Science of the Soul Research Centre, 2003.

Descartes, René. *The Passions of the Soul*. Indianapolis: Hackett, 1989.

De Smet, Daniel. "The Demon in Potentiality and the Devil in Actuality: Two Principles of Evil according to 4th/10th Century Ismailism." *Arabica* 69 (2022): 601–25.

Desparmet, Joseph. *Le mal magique: ethnographie traditionnelle de la Mettidja.* Algiers: Impr. J. Carbonel, 1932.

De Vaux, Carra. *L'abrégé des merveilles*. Paris: Klinsieck, 1898.

al-Dhubiyānī, Nābighah. *Diwān al-Nābighah al-Dhubiyānī.* Cairo. Dār al-Maʿarif, n.d.

Diamond, Stephen. *Anger, Madness, and the Daimonic: The Psychological Genesis of Violence, Evil, and Creativity.* Albany: State University of New York Press, 1996.

al-Dirbī, ʾAḥmad. *Kitāb al-Mujaribāt.* Istanbul: M. Durmuş Gökçen Estate, n.d.

al-Diyārbakrī, Ḥusayn. *Tārikh al-khamīs fī ʾaḥwāl ʾanfus al-nafīs,* vol. 1. Edited by Husayn b. Muhammad Ibn al-Hasan. Cairo: 1866.

Doherty, Lillian Eileen. *Siren Songs: Gender, Audiences and Narrators in the Odyssey.* Ann Arbor: University of Michigan Press.

Dols, Michael. *The Madman in Medieval Islamic Society.* Oxford: Oxford University Press, 1992.

Donaldson, Bessie Allen. "The Belief in Jinn among the Persians." *The Muslim World* 20 (1930): 185–94.

Doufikar-Aerts, Faustina. "Dionysus, Enoch and Zakhraf: Deity, Prophet and King of the Jinn. Metamorphoses of the Golden Letter." *Medioevo romanzo e orientale* 8 (2010): 115–28.

Doutté, Edmond. *Magie et religion dans l'Afrique du Nord.* Algiers: Typographie Adolphe Jourdan, 1908.

Elmore, Gerald. "Fabulous Gryphon (ʿAnqāʾ Mughrib) on the Seal of the Saints and the Sun Rising in the West." PhD diss., Yale University, 1995.

Elmore, Gerald. "Ibn al-ʿArabī Testament on the Mantle of Initiation." *Journal of the Muhyiddin Ibn Arabi Society* 26 (1999): 1–33.

Elmore, Gerald. "Qur'ānic Wisdom, Propheology Ibn ʿArabī's Fuṣūṣ al-ḥikam." *Journal of the Muhyiddin Ibn Arabi Society* 42 (2007): 71–111.

Elsby, Charlene. "Socrates's Demonic Sign (Daimonion Sēmeion)." In *Philosophical Approaches to Demonology,* edited by Benjamin W. McCraw and Robert Arp, 95–109. London: Routlege, 2017.

Erlwein, Hannah. *Arguments for God's Existence in Classical Islamic Thought: A Reappraisal of the Discourse.* Berlin: De Gruyter, 2019.

Fahd, Toufy, and Andrew Rippin. "Shayṭān." In *Encyclopaedia of Islam,* 2nd ed. Edited by P. Bearman, Th. Bianquis, C. E. Bosworth, E. van Donzel, and W. P. Heinrichs. http://dx.doi.org/10.1163/1573-3912_islam_COM_1054. Accessed January 7, 2022.

Fahd, Toufy. *Anges, démons et djinns en Islam.* Paris: Seuil, 1971.

Fahmi, Mustafa. *ʾAsrār al-jinn.* Cairo: al-Maṭbaʾ al-ʾAṣriyya, 1935.

Fanger, Claire. *Rewriting Magic: An Exegesis of the Visionary Autobiography of a Fourteenth-Century French Monk.* University Park: Penn State University Press, 2015.

Fartacek, Gebhard. *Unheil durch Dämonen: Diskurse über das Wirken der Ginn: Eine sozialanthropologische Spurensuche in Syrien.* Köln: Böhlau Verlag, 2010.

Ferris, David. *Silent Urns: Romanticism, Hellenism, Modernity*. Stanford, CA: Stanford University Press, 2000.

Fodor, Alexander. *Amulets from the Islamic World: Catalogue of the Exhibition Held in Budapest in 1988*. Budapest: Eötövos Loránd University Chair for Arabic Studies, 1990.

Gallorini, Louise. "The Symbolic Functions of Angels in the Qurʾān and Sufi Literature." PhD diss., American University of Beirut, 2021.

Gaudefroy-Demombynes, Maurice. *Mahomet*. Paris: Editions Albin Michel, 1957.

Geiger, Abraham. *Judaism and Islam: A Prize Essay*. Ithaca, NY: Cornell University Library, 2009.

al-Geyoshi, Muhammad Ibraheem. "al-Tirmidhi's Conception of the Areas of Interiority." *Islamic Quarterly* 16 (1972): 168–88.

al-Geyoshi, Muhammad Ibraheem. "Al-Tirmidhi's Conception of the Struggle between Qalb and Nafs." *Islamic Quarterly* 18 (1974): 3–14.

al-Ghazālī, ʾAbū Ḥāmid. *al-Ḥikma fī al-makhlūqāt Allāh*. Edited by Muhammad Rashid Rida al-Qabbani. Beirut: Tawzīʿ Dār ʾIḥyāʾ al-ʿUlūm, 1978.

al-Ghazālī, ʾAbū Ḥāmid. *Kitāb sharḥ ʿajāʾib al-qalb: The Marvels of the Heart: Book 21 of ʾIḥyāʾ ʿulūm al-dīn*. Translated by Walter James Skellie. Louisville, KY: Fons Vitae, 2010.

al-Ghazālī, ʾAbū Ḥāmid. *Mukhtaṣar ʾiḥyāʾ ʿulūm al-dīn*. Edited by Marwan Khalaf. Lympia: Spohr Publishers Limited, 2014.

al-Ghazālī, ʾAbū Ḥāmid. *Revival of Religious Sciences: ʾIḥyāʾ ʿulūm al-dīn*. Translated by Mohammad Mahdi al-Sharif. Beirut: Dār al-Kutub al-ʾIlmiyya, 2011.

al-Ghazālī, ʾAbū Ḥāmid. *The Incoherence of the Philosophers: A Parallel English-Arabic Text Translated, Introduced, and Annotated by Michael E. Marmura*. Provo, UT: Brigham Young University Press, 2000.

al-Ghazālī, ʾAbū Ḥāmid. *ʾIḥyāʾ ʿulūm al-dīn*, 5 vols. Cairo: Maṭbaʿat al-Istiqāma, n.d.

Gieseler-Greenbaum, Dorian. "Porphyry of Tyre on the Daimon, Birth and the Stars." *Neoplatonic Demons and Angels*, edited by Luc Brisson, Seamus O'Neill, and Andrei Timotin, 102–39. Leiden: Brill, 2018.

Gieseler-Greenbaum, Dorian. *The Daimon in Hellenistic Astrology: Origins and Influence*. Boston: Brill, 2016.

Goldziher, Ignaz. "Die Ginnen der Dichter." Zeitschrift der Deutschen Morgenländischen *Gesellschaft* 45 (1891): 685–90.

Golia, Maria. *Cairo, City of Sand*. London: Reaktion Books, 2004.

Graham, William. "The Earliest Meaning of Qur'ān." *Die Welt des Islams* 23 (1984): 361–77.

Gruber, Christiane. "In Defence and Devotion: Affective Practices in Early Modern Turco-Persian Manuscript Paintings." In *Affect, Emotion, and*

Subjectivity in Early Modern Muslim Empires: New Studies in Ottoman, Safavid, and Mughal Art and Culture, edited by Kishwar Rizvi, 95–123. Leiden: Brill, 2017.

Grunebaum, Gustave Edmund. "Observations on the Muslim Concept of Evil." *Studia Islamica* 31 (1970): 117–34.

Hadromi-Allouche, Zohar. "Between Pure Milk and the Froth: Images of the Devil in the Muslim Tradition (Ḥadīth)." PhD diss., SOAS University London, 2006.

Hakim, Suad. "Ibn 'Arabī's Metaphysics of the Human Body." *Journal of the Muhyiddin Ibn Arabi Society* 59 (2016). https://ibnarabisociety.org/the-paths-to-god-souad-hakim/.

al-Ḥalabī, Nūr ad-Dīn ʿAlī. *ʿIqd al-marjān fī-mā yataʿallaq bil-jānn*. Cairo: Maktabat Ibn Sīnā, 1988.

al-Ḥalwatī, Muḥammad ʾAbī al-Mawāhab. *Kitāb mafātīḥ al-kunūz*. Cairo: 1988.

Hamadhānī, Yaʿqūb. *Sifāt jazīrat al-ʿarab*. Edited by David Heinrich Müller. Amsterdam: Oriental Press, 1968.

Harendrachandra, Paul. *Jalālu'd-dīn Rūmī and his Taṣawwuf*. Calcutta: Sobharani Paul, 1985.

Hassig, Debra. *Medieval Bestiaries: Text, Image, Ideology*. Cambridge: Cambridge University Press, 1995.

Hawting, Gerald. *The Idea of Idolatry and the Emergence of Islam: From Polemic to History*. Cambridge: Cambridge University Press, 2006.

Hegedus, Tim. *Early Christianity and Ancient Astrology*. New York: Peter Lang, 2007.

Henninger, Joseph. "Beliefs in Spirits among the Pre-Islamic Arabs." In *Magic and Divination in Early Islam*, edited by Emilie Savage-Smith, 1–54. Burlington: Ashgate, 2004.

Henninger, Joseph. "La religion bédouine préislamique." *L'antica Società Beduina, Studi Semitici* 2 (1959), 115–40.

Hentschel, Kornelius. *Geister, Magier und Muslime: Dämonenwelt und Geisteraustreibung im Islam*. Munich: Diederichs, 1997.

Hirtenstein, Stephen, ed. *Muhyiddin Ibn ʿArabī: A Commemorative Volume*. Dorset: Element Books Limited, 1993.

Hornblower, George Davis. "Traces of a Ka-Belief in Modern Egypt and Old Arabia," *Islamic Culture* 1 (1927): 426–30.

Hoyland, Robert. *Arabia and the Arabs from the Bronze Age to the Coming of Islam*. Abingdon: Routlege, 2001.

al-Hujwīrī, ʾAbū al-Ḥasan ʿAlī. *Kash al-Maḥjūb: The Oldest Persian Treatise on Sufism*. Translated by Reynold A. Nicholson. London: Luzac & Co, 1959.

Iafrate, Allegra. *The Long Life of Magical Objects: A Study in the Solomonic Tradition*. University Park: Penn State University Press, 2019.

Ibn al-Jawzī, ʿAbd al-Raḥmān b. ʿAlī. *al-Muntaẓam fī tārīkh al-mulūk wal-ʾumam.* Beirut: Dār al-Kutub al-ʾilmiya, 1992.

Ibn al-Kalbī, Hishām b. Muḥammad. *Kitāb al-ʾAṣnām.* Cairo, Dār al-kutub al-miṣriyya, 1995.

Ibn Barrajān, ʿAbd al-Salām b. ʿAbd al-Raḥmān. *Tafsīr Ibn Barrajān: Tanbīh al-afhām ilā tadabbur al-kitāb al-ḥakīm wa-taʿarruf al-āyāt wa-l-nabaʾ al-ʿaẓīm.* 5 vols. Edited by Ahmad Farid Mazyadi. Beirut: Dār al-Kutub al-ʿIlmiyya, 2013.

Ibn Faḍlān, ʾAḥmad. *Riḥlat Ibn Faḍlān Ilā Bilād al-Turuk wa al-Rūs wa al-Ṣaqāliba.* Edited by Shakir Luaybi. Abu Dhabi: Dār al-Suwaydī li-l-Nashr wa al-Tawzīʿ, 2003.

Ibn Fāris, ʾAḥmad. *Muʿajam maqāyīs al-lugha,* vol. 1. Cairo: Dār ʾiḥyāʾ al-kutub al-ʿarabiya, 1941.

Ibn Ḥazm, ʿAlī b. Aḥmad. *Kitāb al-fiṣal fī l-milal wa-l-ahwāʾ wa-l-niḥal.* Bagdad: Maktaba al-Muthannā, 1964.

Ibn Kathīr, ʾIsmāʿīl b. ʿUmar. *The Signs before the Day of Judgment.* London: Dar al-Taqwa, 1992.

Ibn Kathīr, ʾIsmāʿīl b. ʿUmar. *Tafsīr al-Qurʾān al-ʿazīm,* vol. 14. Cairo: 2000.

Ibn Khaldūn, ʾAbū Zayd. *al-Muqaddima.* Tunis: Dār al-Qalam, 1984.

Ibn Manẓūr, Muḥammad b. Makram. *Lisān al-ʿarab.* 15 vols. Beirut: Dār ṣādir, n.d.

Ibn Nadīm, ʾAbū al-Faraj b. ʾIsḥāq. *The Fihrist of Ibn Nadīm.* Edited and translated by Bayard Dodge. New York: Columbia University Press, 1970.

Ibn Qutayba, ʿAbdallāh b. Muslim. *Taʾwīl mushkil al-Qurʾān.* Edited by Ahmad Saqr. Cairo: ʿĪsā al-Bābī al-Ḥalabī, 1954.

Ibn Rushd, ʾAbū al-Walīd Muḥammad. *Incoherence of the Incoherence: Tahafut al-Tahafut.* Translated by Simon van den Bergh. London: Think: 2018.

Ibn Saʿd, Muḥammad. *Kitāb al-Ṭabaqāt al-kabīr,* vol. 1. Edited by Ali Muhammad Umar. Cairo: Maktabat al-Khānjī, 2001.

Ibn Shuhaid, ʾAbū ʿAmīr. *Risālat at-tawābī wa z-zawābī: The Treatise of Familiar Spirits and Demons.* Translated by James T. Monroe. Leiden: Brill, 1971.

Ibn Taymiyya, Taqī ad-Dīn. *Īḍāḥ ad-dalāla fī ʿumūm ar-risāla.* Cairo: Maṭbaʿa al-Sharq, 1924.

Ibn Waṣīf Shāh, ʾIbrāhīm. *ʾAkhbār al-zamān.* Cairo: Maṭbaʿat ʿAbd al-Ḥamīd Aḥmad Ḥanafī, 1938.

Ibn ʿAbd Rabbih, ʾAḥmad b. Muḥammad. *Al-ʿIqd al-farīd: The Unique Necklace,* vol. 1. Edited and translated by Issa J. Boullata and Roger M. A. Allen. Reading: Garnet, 2006.

Ibn ʿĀbidīn, Muḥammad. *Radd al-Muhtār ʿala al-Durr al-Mukhtār,* vol. 9. Beirut: Dār al-Kutub al-ʿIlmīyya, 2003.

Ibn ʿArabī, Muhyī al-Dīn Abū ʿAbd Allāh. "Al-Tadbīrāt al-Ilāhiya fī Iṣlāḥ al-Mamlaka al-Insāniya." In *Kleinere Schriften des Ibn Arabi nach Handschriften in Upsala und Berlin zum ersten Mal Herausgegeben und mit Einleitung und Kommentar Versehen*, edited by H. S. Nyberg, 101–240. Leiden: Brill, 1914.

Ibn ʿArabī, Muhyī al-Dīn Abū ʿAbd Allāh. *Fuṣūṣ al-ḥikam*. Beirut: Dār al-kutub al-ʿarabī, 1946.

Ibn ʿArabī, Muhyī al-Dīn Abū ʿAbd Allāh. *al-Futūḥāt al-Makkiyya*. 4 vols. Cairo: 1859.

Ibn ʿArabī, Muhyī al-Dīn Abū ʿAbd Allāh. *Divine Governance of the Human Kingdom: Al-Tadbīrāt al-Ilāhiya fī Iṣlāḥ al-Mamlaka al-Insāniya*. Edited by Tosun Bayrak al-Jerrahi al-Halveti. Louisville, KY: Fons Vitae, 1997.

Ibn ʿArabī, Muhyī al-Dīn Abū ʿAbd Allāh. *Rasāʾil Ibn ʿArabī*. Beirut: Dār al-kutub ʿilmiyyah, n.d.

Ibn ʿArabī, Muhyī al-Dīn Abū ʿAbd Allāh. *The Meccan Revelations*. 2 vols. Edited by Michel Chodkiewicz. Michigan: Pir Press, 2002.

Ibn ʿArabī, Muhyī al-Dīn Abū ʿAbd Allāh. *The Seven Days of the Heart: Prayers for the Nights and Days of the Week*. Edited and translated by Stephen Hirtenstein and Pablo Beneito. Oxford: Anqa, 2000.

Ibn ʿArabī, ʾAbū ʿAbd Allāh Muḥammad. "Kitāb Kunh mā lā budda lil-murīd minhu." In *Majmūʿat rasāʾil Ibn al-ʿArabī*, vol. 1, 113–230. Beirut: Dār al-Maḥajjah al-Bayḍāʾ, 2000.

Ibn ʿArabī, ʾAbū ʿAbd Allāh Muḥammad. "Risālat fī al-maʿrifa al-nafs wal-rūḥ." In *Acts of the Fourteenth Congress of Orientalists*, edited by Miguel Asín Palacios, 160–66. Paris: 1905.

Ibn ʿArabī, ʾAbū ʿAbd Allāh Muḥammad. *Contemplations of the Holy Mysteries*. Translated by Stephen Hirtenstein and Pablo Beneito. London: Anqa, 2008.

Ibn ʿArabī, ʾAbū ʿAbd Allāh Muḥammad. *Kitāb al-Isrāʾ ilā al-maqām al-ʾasrā*. Edited by Suʿād Ḥakīm. Beirut: Dandarah lil-Ṭibāʿah wa-al-Nashr, 1988.

Ibn ʿArabī, ʾAbū ʿAbd Allāh Muḥammad. *Kitāb al-khalwa* (MS Carulla #2080). Istanbul: Süleymaniye Library, c. 719 AH.

Ibn ʿArabī, ʾAbū ʿAbd Allāh Muḥammad. *Kitāb Maḥajjat al-bayḍāʾ* (MS Yusuf Aga 4986). Konya: Yusuf Aga Library, 600 AH.

Ibn ʿArabī, ʾAbū ʿAbd Allāh Muḥammad. *Kitāb ʿAnqāʾ mughrib* (MS or. oct. 3266). Berlin: Staatsbibliothek zu Berlin, n.d.

Ibn ʿArabī, ʾAbū ʿAbd Allāh Muḥammad. *Kitāb ʿAnqāʾ mughrib*. N.D.: ʿĀlam al-Fikr, 2019.

Ibn ʿArabī, ʾAbū ʿAbd Allāh Muḥammad. *Mashāhid al-ʾasrār al-qudsiyya wa maṭāliʿ al-ʾanwār al-ʾilahiyya*. Beirut: Dār al-kutub al-ʾilmiyya, 2005.

Ibn ʿArabī, ʾAbū ʿAbd Allāh Muḥammad. *Mawāqiʿ al-nujūm wa-maṭāliʿ ʾahillat al-ʾasrār wa-al-ʿulūm*. Edited by Muhammad Badr al-Din al-Nasani. Cairo: 1907.

Ibn ʿArabī, ʾAbū ʿAbd Allāh Muḥammad. *Prayer for Spiritual Elevation and Protection*. Oxford: Anqa, 2007.

Ibn ʿArabī, ʾAbū ʿAbd Allāh Muḥammad. *Rūḥ al-quds*. Damascus: 1986.

Ibn ʿArabī, ʾAbū ʿAbd Allāh Muḥammad. *Risāla rūḥ al-quds fī muḥāsaba al-nafs*. Damascus: Muʾassasa al-ʿilm, 1964.

al-Ibshīhī, Shihāb al-Dīn. *Kitāb al-Mustaṭraf fī kull fann mustaẓraf*, vol. 2. Edited by Aḥmad Saʿd. Cairo: Maṭbaʿa al-munīrīya, 1952.

al-Iṣfahānī, ʾAbū al-Qāsim. *Kitāb tafṣīl al-Nashʾatayn wa Taḥṣīl al-Saʿādatāyn*. Beirut: Dār al-Gharb al-Islāmī, 1988.

al-Iṣfahānī, ʾAbū al-Qāsim. *ʾAkhbar al-Nisaʾ fī Kitāb al-ʾaghānī*. Beirut: Dār al-Kutub al-ʾilmiya, 1971.

al-Iṣfahānī, ʾAbū Nuʿaym ʾAḥmad b. ʿAbd Allāh. *Dalāʾil al-nubuwwa*. Beirut: Dār al-Nafāʾis, 1986.

al-Iṣfahānī, ʿAbd al-Ḥasan b. ʾAḥmad. *Kitāb al-Bulhān* (MS. Bodl. Or. 133). Oxford, the Bodleian Library, 14th century AD.

Izutsu, Toshihiko. *God and Man in the Qur'an: Semantics of the Qur'anic Weltanshauung*. Pelting Jaya: Islamic Book Trust, 2002.

Izutsu, Toshihiko. "Revelations as Linguistic Concept in Islam, Studies in Medieval Thought." *Journal of the Japanese Society of Medieval Philosophy* 5 (1962): 122–67.

Izutsu, Toshihiko. *The Concept of Belief in Islamic Theology*. Pelting Jaya: Islamic Book Trust, 2001.

Izutsu, Toshihiko. "The Theophanic Ego in Sufism: An Analysis of the Sufi Psychology of Najm al-Din Kubra." *Sophia Perennis* 4 (1978): 23–42.

al-Jāḥiẓ, ʾAbū ʿUthman ʿAmr. *Kitāb al-Ḥayawān*. 7 vols. Edited by ʿA. M. Ibn. Hārūn. Cairo: Muṣṭafā al-Bābī al-Ḥalabī, 1958.

Jausen, Antonin. *Coutumes des Arabes au pays de Moab*. Paris: Maisonneuve, 1948.

Jawād, ʿAlī. *al-Mufaṣṣal fī tārīkh al-ʿarab qabla al-ʾislām*. 6 vols. Beirut: Avand Danesh Ltd., 2006.

al-Jawziyya, Ibn Qayyim Muḥammad. *al-Tafsīr al-qayyim*. Edited by Muḥammad Uways and Muḥammad Ḥāmid al-Fiqī. Beirut: Dar al-kutub al-ʿilmiyah, 1978.

al-Jayyānī, ʾAbū Ḥayyān. *Al-Baḥr al-muḥīṭ*, vol. 1. Riyadh: Maktabat al-Nashr al-Ḥadītha, 1960.

al-Jazwī, ʾAbī al-Faraj. *The Devil's Deceptions: A Complete Translation of the Classical Text* Talbīs Iblīs. Birmingham: Dār as-Sunnah, 2014.

Jeffery, Arthur. *The Foreign Vocabulary of the Qur'an*. Leiden: Brill, 2007.

al-Jīlānī, ʿAbd al-Qādir. *al-Ghunyā al-ṭālibī ṭarīq al-ḥaqq*. Cairo: Muṣṭafa al-Bābī al-Ḥalabī, 1956.

al-Jīllī, ʿAbd al-Karīm, *al-ʾInsān al-kāmil fī maʿarifa al-ʾawārikh wal-ʾawāʾil, Beirut: Dār al-Kutub al-ʾIlmiya*, 1971.

al-Jīllī, ʿAbd al-Karīm. *al-Insān al-kāmil*. Cairo: 1886.

Kabbani, Hisham. *Angels Unveiled: A Sufi Perspective*. Fenton: Islamic Supreme Council of America, 2011.

Kant, Immanuel. *Groundwork of the Metaphysics of Morals*. Translated by H. J. Paton. London: Harper Torchbooks, 1956.

Katajala-Peltomaa, Sarii. *Demonic Possession and Lived Religion in Later Medieval Europe*. Oxford: Oxford University Press, 2020.

al-Karmī, Marʿī Ibn Yūsuf al-Ḥanbalī. *Shifāʾ al-Ṣudūr fī Ziyārat al-Mashāhid wa al-Qubūr*. Mecca: Maktabat Narrār Muṣṭafā al-Bāz, 1998.

al-Kāshāni, Muḥammad b. Murtaḍā. *Tafsīr al-ṣāfī*. Beirut: al-Muʾassasa al-ʿalamī lil-maṭbūʿāt, 1982.

al-Kāshānī, ʿAbd al-Razzāq. *Tafsīr al-Kāshānī*, vol. 1. Translated by Feras Hamza. Louisville, KY: Fons Vitae, 2017.

Keating, Geoffrey. *The History of Ireland: From the Earliest Period to the English Invasion*. New York: James B. Kirker, 1866.

Kennedy, Philip. "Some Demon Muse: Structure and Allusion in al-Hamadhānī's *Maqāma Iblīsiyya*." *Arabic and Middle Eastern Literature* 1 (1999): 115–35.

Khalil, Atif. "White Death: Ibn al-ʿArabī on the Trials and Virtues of Hunger and Fasting." *Journal of the American Oriental Society* 141 (2021): 577–86.

Khan, Hazrat Inyat. *The Heart of Sufism*. Boston: Shambhala, 1999.

al-Kharrāz, ʾAbū Saʿīd. *Rasāil al-Kharrāz*. Baghdad: Maṭbaʿa al-majmaʿ al-ʿilmī al-ʿirāqī, 1967.

Kister, Meir. "Adam: A Study of Some Legends in Tafsīr and Ḥadīth Literature." *Israel Oriental Studies* 13 (1993): 113–74.

Kitāb al-Mandal al-Sulaymānī: Magical Prayers and Amulets to Control Jinn (MS Ar.286). Addis Ababa: Institute of Ethiopian Studies, c. 1900.

Kitāb al-Mandal al-Sulaymanī (MS 2774) Saana: Dār al-Makhṭūtāt, n.d.

Klar, M. O. "And We Cast upon His Throne a Mere Body." *Journal of Qur'anic Studies* 6 (2004): 103–26.

Knyush, Alexander. *Ibn Arabi in the Later Islamic Tradition*. Albany: State University of New York Press, 1999.

Krawietz, Brigit. "Ten Theses on Working with Jinn (Demons) in Islamic Studies." In *Studying the Near and Middle East at the Institute for Advanced Study, Princeton, 1935–2018*, edited by Sabine Schmidtke, 331–37. Piscataway, NJ: Gorgias Press, 2018.

Kubrā, Najm al-Dīn. *Fawā'iḥ al-jamāl wa-fawātiḥ al-jalāl*. Edited by Fritz Meier. Wiesbaden: Steiner, 1957.

Kurk, Remke. "Elusife Giraffes: Ibn 'Abi l-Ḥawāfir's Badā'iʿ al-Akwān and Other Animal Books." In *Arab Painting: Text and Image in Illustrated Arabic Manuscripts*, edited by Anna Contadini, 49–64. Leiden: Brill, 2008.

Lane, Edward William. *An Account of the Manners and Customs of the Modern Egyptians: Written in Egypt During the Years 1833–35*, vols. 1–2. London: Charles Knight & Co., 1836.

al-Lamaṭī, 'Aḥmad b. al-Mubārak. *Al-Dhahab al-Ibrīz min Kalām Sayyidī ʿAbd al-ʿAzīz al-Dabbāgh: Pure Gold from the Words of Sayyidī ʿAbd al-ʿAzīz al-Dabbāgh*. Edited and translated by John O'Kane and Bernd Radtke. Leiden: Brill, 2007.

Laughlin. Vivian. "A Brief Overview of al Jinn within Islamic Cosmology and Religiosity." *Journal of Adventist Mission Studies* 11 (2015): 67–78.

Lawrence, Bruce. *The Qur'an: A Biography*. New York: Grove Press, 2007.

Leaman, Oliver. *The Qur'an: A Philosophical Guide*. London: Bloomsbury, 2016.

Le Coq, Albert. *Volkskundliches aus Ost-Turkistan*. Berlin: D. Reimer, 1916.

Liber XXIV Philosophorum: Book of the XXIV Philosophers, editio minima. London: Matheson Trust, 2015.

Liebling, Robert. *Legends of the Fire Spirits: Jinn and Genies from Arabia to Zanzibar*. Berkeley, CA: Counterpoint, 2010.

Lory, Pierre. "Sexual Intercourse between Humans and Demons in the Islamic Tradition." In *Hidden Intercourse: Eros and Sexuality in the History of Western Esotericism*, edited by Wouter J. Hanergaaf and Jeffrey Kripal, 49–64. Leiden: Brill, 2008.

MacDonald, Duncan. "Ḏjinn." In *Encyclopedia of Islam*, 2nd ed. Edited by P. Bearman, T. Bianquis, C. E. Bosworth, E. van Donzel, and W. P. Heinrichs. http://dx.doi.org/10.1163/1573-3912_islam_COM_0191.

MacDonald, Duncan. "G͟hūl." In *Encyclopaedia of Islam*, 1st ed. Edited by M. Th. Houtsma, T. W. Arnold, R. Basset, and R. Hartmann. http://dx.doi.org/10.1163/2214-871X_ei1_SIM_2495.

MacDonald, Duncan. "Ḳarīn." In *Encyclopaedia of Islam*, 2nd ed. Edited by P. Bearman, Th. Bianquis, C. E. Bosworth, E. van Donzel, and W. P. Heinrichs. http://dx.doi.org/10.1163/1573-3912_islam_SIM_3933.

MacDonald, Duncan. *Religious Attitude and Life in Islam*. Chicago: University of Chicago Press, 1909.

Majmūʿ min kull fann yabḥarh annahu jawāhir al-kalām min shiʿr wa-mithl wa-qawā'id min kull fāḍil wa-ākhir al-kitāb asmā'wa-adʿiyāt min kull shai' (MS Staatsbibliothek zu Berlin 174 Bl). Berlin: Staatsbibliothek zu Berlin, 1783.

al-Masʿūdī, ʾAbū al-Ḥasan ʿAlī, *ʾAkhbār al-zamān*, vol. 1. Beirut: Dār al-ʾAndalus lil-Ṭibāʿa wa-al-Nash, 1996.

al-Masʿūdī, ʾAbū al-Ḥasan ʿAlī. *Murūj al-Dhahab wa-Maʿādin al-Jawhar*, vol. 2. Edited by Charles Pellat. Beirut: 1965.

al-Māturīdī, ʾAbū Manṣūr. *Kitāb al-Tawḥīd*. Beirut: Dar El-Machreq Éditeurs, 1970.

Al-Mayhānī, Muḥammad b. al-Munawwar. *ʾAsrār al-tawḥīd*. Tehran: Amīr Kabīr, 1914.

al-Maʿarrī, ʾAbū al-ʿAlāʾ. *Risālat al-ghufrān*. Edited by Aisha al-Rahman. Cairo: Dār al-maʿarif, 1950.

Meier, Fritz. "Some Aspects of Inspiration by Demons in Islam." In *The Dream and Human Societies*, edited by G. E. von Grunebaum and Roger Caillois, 421–31. Berkeley: University of California Press, 1966.

Meier, Fritz. "Ein arabischer bet-ruf." In *Bausteine I: Ausgewählte Aufsätze zur Islamwissenschaft*, edited by Fritz Meier, 581–628. Stuttgart: Franz Steiner Verlag, 1992.

Miller, Jeanne. "More Than the Sum of Its Parts: Animal Categories and Accretive Logic in Volume One of al-Jāḥiẓ's Kitāb al-Ḥayawān." PhD diss., New York University, 2013.

Moleiro, Manuel, ed. *The Book of Felicity*. Barcelona: M. Moleiro Editor, S.A., 2007.

Mollenauer, Lynn. *Strange Revelations: Magic, Poison, and Sacrilege in Louis XIV's France*. University Park: Penn State University Press, 2007.

Moreman, Christopher. "Rehabilitating the Spirituality of Pre-Islamic Arabia: On the Importance of the Kahin, the Jinn, and the Tribal Ancestral Cult." *Journal of Religious Philosophy* 41 (2016): 1–21.

Morisson, Elizabeth, ed. *The Book of Beasts: The Bestiary in the Medieval World*. Los Angeles: J. Paul Getty Museum, 2019.

Morris, James Winston. "Listening for God: Prayer and the Heart in the al-Futūḥāt." https://ibnarabisociety.org/listening-for-god-part-3-james-morris/. Accessed online on 14. May.

Morris, James Winston. *The Reflective Heart: Discovering Spiritual Intelligence in Ibn 'Arabi's Meccan Illuminations*. Louisville, KY: Fons Vitae, 2005.

Murata, Sachiko. "Angels." In *Islamic Spirituality, the Foundations*, edited by S. H. Nasr, 324–45. New York: Crossroad, 1987.

Murata, Sachiko. *Chinese Gleams of Sufi Lights: Wang Tai-yü' s Great Learning of the Pure and Real and Liu Chih's Displaying the Concealment of the Real Realm*. Albany: State University of New York Press, 2000.

Murata, Sachiko. "Good and Evil in Islamic Neoconfucianism." In *The Passions of the Soul in the Metamorphosis of Becoming*, edited by Anna-Teresa Tymieniecka, 125–34. London: Springer, 2003.

Murata, Sachiko. "Masculine-Feminine Complemetarity in the Spiritual Psychology of Islam." *Islamic Quarterly* 33 (1989): 165–86.

Murata, Sachiko. "Reading Islamic Texts from the Standpoint of Ying and Yang." In *Islam and Confucianism. A Civilizational Dialogue,* edited by Osman Bakar, 95–117. Kuala Lumpur: University of Malaya Press, 1997.

Murata, Sachiko. *Tao of Islam: A Sourcebook on Gender Relationships in Islamic Thought*. Albany: State University of New York Press, 1992.

al-Nābulsī, ʿAbd al-Ghanī. *Hadiyyat al-Murād fī Sharḥ Hadiyyat Ibn al-ʿImad*. Edited by Abd al-Razzaq Halabi and Abd al-Rahman b. Muhammad Imadi. Limassol: Al-Jaffan & al-Jabi, 1994.

Nasr, Seyyed Hossein. "God Is the Absolute Reality and All Creation His Tajallī (Teophany)." In *Wiley Blackwell Companion to Religion and Ecology,* edited by John Hart, 3–11. London: John Wiley and Sons, 2017.

Nasr, Seyyed Hossein. "Happiness and the Attainment of Happiness." *Journal of Law and Religon* 29 (2014): 76–91.

Nasr, Seyyed Hossein. *The Need for a Sacred Science*. Albany: State University of New York Press, 1993.

Nasr, Seyyed Hossein. *Islamic Spirituality: Foundations*. London: Crossroads, 1997.

Nasr, Seyyed Hossein. *The Garden of Truth: The Vision and Promise of Sufism, Islam's Mystical Tradition*. New York: HarperCollins, 2007.

Nasser, Lana. "The Jinn: Companion in the Realm of Dreams and Imagination." In *Dreaming in Christianity and Islam: Culture, Conflict and Creativity,* edited by Karl Bulkeley, Kate Adams, and Patricia M. Davis, 143–55. London: Rutgers University Press, 2005.

Nathan, Tobie. *Nous ne sommes pas seuls au monde: Les enjeux de l'ethnopsychiatrie*. Paris: Points, 2001.

Nawfal, ʿAbdul Rāziq. *ʿĀlam al-jinn wal-malāʾik.* Cairo: 1968.

Nicholson, Reynold. *Studies in Islamic Mysticism*. London: Routlege, 1921.

Nicholson, Reynold. *The Mystics of Islam*. Bloomington, IN: World Wisdom Inc., 2002.

al-Niffari, *Trois auvres inédites de mystiques musulmans.* Beirut: Dār almashriq, 1973.

Noble, Michael. *Philosophizing the Occult: Avicennan Psychology and "The Hidden Secret" of Fakhr al-Dīn al-Rāzī*. Berlin: De Gruyter, 2021.

Nokso-Koivito, Inka. "Microcosm-Macrocosm Analogy in Rasāʾil Ikhwān aṣ-Ṣafāʾ and Certain Related Texts." PhD diss., University of Helsinki, 2014.

Nünlist, Tobias. "Demonology in Islam." In *The History of Evil in the Medieval Age 450–1450 CE Volume II,* edited by Andrew Pinsent, 152–70. London: Routlege, 2018.

Nünlist, Tobias. "Von Berittenen und Gerittenen: Aspekte des Dämonenglaubens im Bereich des Islams." *Asiatische Studien / Études Asiatiques* 1 (2011): 145–72.

Nünlist, Tobias. *Dämonenglaube im Islam*. Berlin: De Gruyter, 2015.

Olomi, Ali. "Jinn in the Qur'an." In *The Routledge Companion to the Qur'an*, edited by George Archer, Maria M. Dakake, and Daniel A. Madigan, 145–52. London: Routlege, 2021.

Omsby, Eric. *Between Reason and Revelation: Twin Wisdoms Reconciled: An Annotated English Translation of Nāṣir-i Khusraw's Kitāb al-Jāmiʿ al-ḥikmatayn*. London: I. B. Tauris, 2012.

Ossa-Richardson, Anthony. "Possession or Insanity? Two Views from the Victorian Lunatic Asylum." *Journal of the History of Ideas* 74 (2013): 553–75.

Padwick, Constance. "Notes on the Jinn and the Ghoul in the Peasant Mind of Lower Egypt." *Bulletin of the School of Oriental Studies* 3 (1924): 421–46.

Papas, Alexandre. "Dog of God: Animality and Wildness among Dervishes." In *Islamic Alternatives: Non-mainstream Religion in Persianate Societies*, edited by Shahrokh Raei, 121–38. Wiesbaden: Harrasowitz Verlag, 2017.

Parman, Talat. "The Demon as Human Double." In *I, Mehmed Siyah Kalem, Master of Humans and Demons*, edited by Yayına Hazırlayan, 129–34. Ankara: Kültür ve Turizm Bakanlığı, 2004.

Partridge, Esmé. *Al-Kindi's Theory of Magical Arts. A Commentary of al-Kindi's Treatise "On Rays."* London: 2018.

Perdigon, Sylvian. "Bleeding Dreams: Miscarriage and the Bindings of the Unborn in the Palestinian Refugee Community of Tyre, South Lebanon." In *Living and Dying in the Contemporary World*, edited by Veena Das and Clara Han, 142–58. Berkeley: University of California Press, 2015.

Philips, Abu Ameenah Bilal. *Ibn Taymiyah's Essay on the Jinn*. Riyadh: International Islamic Publishing House, 1989.

Philips, Abu Ameenah Bilal. *The Exorcist Tradition in Islam*. Birmingham: Al-Hidaayah Publishing & Distribution, 2008.

Picatrix: A Medieval Treatise on Astral Magic. Translated by Dan Attrell and David Porreca. University Park: Penn State University Press, 2019.

Pinault, David. *The Shiites: Ritual and Popular Piety in a Muslim Community*. London: Bloomsbury, 1992.

Plato. *The Dialogues of Plato*, vol. 3. Oxford: Clarendon Press, 1871.

Porter, Venetia. "The Use of the Arabic Script in Magic." *Proceedings of the Seminar for Arabian Studies* 40 (2010): 131–40.

Powers, John. *Introduction to Tibetan Buddhism: A Revised Edition*. Ithaca, NY: Snow Lion, 2007.

Probert, Garcia. "Exploring the Life of Amulets in Palestine: From Healing and Protective Remedies to the Tawfik Canaan Collection of Palestinian Amulets." PhD diss., University of Leiden, 2021.

al-Qayṣarī, Dāʾūd. *Muqaddima. Foundations of Islamic Mysticism: Qayṣarī's Introduction to Ibn ʿArabī's Fuṣūṣ al-ḥikam: A Parallel English-Arabic Text*. Edited and Translated by Mukhtar Ali. New York: Spiritual Alchemy Press, 2012.

al-Qazwīnī, ʾAbū Yaḥyā Zakariyyāʾ. *ʿAjāʾib al-makhlūqāt wa-gharāʾib al-mawjūdāt*. Die Wunder des Himmels und der Erde. Translated by Alma Giese. Munich: Edition Erdmann, 2004.

al-Qazwīnī, ʾAbū Yaḥyā Zakariyyāʾ. *ʿAjāʾib al-makhlūqāt wa-gharāʾib al-mawjūdāt* (MS Garrett no. 82G). Princeton, NJ: Princeton University Library, 1822.

al-Qazwīnī, ʾAbū Yaḥyā Zakariyyāʾ. *ʿAjāʾib al-makhlūqāt wa-gharāʾib al-mawjūdāt* (St Andrews ms32(0)). Edinburgh: University of St Andrews Library Special Collections, c. 1203–1283.

al-Qurṭubī, Muḥammad b. ʾAḥmad. *Tafsīr al-Qurṭubī*. Cairo: Dār al-Shaʿab, 1925.

al-Qushayrī, ʿAbd al-Karīm. *Epistle on Sufism: Al-Risala Al-qushayriyya Fi ʿilm Al-tasawwuf Billingual Edition*. 2 vols. Edited and translated by Alexander D. Knysh. London: Garnet, 2007.

Racius, Edgunas. "Islamic Exegeses of the Jinn—Their Origin, Kinds and Substance and Their Relation to Other Beings." *Studia Orientalia Electronica* 85 (2014): 127–38.

Rašić, Dunja. *The Written World of God: The Cosmic Script and the Art of Ibn ʿArabī*. Oxford: Anqa, 2021.

al-Rawi, Ahmed. "The Arabic Ghoul and Its Western Transformation." *Folklore* 120 (2009): 292–99.

al-Rāzī, Fakhr al-Dīn. *Sharḥ al-ʾishārāt wal-tanbīhāt*. Tehran: Anjoman-i Āthār-i wa Mafākhir-i Farhangī, 2005.

al-Rāzī, Najm al-Dīn. *Mirṣād al-ʿibād min al-mabdaʾ ʿila al-maʿād*. In *The Path of God's Bondsmen from Origin to Return: A Sufi Compendium*. Edited and Translated by Hamid Algar. Delmar: Caravan Books, 1982.

al-Rāzī, ʾAbū Bakr Muḥammad. *Rasāʾil al-falsafiyya*. Edited by Paul Kraus. Cairo: 1939.

Regourd, Anne. "Images de djinns et exorcisme dans le Mandal al-Sulaymānī." In *Images et magie: Picatrix entre Orient et Occident*, edited by Jean Patrice Boudet, Anna Caiozzo, and Nicolas Weill-Parot, 253–94. Paris: Honoré Champion Éditeur, 2011.

Ridgeon, Lloyd. "A Sufi Perspective of Evil." *Journal of the British Institute of Persian Studies* 36 (1998): 113–22.

Roberts, Avens. "The Image of the Devil in C. G. Jung's Psychology." *Journal of Religion and Health* 16 (1977): 196–222.

Ronis, Sara. *The Demons in the Details: Demonic Discourse and Rabbinic Culture in Late Antique Babylonia.* Oakland: University of California Press, 2022.

Rouget, Gilbert. *Music and Trance: A Theory on the Relations between Music and Possession.* Chicago: University of Chicago Press, 1985.

Rubin, Uri. *The Eye of the Beholder: The Life of Muḥammad as Viewed by the Early Muslims—A Textual Analysis*. Princeton, NJ: The Darwin Press, 1995.

Rührdanz, Karin. "Ein Illustrierter iatromagischer Text als Bestandteil von ʿAjāʾib al-makhlūqāt-Handschriften: vom Staunen über die Wunder der Schöpfung zur Magischen Praxis." *TUBA* 26 (2002): 183–93.

Rustom, Mohammed. "Qur'anic Exegesis in the Later Islamic Philosophy: Mullā Ṣadrā's *Tafṣīr Sūrat al-Fātiḥa*." PhD diss., University of Toronto, 2009.

Rustom, Muhammad, and Muhammad Faruque. *From the Divine to the Human: Contemporary Islamic Thinkers on Evil, Suffering, and the Global Pandemic.* London: Routlege, 2023.

Sabzawārī, Ismaʿīl b. Muḥammad. *Kitāb al-majmaʿ al-nūrayn mashhūr ba ḥayawān*. Teheran: Kitābfurūshī-i ʿIlmiyya-i islāmiyya, n.d.

Sabzvārī, Muḥammad ʿAlī. *Tuḥfah Yi-ʿAbbāsī: The Golden Chain of Sufism in Shī'ite Islam*. Translated by Muhammad. H. Fagfoory. Lanham, MD: University Press of America, 2007.

al-Safi, Ahmed. *Traditional Sudanese Medicine*. Khartoum: Azza House, 2007.

Saif, Liana. "Between Medicine and Magic: Spiritual Aetiology and Therapeutics in Medieval Islam." In *Demons and Illness from Antiquity to the Early Modern Period,* edited by Siam Bhayro, 313–38. Leiden: Brill, 2017.

Saniotis, Arthur. "Sacred Worlds: An Analysis of Mystical Mastery of North Indian Faqirs." PhD thesis, Adelaide University, 2002.

al-Sarāī, Maḥmud b. ʿAlī. *Nahj al-farādīs* (14/2014). Copenhagen: The C. L. David Foundation and Collection, The David Collection, c. 1465.

Schaefer, Karl. *Enigmatic Charms: Medieval Arabic Block Printed Amulets in American and European Libraries and Museums*. Leiden: Brill, 2006.

Schimmel, Annemarie. *Deciphering the Signs of God.* New York: Sunny Press, 1994.

Schimmel, Annemarie. *Mystical Dimensions of Islam*. Chappel Hill: University of North Carolina Press, 1975.

Scholem, Gershom. "Some Sources of Jewish-Arabic Demonology." *Journal of Jewish Studies* 16 (1965), 1–13.

Schöller, Gregor. *The Oral and the Written in the Early Islam*. London: Routlege, 2006.

Schöller, Marco. "His Master's Voice: Gespräche mit Dschinnen im heutigen Ägypten." *Die Welt des Islams New Series* 41 (2001): 32–71.

Sells, Michael *Approaching the Qur'an: The Early Revelations*. London: White Cloud Press, 2007.

Sells, Michael. "Bānat Suʿād: Translation and Introduction." *Journal of Arabic Literature* 21 (1990): 140–54.

Sells, Michael. "Bewildered Tongue: The Semantics of Mystical Union in Islam." In *Mystical Union in Judaism, Christianity and Islam*, edited by Moshe Idel, 87–124. New York: Continuum, 1999.

Senger, Gerda. *Women and Demons: Cult Healing in Islamic Egypt*. Leiden: Brill, 2003.

Shadrach, Nineveh. *The Book of the Deadly Names*. Vancouver: Ishtar, 2007.

Shaffer, Matt. *Djinns, Stars and Warriors: Mandinka Legends from Pakao, Senegal*. Leiden: Brill, 2003.

Shah, Idries. *The Commanding Self*. London: Idries Shah Foundation, 2019.

al-Shamy, Hasan. "Belief Characters as Anthropomorphic Psychosocial Realities: The Egyptian Case." *al-Kitāb al-Sanawī li-ʿIlm al-Ijtimāʿ* 3 (1982): 1–14.

al-Shamy, Hasan. "Mental Health in Traditional Culture: A Study of Preventive and Therapeutic Folk Practices in Egypt." *Catalyst* 6 (1972): 13–28.

al-Shamy, Hasan. "Twins/Zwillinge: A Broader View: A Contribution to Stith Thompson's Incomplete Motif System—a Case of the Continuation of Pseudoscientific Fallacies." *Humanities* 10 (2020): 1–28.

al-Shamy, Hasan. *Religion among the Folk in Egypt*. Westport: Praeger, 2009.

al-Sharānī, ʿAbd al-Wahhāb. *Lawāqiḥ al-ʾanwār fī ṭabaqāt al-ʾakhyār*. Beirut: Dār al-Fikr, 1954.

al-Sharnūbī, ʿAbd al-Majīd *Sharḥ Tāʾiyyat al-sulūk ilā malik al-mulūk*. Beirut: al-Maktaba al-ʿAṣriyya, 2011.

Shaw, Wendy. *What is Islamic Art? Between Religion and Perception*. Cambridge: Cambridge University Press, 2019.

Shazad, Qaiser. "Ibn 'Arabī's Metaphysics of the Human Body." *Islamic Studies* 46 (2007): 499–525.

Sherman Jackson, *Islam and the Problem of Black Suffering*. Oxford: Oxford University Press, 2009.

al-Shibilī, Badr al-Dīn. *Kitāb ʾākām al-marjān fī ʾaḥkām al-jānn*. Edited by Badeen Edward. Beirut: Dār al-Fārābī, 2017.

Shīrāzī, Ṣadr al-Dīn. *Divine Manifestations: Concerning the Secrets of the Perfecting Sciences*. London: Islamic College for Advanced Studies, 2010.

al-Sīnūbī, Nābī b. Turkhan. *Ḥayāt al-qulūb fī al-maw ʿiza* (Ms. R-5114). Sarajevo: Gazi Husrev-beg Library, 1877.

Smith, William Robert. *Lectures on the Religion of the Semites*. New York: Meridian Library, 1927.

Steingass, Francis Joseph. *A Comprehensive Persian-English Dictionary, Including the Arabic Words and Phrases to Be Met with in Persian Literature*. London: Routledge, 1892.

Stephan, Stephan H. "Lunacy in Palestine Folklore," *Journal of the Palestine Oriental Society* 5 (1925): 1–16.

Stroumsa, Sarah. *Freethinkers in Medieval Islam: Ibn Al-Rawāndī, Abū Bakr Al-Rāzī and Their Impact on Islamic Thought*. Leiden: Brill, 1999.

Suhrawardī, Shahāb ad-Dīn. *The Philosophy of Illumination: A New Critical Edition of the Text of Ḥikmat al-Ishrāq with English Translation, Noted, Commentary and Introduction by John Walbridge and Hossein Ziai*. Provo, UT: Brigham Young University Press, 1999.

Suhrawardī, Shahāb ad-Dīn. *Treatises of Shihabuddin Yahya al-Shuhrawardi*. London: Octagon Press, 1982.

al-Suyūṭī, Jalāl al-Dīn. *al-Ṭibb al-nabī or Medicine of the Prophet*. Translated by Cyril Elgood. *Osiris* 14 (1962): 33–192.

al-Suyūṭī, Jalāl al-Dīn. *Laqṭ al-marjān fī ʿaḥkām al-jānn*. Cairo: Maktaba al-Turāth al-Islāmī, 1991.

al-Ṭabarī, Muḥammad b. Jarīr. *Ṭafsīr al-Tabarī: Jāmiʿ al-bayān ʿan taʾwīl āy al-Qurʾān*. Cairo: Maṭbaʿat al-yamanīya, 1903.

al-Ṭabarī, ʾAbū Jaʿfar Muḥammad. *The History of al-Ṭabarī Volume 1: General Introduction and From the Creation to the Flood*. Translated by Franz Rosenthal. Albany: State University of New York Press, 1989.

Ṭabasī, Muḥammad b. ʾAḥmad. *al-Shāmil fī al-bahr al-kāmil fī al-dawr al-ʿāmil fī ʾuṣūl al-taʿzīm wa-qawāʿid al-tanjīm* (MS Princeton 160). Princeton, NJ: Princeton University Library, c. 16th–17th century.

al-Ṭabāṭabāʾī, Muḥammad. *al-Makhluqāt al-khafiya fī al-Qurʾān*. Beirut: Dār al-ṣafwān, 1995.

at-Tādilī, Ibn al-Zayyāt Yūsuf. *al-Tashawwuf ilā rijāl at-taṣawwuf*. Rabat: Maṭbūʿāt Ifrīqiyā al-Shimāliyya al-Fanniyya, 1958.

al-Tahanāwī, Muhammad b. ʿAlī. *Mawsūʿat istilāḥāt al-ʿulūm al-islāmiya*. Beirut: Dār al-khayyāt, 1969.

Takeshita, Masataka. "Ibn ʿArabi's Theory of the Perfect Man and Its Place in the History of Islamic Thought." PhD diss., University of Chicago, 1986.

Tales of the Marvelous, News of the Strange. Translated by Robert Irwin, Malcom C. Lyons, and Coralie Bickford-Smith. London: Penguin Classics, 2014.

Taneja, Anand Vivek. *Jinneology: Time, Islam, and Ecological Thought in the Medieval Ruins of Delhi*. Stanford, CA: Stanford University Press, 2017.

Tehrani, Husayn Husayni. *Lubb al-Lubb: A Short Treatise on Wayfaring*. London: Createspace Publishing Platform, 2014.

Teixidor, Javier. *The Pantheon of Palmyra*. Leiden: Brill, 1979.

Temple, Richard Carnac, ed. *North Indian Notes and Queries Volumes 1–3*. Allahabad: Pioneer Press, 1891.

Tengour, Esma. "Représentations et croyances dans l'Arabie du VIIe siècle." *Open Editions Journals* 53 (2011), accessed January 15, 2022. https://journals.openedition.org/insaniyat/12994.

Teuma, Edmund. "The Nature of Iblis in the Qur'an, as Interpreted by the Commentators." *Melita Theologica* 31 (1980): 10–21.

Thomas, Keith. *Religion and the Decline of Magic: Studies in Popular Beliefs in Sixteenth- and Seventeenth-Century England*. London: Penguin, 1991.

al-Tilimsānī, Ibn al-Ḥājj. *Kitāb shumūs al-ʾanwār wa-kunūz al-ʾasrār al-kubrā*. Cairo: Maktaba wa-maṭbaʿat al- Ḥājj ʿAbbās b. ʿAbd al-Salām, n.d.

Tremearne, Arthur. *The Ban of the Bori: Demons and Demon-Dancing in West and North Africa*. London: Heath, Cranton & Ouseley Ltd., 1914.

Trimingham, J. Spencer. *Islam in the Sudan*. Oxford: Oxford University Press, 1949.

Tritton, A. S. "Spirits and Demons in Arabia." *Journal of the Royal Asiatic Society of Great Britain and Ireland* 4 (1934): 715–27.

al-Tūnisī, Muḥammad. *In Darfur: An Account of the Sultanate and Its People: A Bilingual Arabic Edition*. Edited and translated by Humphrey Davies and R. S. O'Fahey. New York: New York University Press, 2018.

Ṭūsī, Muḥammad b. Maḥmūd. *ʿAjāyib-nāma: ʿAjāʾib al-makhlūqāt wa gharāʾib al-mawjūdāt*. Tehran: Nashr-i Markaz, 1996.

Ṭūsī, Muḥammad b. Maḥmūd. *ʿAjāʾib al-makhlūqāt wa gharāʾib al-mawjūdāt* (MS Sam Fogg 14229). London: Sam Fogg Gallery, The Art of the Middle Ages, 1704.

Ṭūsī, Muḥammad b. Maḥmūd. *ʿAjāʾib al-makhlūqāt wa gharāʾib al-mawjūdāt* (Walters Ms. 593). Palo Alto, CA: Stanford University Library, 1501.

Ṭūsī, Muḥammad b. al-Ḥasan. *Al-ʾIstibṣār fī mā ʾukhtulif min al-ʾakhbār*, vol. 2. Tehran: Dār al-kutub al-Islamiyya, 1970.

al-Tustarī, Sahl. *Tafsīr al-Tustarī: The Great Commentary of the Holy Qur'an*. Edited and translated by Anabel Keeler and Ali Keeler. Louisville, KY: Fons Vitae, 2011.

Upton, Charles. *Vectors of Counter-Initiation: The Course and Destiny of Inverted Spirituality*. New York: Sophia Perennis, 2012.

Valiuddin, M. *Contemplative Disciplines in Sufism.* Hague: East-West Publications, 1980.

Van der Lught, Mara. *Dark Matters: Pessimism and the Problem of Suffering.* Princeton, NJ: Princeton University Press, 2021.

Van Vloten, Gerlof. "Dämonen, Geister und Zauber bei den alten Arabern." *Wiener Zeitschrift für die Kunde des Morgenlandes* 8 (1894): 59–73.

Virani, Shafijique. *The Ismailis in the Middle Ages: A History of Survival, a Search for Salvation.* New York: Oxford University Press, 2007.

Viré, F., "Ḳird." In *Encyclopaedia of Islam,* 2nd ed. Edited by P. Bearman, Th. Bianquis, C. E. Bosworth, E. van Donzel, and W. P. Heinrichs. Accessed January 14, 2022. http://dx.doi.org/10.1163/1573-3912_islam_SIM_4386.

Von Franz, Marie Louise. "Daimons and the Inner Companion." In *Angels and Mortals: Their Co-Creative Power,* edited by Maria Parisen. London: Quest Book the Theosophical Publishing House, 1990.

Von Franz, Marie Louise. *Projection and Re-Collection in Jungian Psychology: Reflections of the Soul.* Chicago: Open Court Publishing Company, 1985.

Von Franz, MarieLouise. *Spiegelungen der Seele.* Küsnacht: Stiftung für Jungische Psychologie, 2005.

Waardenburg, Jacques. "Changes of Belief in Spiritual Beings, Prophethood and the Rise of Islam." In *Struggles of God,* edited by Hans Kippenberg, 259–90. Berlin: De Gruyter, 1984.

Waardengurg, Jacques. *Islam. Historical, Social and Political Perspectives.* Berlin: DeGruyter, 2002.

Walad, Bahāʾ al-Dīn Muḥammad. *Walad-nāmeh.* Tehran: 1937.

Walker, Daniel. *Spiritual and Demonic Magic.* University Park, PA: Penn State University Press, 2000.

al-Wansharīsī, Aḥmad b. Yaḥyā. *al-Miʿyār al-muʿrib wal-jāmiʿ al-mughrib ʿan fatāwī ahl Ifrīqiya wal-Andalus wal-Maghrib.* Edited by Muḥammad Ḥajjī. Beirut: Dār al-gharb al-islāmī, 1981.

Wedel, Theodore. *Astrology in the Middle Ages.* New York: Dover, 2005.

Welch, Alford. "Allah and Other Supernatural Beings." *Journal of the American Academy of Religion* 47 (1979): 733–53.

Wellhausen, Julius. *Reste arabischen Hidentums.* Berlin: G. Reimer, 1897.

Werth, Megan. *Spirit possession.* "Exploring the Role of Textual Transmission." PhD diss., Wright State University, 2012.

Westermarck, Edward. "The Nature of the Arab Ginn, Illustrated by the Present Beliefs of the People of Morocco," *Journal of the Anthropological Institute of Great Britain and Ireland* 24 (1899): 252–69.

Westermarck, Edward. *Ritual and Belief in Morocco,* vol. 1. London: Macmillan and Co., 1926.

Wheeler, Brannon. *Mecca and Eden: Rituals, Relics and Territory in Islam.* Chicago: University of Chicago Press, 2006.
Winkel, Eric. *Changes. The Third of the Six Sections of the Openings Revealed in Makkah.* London: Futuhat Project, 2017.
Winkler, Heinrich. *Salomo und die Ḳarīna.* Stuttgart: Verlag von W. Kohlhammer, 1931.
Wójcik-Owczarek, Katarzyna. "A Few Words on the Sisinnios-type of Gello Story." Scripta.
Yāqūt, Shihāb al-Dīn. *Muʿjam al-buldān.* Beirut: Dār ṣādr, n.d.
Yasien, Mohamed. "The Cosmology of Ikhwān al-Ṣafā', Miskawayh and al-Iṣfahānī," *Islamic Studies* 34 (2000): 657–79.
Yazaki, Saeko. *Islamic Mysticism and Abu Talib Al-Makki: The Role of the Heart.* London: Routlege, 2012.
Yılmaz, Hüseyin. *Caliphate Redefined: The Mystical Turn in Ottoman Political Thought.* Princeton, NJ: Princeton University Press, 2018.
Young, Peter. "Concerning the Station of Purity." *Journal of the Muhyiddin Ibn Arabi Society* 8 (1989): 33–41.
Yousef, Muhammed Haj. *Ibn ʿArabī—Time and Cosmology.* London: Routlege, 2008.
Zadeh, Travis. "Commanding Demons and Jinn: The Sorcerer in Early Islamic Thought." In *No Tapping around Philology: A Festschrift in Honor of Wheeler McIntosh Thackston Jr.'s 70th Birthday,* edited by Alireza Korangy and Dan Sheffield, 131–60. Wiesbaden: Harrassowitz Verlag, 2014.
Zadeh, Travis. "Magic, Marvel and Miracle in Early Islamic Thought." In *The Cambridge History of Magic and Witchcraft in the West,* edited by David J. Collins, 235–67. Cambridge: Cambridge University Press, 2015.
Zadeh, Travis. *Wonders and Rarities. The Marvelous Book that Traveled the World and Mapped the Cosmos.* Cambridge: Harvard University Press, 2023.
Zādih, Tash Kubrī. *Miftāḥ as-saʿāda wa-miṣbāḥ al-siyāda,* vol. 1. Cairo: Dār al-kutub, 1968.
al-Zain, Amira. "The Evolution of the Concept of Jinn from Pre-Islam to Islam." PhD diss., Georgetown University 1995.
al-Zain, Amira. *Islam, Arabs and the Intelligible World of Jinn.* Syracuse, NY: Syracuse University Press, 2009.
al-Zamakhsarī, ʾAbū al-Qāsim. *ʾAsās al-balāgha.* Beirut: n.d, 1955.
Zaydān, ʿAbd al-Karīm. *Al-ʾAʾmāl al-kāmila.* Beirut: Dar al Jil, 1988.
Zbinden, Ernst. *Die Djinn des Islam und der altorientalische Geisterglaube.* Bern: Verlag Paul Haupt, 1953.
Zildic. "Friend and Foe: The Early Ottoman Reception of Ibn ʿArabī." PhD diss., University of California, 1991.

Zvi, Mark. "Dybbuk and Devekut in the Shivhe ha-Besht: Toward a Phenomenology of Madness in Early Hasidism." In *Spirit Possession in Judaism: Cases and Contexts From the Middle Ages to the Present,* edited by Matt Goldish, 257–305. Detroit, MI: Wayne State University Press, 2003.

Zwemer, Samuel. "The Familiar Spirit or Qarina." *The Muslim World* 6 (1916): 360–74.

Zwemer, Samuel. *The Influence of Animism on Islam: An Account of Popular Superstitions*. London: Central Board of Missions, 1920.

Zwettler, Michael. "A Mantic Manifesto: The Sura of 'The Poets' and the Qur'anic Foundations of Prophetic Authority." In *Poetry and Prophecy. The Beginnings of a Literary Tradition,* edited by James L. Kugel, 75–120. Ithaca, NY: Cornell University Press, 1990.

Index

ʾAbū Dibāj, 65, 116–17
ʾAbū Hadrāj (jinni), 72
ʾAbū Madyan, 125
ʾAbū Thumāmah, 56–57
Adam (prophet), 12, 18, 30–31, 34, 39, 41, 43, 45, 63, 67–68, 72, 75, 77, 103, 106–109, 112–13
ʾAḥmar, the Red King, 43, 67, 69–70, 147
air, 29, 32, 35–36, 38, 40, 42, 83, 86
Aisha (the wife of Muhammad), 32 100–101
Akbarian, 1, 15–16, 19, 20–22, 24–25, 27, 39–40, 45, 62–63, 71, 83, 87, 93, 96, 103, 127–28, 131n, 137n, 144n, 165n, 171n
Akbarian School, 1, 20, 88, 131n
Albasty, 135n
ʿAlī b. ʾAbī Ṭālib, 78, 105, 164n
ʿAmr al-Jinnī, 15, 87
ʿAnāq bt. Adam, 75
Angels, 2, 10, 22, 24, 28–32, 34–35, 39, 48, 51, 60, 67–68, 71, 74, 76, 86, 94, 95, 99, 101, 104, 108–10, 114, 116, 120, 124, 143n, 144n, 166n, 169n
anger (*ghaḍab*), 15, 88, 106, 122, 150, 166n, 161n, 165n
Aristotle, 3, 5, 86, 143n
al-Ashʿarī, Abū al-Ḥasan, 39
ʿAṭṭār, 43, 103, 127, 129, 144n, 147n, 159n, 172n
Avicenna (Ibn Sīnā), 29, 54, 150, 158, 165n
azif (jinn music), 74

Balʿām b. Bāʿūr, 118
Banū al-Qāwāʿid tribe, 65–66
Banu Mulayḥ tribe, 57
Banū Sāsān tribe, 57
Barqān, the king of jinn, 70
barzakh
  as border, 6
  as the intermediate World of Jabarut, 5–6, 127, 81, 113, 133n
  See Jabarut
Bashīr (jinni), 66
Bātin (the invisible, subtle), 6
Bilquis, the queen of Sheba, 63
al-Bīrūnī, Muḥammad b. ʾAḥmad, 5
al-Bistāmī, ʾAbū Yazīd, 123
Bīwarāsp, the Wise, 17, 70, 76
blood clot (*ʿalaqa*), 103–105, 164n
Bosnevi, Abdullah, 39, 63, 137
Brethren of Purity (*ʾIkhwān al-Ṣafā*), 17, 25, 30, 58, 68, 70, 138–40, 142, 146

al-Buqaʿiyy, ʾIbrahīm, 63

cats, 1, 14, 38
clarified causes (*al-ʿilal*), 100
Conquest of the City (*fatḥ al-madīna*), 82

al-Ḍaḥḥāk (sorcerer), 76
daimones (servants of *theoi*), 67–68, 154n
Dajjāl, the Antichrist, 63
al-Damīrī, Kamāl al-Dīn, 29, 31, 53, 63, 70, 141n, 147n
Descartes, René, 3
devil (*al-shayṭān*), 12, 15–16, 22, 28, 33–34, 39, 40–44, 52, 58, 68, 75, 87, 91, 93–94, 96–97, 99, 101, 103, 114, 120, 124, 144n, 148n, 150n, 161n, 173n
  Iblis, 2, 20, 22, 34, 38, 40–42, 51, 74–75, 77, 86, 91–92, 96–97, 100, 104–107, 109–11, 114, 116, 119–20, 122, 124–25, 128–29, 131n, 133n, 137n, 149n, 146n, 147n, 155n, 157n, 159n, 160n, 165n, 166n, 169n, 171n, 172n
  The Devil Within, 11–12, 19, 27, 40–42, 82, 84, 96, 98, 101, 104–105, 107–108, 117, 124–25
  Jānn, 30, 42–44
  Lucifer, 7
Dhikr (remembrance of God), 122–23
al-Dhubiyānī, al-Nābighah, 71
Dhū al-Rummah, 74
al-Diyārbakrī, Ḥusayn, 31
dogs, 1, 10, 36, 38, 44, 46, 88, 123, 136n

Earths
  Earth of Devotions (*ʿarḍ al-ʾibādāt*), 45
  Earth of Exorbitance (*ʿarḍ al-ṭaghyān*), 46
  Earth of Impiety (*ʿarḍ al-ʾilḥād*), 46
  Earth of Lust (*ʿarḍ al-shahwa*), 46
  Earth of Misery (*ʿarḍ al-shaqāwa*), 46
  Earth of Nature (*ʿarḍ al-ṭab*), 45
ego (*ʾanāniyya*), 88, 93, 106
epilepsy (*ṣarʿ*), 54, 137n

fairies, 28, 58–59
al-Farazdaq (poet), 73
fire, 12, 22, 28–29, 31–33, 35–36, 40–41, 44, 49, 58, 64, 68, 83, 86–87, 95–96, 104–105, 108, 114, 118, 127, 168n

Gabriel (Jibrāʾīl), the archangel, 39, 60, 71, 95, 99, 104–105, 169
Gello, 135
genius spirit (pl. *genii*), 28, 141n
al-Ghazālī, ʾAbū Ḥāmid, 3, 23, 25, 30, 38, 43, 64, 74, 158n
al-Ghazālī, ʾAḥmad, 22
God, 1–5, 11–12, 15–16, 18–23, 27, 29–35, 39, 41–42, 44–45, 52–53, 56–57, 59, 67, 70, 73–77, 79, 82–89, 91, 93–95, 97–101, 103–104, 106–14, 117–30, 137n, 138n, 139n, 144n, 146n, 150n, 151n, 154n, 157n, 158n, 160n, 162n, 164n, 166n, 167n, 172n, 173n, 178n, 181n
  The Deceiver (*al-Mākir*), 4, 139n
  The One Who Leads Astray (*al-Mudhill*), 4, 16, 20–21, 39, 79, 111, 139, 159n
  The Sublimely Subtle (*al-Laṭīf*), 39–40
  The Merciful (*al-Raḥman*), 110–11

Great City (*al-madīna al-kubra*), 21, 81–83, 86, 140n, 157n

Hadhad, the king, 63
ḥadīth qudsī, 2–3, 82
Hajal (jinni), 73
Hāmah b. ʾAlhām, 34–35
Ḥārith, 30–31, 42
Harun (Hārūn), 67
Ḥasān b. Thābit, 73
Hawbar (jinni), 73
hermaphrodite (*khunthā*), 42–43
human body (*jism*), 53, 81, 83–86, 89, 96–99, 119, 121, 135, 149n, 160n, 163n, 164n, 165n, 170n, 172n, 173n
human self (*huwiyya*), 88, 129
hypocrite (*munāfiq*), 100

Ibn ʿArabī, Muhyī d-Dīn, 1–7, 15–16, 18–25, 27–28, 30–37, 39–40, 42–43, 45, 49, 52–55, 60–61, 63–65, 67–68, 71, 73, 75–78, 81–89, 91, 93–101, 103–16, 118–29, 133n, 136n, 138n, 139n, 140n, 143n, 144n, 145n, 147n, 152n, 153n, 157n, 159n, 162n, 164n, 165n, 167n, 170n
  Greatest Shaykh (*al-shaykh al-ʾakbar*), 2
  Seal of Sainthood (*khatam al-wilāya*), 2
  Reviver of Faith (*muḥyiddin*), 2
  heretic, 2
Ibn Barrajān, ʿAbd al-Salām, 29, 127, 172n
Ibn Manẓūr, Muḥammad b. Makram, 28, 60, 62, 65, 143n
Ibn Rushd, ʾAbū al-Walīd Muḥammad, 69
Ibn Shuhaid, ʾAbū ʿAmīr, 73, 153n, 156n
Ibn Taymiyya, Taqī ad-Dīn, 2, 57, 116, 144n
Ibrahim (Ibrāhīm), 67
Idris (Idrīs), 67
ʾilhām (the Divine inspiration), 93, 162n
illumination (*ḍiyāʾ*), 103
al-Iṣfahānī, Abū al-Faraj, 58, 69, 72, 135n
ʾIsmāʿīl (jinni), 65, 116

al-Jāḥiẓ, ʾAbū ʿUthman ʿAmr, 4, 7, 29, 49, 51
al-Jawzī, ʾAbī al-Faraj, 56, 58, 78
Jesus (ʿĪsā), 67, 107, 128, 166n, 172n, 173n
al-Jīlī, ʿAbd al-Karīm, 31, 45
jinn, 1, 4–13, 15–20, 22–25, 27–79, 81–83, 86–88, 90–101, 103–104, 106–108, 110–21, 123–29, 132n, 133n, 134n, 135n, 137n, 142n, 144n, 145n, 148n, 151n, 152n, 154n, 156n, 157n, 163n, 167n, 169n, 172n
  ḥinn, 46, 48–49
  shiqq, 46, 114, 153n, 167n
jinn conjurors
  See Men of the Limit
jinn doppelgangers (*quranāʾ*), 9–17, 19–24, 27, 30, 32, 34, 36, 39–40, 42–45, 49, 51–55, 57, 60–62, 64–66, 68–70, 73–76, 79, 82–83, 86–89, 93–94, 96–98, 100–101, 103–104, 106–108, 111–16, 119–27, 136n, 145n, 173
  ghoul, 7, 34, 46, 49–50, 51, 113, 148n, 167n
  ifrit, 34, 46, 49, 139n, 149n
  siʿlāh, 7, 46–47, 73, 148n
  dalhāth, 48
  mārid, 46, 48–49

jinn doppelgangers *(continued)*
  nasnās, 5, 47, 71, 87, 148n, 153n
  mārij, 32–33, 143n
  abqarī, 49
  buhma, 49
  alyas, 49
jinnealogy, 8, 19, 25, 66, 70, 133n
jinn of Niṣībīn, 65, 154n
jñāna (wisdom), 29
jurisprudents (*fuqahā'*), 3, 8, 70
al-Jurjānī, ʿAlī, 84, 131n

ka double, 10–11
kāfir (polytheist), 7, 15, 28, 56–57, 65
Kamṭam, the Lord of the West, 68
ḳarīneh
  See jinn doppelgangers
Kaʿab b. Zuhayr, 50
Khadija, 95
Khāḳān tribe, 65
Khālid b. al-Walīd, 55
al-Khannās, 43, 105, 147n
khawāṭir (passing thoughts and inrushes), 93, 95, 162n
al-Khawwas, Ibrahim, 123
Kubrā, Najm al-Dīn, 34, 122–23, 135, 139n, 144n, 170n
Kuthayyit ʿAzzah (poet), 73
Lilith, 12, 43, 135n

Lo Gue, the dance, 126
lust (*shahwah*), 16, 38, 46, 88, 91, 110, 160n

macrocosm (*ʿālam kabīr*), 22, 24–25, 81, 140n, 158n
magic, 17–18, 23, 35, 38, 54, 57, 68, 74–75, 87, 104, 105, 119, 169n
  nigromancia, 74
  siḥr, 74
  science of Mystery (*ʿulūm al sirr*), 75
  sīmīyā', 75–76

Māhān tribe, 65
majnūn (a possessed, insane person), 54–55
al-Makkī, ʾAbū Ṭālib, 22, 96
Malakūt (*ʿalām al-malakūt*), 5, 81, 132n
Mani, 5, 57, 87
Manicheism, 11
al-Masʿūdī, ʾAbū al-Ḥasan ʿAlī, 5, 46
Maqrūn (victims of jinn doppelgangers), 53
Maymūn, the king of jinn, 67
Māzar, the Lord of the East, 68
Mazdeism, 11
Men of the Limit (*rijāl al-ḥadd*), 113–15, 118–19
microcosm (*ʿālam ṣaghīr*), 22, 25, 81–82, 140n
Moses (Mūsā), 67, 75, 98, 118
Mudhab, the king of jinn, 67, 70
muḥaddith (scholar of hadith), 2
Muhammad (prophet), 11, 19, 32–34, 39, 45, 48, 54, 57, 71, 74, 78–79, 89, 99, 105–106, 113, 117–18, 129–30, 133, 139, 154n, 159n, 165n
mujawiz (a bachelor; a man married to his *qarīn*), 62
Mulk (*ʿalām al-mulk*), 81, 128, 132n
Murra b. al-Hārith, the jinni, 74

Nahhada, 153n

Paradise (*janna*), 12, 28, 34, 53, 76, 90, 107, 127, 129, 144n, 147n, 165n, 172n
People of God (*ʾahlu allah*), 19, 103
People of Reflection (*ʾahl al-naẓār*), 77
perdition (*al-bawār*), 33, 51
Perfect Human (*al-ʾinsān al-kāmil*), 89

personal judgement (*ra'y*), 100
pigs, 107, 163n
Plato, 3, 11, 68, 132n
Plutarch, 11
Pseudo-Majriti, 68, 75, 88

Qanṭarūn, 34, 144n
qarīn
  See jinn doppelgangers
Qarīna, 13–14, 24, 38, 60, 105, 120, 135n, 136n
Qasūra, the Lord of the South, 68
al-Qazwīnī, 'Abū Yaḥyā Zakariyyā', 3, 47–51, 59, 71, 143n, 148n, 167n
Qur'an, 1, 3, 6, 8, 12, 15, 24, 28–32, 44, 55, 57, 78–79, 83, 85–86, 88, 90, 93, 95–96, 103, 112, 122, 123, 125, 134n, 144n, 148n
al-Qushayrī, ʿAbd al-Karīm, 78, 87, 123

rabies, 54
al-Rāzī, 'Abū Bakr, 86, 88
Red Feast, 121
religious scholars (*ʿulamā'*), 16, 20, 30–32
revelation (*kashf*), 3, 22–23, 30, 32, 40–41, 54, 78, 93, 95, 122
Rūmī, Jalāl al-Dīn, 25, 51, 86, 113, 167n

Ṣakhr, 38, 65, 70–71, 76, 114, 121, 145n
Sarīʿ (jinni), 66
Satya Yuga, 30
science of meanings (*ʿilm al-maʿāna*), 15
al-Shabībī, 'Abū Muḥammad, 71
Sharia, 2, 71, 78, 94, 98, 101, 109–10, 122
al-Shiblī, Badr al-Dīn, 8, 44, 45, 53, 142n, 146n
Shiniqanaq, the jinn chieftain, 73
Shīrāzī, Ṣadr al-Dīn, 77, 144n
Siyāh Qalam, 92
Snakes, 36, 44, 46, 52–53, 64, 88, 91, 97, 107, 116, 118
  al-'arqām, 53
Solomon, 18–19, 38–39, 65, 70–71, 74, 76, 113–15, 121, 139n, 145n, 149n, 153n, 155n
soul (*nafs*), 2, 10–11, 17, 20–22, 25, 28, 32, 34, 38, 44, 51, 55, 62, 68, 81–94, 96, 101, 103, 105–106, 109–11, 114, 119–23, 129, 131n, 139n, 140n, 158n, 159n, 160n, 161n, 162n, 164n, 165n, 169n
  the lower soul (*al-nafs al-'ammārah*), 17, 20–22, 34, 38, 44, 51, 82–83, 88–90, 93, 96, 103, 105, 109–11, 122, 129, 131n, 139n, 161n, 164n, 165n
  the blaming soul (*al-nafs al-lawwāmah*), 85
  the serene soul (*al-nafs al-muṭma'inna*), 85, 162n
  the animal soul (*al-nafs al-ḥayawāniyya*), 85, 88–89
  the vegetable soul (*al-nafs al-nabātiyya*), 85, 88, 165n
  the rational soul (*al-nafs-al-nāṭiqa*), 88, 161n
  the desiring soul (*al-nafs al-shahwaniyya*), 88, 90
  the wrathful soul (*al-nafs al-ghadabiyya*), 88–90, 99, 165n
  the demonic soul (*al-nafs al-'iblīsiyya*), 89
spirit (*rūḥ*)
  the Divine spirit (*al-rūḥ al-ilāhī*), 33, 83–86

spirit *(continued)*
the human spirit (*rūḥ al-insān*), 81–87, 106, 127
the animal spirit (*al-rūḥ al-ḥayawānī*), 88, 102
Suhrawardī, Shahāb al-Dīn, 40, 86, 159n
Sunnah, 3, 8, 15, 134n
al-Suyūṭī, Jalāl al-Dīn, 11, 52, 78, 119, 148n

tābi' (jinni companion), 9–12, 25, 51–52, 61–62, 73, 75, 76, 94, 114, 127, 144n, 153n
Tābi'a, 12–13, 135n, 136n
Tadmur (Palmira), 71
Tajallī (the Divine self-disclosure), 111–12, 172n
talisman, 106, 116, 119, 148, 168n
Ṭaykal, the Lord of the North, 69
the Forefather of Jinn (*'abū al-jinn*), 30–32, 35, 40, 42–43, 46, 142n, 147n
the Greater Jihad (*al-jihād al-'akbar*), 21, 103, 140n
theoi (gods), 67–68
Thomas of Chobham, 4
Tiberias, 71–72
Tirān tribe, 65
al-Tirmidhī, al-Ḥakīm, 96, 159n
Torah, 18, 108, 166n
al-Tustarī, Sahl, 97, 106
travel literature (*'adab al-riḥlāt*), 5
Treta Yuga, 30

'Umm al-Ṣibyān, 12–14, 65, 135n, 136n, 169n
'Umar b. al-Khaṭṭāb, 138
unseen (*al-ghayb*), 5, 7, 28–30, 38, 62, 64, 85, 97, 118, 129, 145n, 162n
al-'Uzzā, 55–56, 58

veil (*ḥijāb*), 1, 20–21, 28, 81–82, 97, 112, 121–22
Virgil, 11
visible world
See Mulk

waswās (whispers of jinn), 7, 9, 16, 38, 41, 46, 49, 51, 65, 67, 87, 93, 95–96, 98, 108, 111, 124, 147n, 166n
water, 31–33, 35, 47, 51, 58, 83–84, 98, 114, 119, 125, 136–37, 168n
whimsical behaviour (*hawā*), 88, 91
Wonders (*'ajā'ib*), 3–6, 20, 128–29

Yahya (Yaḥyā), 67
Yūnāq, 34, 144n

ẓāhir (the visible, apparent), 6
Zaqqum, 90–91
Zuhair b. Numair (jinni), 73, 153n, 156n

www.ingramcontent.com/pod-product-compliance
Lightning Source LLC
Chambersburg PA
CBHW021942250225
22368CB00011B/93
* 9 7 8 1 4 3 8 4 9 6 8 8 7 *